# POLARIS!

# POLARIS!

*by James Baar and William E. Howard*

HARCOURT, BRACE & WORLD, INC., NEW YORK

F.11.67

*Library of Congress Catalog Card Number: 60-12731*
*Printed in the United States of America*

*The eight pages of photographs, appearing between pages*
*118 and 119, are reproduced by courtesy and with permis-*
*sion of the following:*
*James Baar—page two, top right, middle left, middle*
*right, bottom left, bottom right; page three, top left,*
*middle, bottom left*
*Electric Boat Division, General Dynamics Corporation—*
*page seven, middle, bottom right*
*Lockheed Missiles and Space Division—page five, top left,*
*top right*
*Muray Associates—page one, top right*
*Sperry Gyroscope Company—page one, bottom*
*United States Air Force—page five, bottom right; page*
*six, bottom*
*United States Navy—page two, top left; page four, top*
*left, top center, top right, bottom; page five, bottom left;*
*page six, top left, top center, top right; page seven,*
*top right; page eight*

*Polaris is a powerful weapon of war, born of grave necessity in an age of troubles. It was brought into being by the remarkable ingenuity of Americans in the hope that its existence would deter war and, through an honorable peace, preserve our freedom. To those who conceived and built the Polaris system and to the men who sail the Polaris submarines, this book is gratefully dedicated.*

# Foreword

Many of the conclusions in this book are controversial. They are based in part on facts drawn from scores of interviews with many persons involved in the Polaris program, among them government officials, scientists, engineers, military men, businessmen, and congressmen. However, these conclusions are ours and, unless otherwise stated, they should not be construed as necessarily representing the opinions of others.

We extend our thanks to all those who took valuable time from their busy lives to give us help in gathering material for this book. We are particularly grateful to Commander Kenneth W. Wade of the Navy's Special Projects Office for aiding us in contacting so many of the people who created the Polaris system.

JAMES BAAR
WILLIAM E. HOWARD

Washington, D.C.

# Contents

# POLARIS!

# 1    Spoils of War

Ernst Steinhoff conceived the idea while talking to his brother, a U-boat commander. The United States had just entered the war. Already it was funneling tremendous amounts of weapons, food, and oil to Russia. It was sending men, tanks, and supplies to North Africa. American harbors were disgorging a never-ending stream of ships across the Atlantic. For every merchantman sent to the bottom with a German torpedo, it seemed as if two took its place.

To Steinhoff, a brilliant young engineer, the German Admiralty was trying to dam up the stream in the wrong place: in the middle of a huge ocean. No matter how vigilant the U-boats, some ships in a convoy generally slipped through, and every one that made it only delayed the conquest of Europe and Asia by Hitler's *Wehrmacht*.

The sensible thing, Steinhoff told his brother, was to cut off the supplies at their source, snip the umbilical cord. But how, was the rejoinder, when there were no airplanes capable of spanning the ocean to bomb American cities. Surely no naval vessel could inflict enough damage with guns to warrant the risk of being sunk by defending battleships and shore batteries. It was impossible. Ernst disagreed. He thought he had a way, if his brother would consent to lending his submarine for a little experiment.

Skeptically, the U-boat skipper nodded permission. Ernst had always been somewhat eccentric, but since he was involved in some highly secret work for the Army, perhaps his idea was worth exploring. The U-boat was undergoing overhaul in the port of Swinemünde in Poland on the Baltic Sea. Swinemünde was just a few miles from Peenemünde, a stretch of empty beach on the German coast, where Ernst Steinhoff and a group of scientists and engineers had been established in a closely guarded research center to work on a new weapon—a long-range rocket. Ernst returned to his laboratory and conferred with Peenemünde's commander, Capt. Walter Dornberger, who at once became intrigued. The men at the research center were always eager to experiment with new ideas. So it was arranged. A few days later a group of technicians from Peenemünde went to Swinemünde, bringing with them several large mortar tubes, each about four and one half feet long. These were hoisted aboard the submarine and bolted to the deck. Waterproof cables were run from them and connected to a firing switch inside the submarine. When all was secure, some long projectiles were carried aboard and gingerly lowered into the mortar tubes.

The system was given a last checkover and, with Dornberger aboard, the U-boat moved out into the Baltic, the mortars protruding from the bow like leaning fence posts. The submarine cruised to Griefswalder Oie, a small island off Peenemünde used for testing rockets, dived a short distance offshore, and leveled off at a depth of 74 feet. Ernst Steinhoff watched from shore. Standing with him was Dornberger's young assistant, Dr. Wernher von Braun.

Suddenly, not far from where the conning tower had disappeared under a panache of white foam, a small rocket ripped from the waves. It flashed through the air in a high arc and struck a target area in the water two miles away.

German scientists running the secret Nazi rocket program had fired the world's first ballistic missile from a submerged submarine. The year was 1942.

The successful shot was followed by another and another that day off Peenemünde. Twenty in all were launched, proving to the rocketmen, and Steinhoff's brother, that it was possible to give a submerged submarine the power to strike distant land targets. Here was a new weapon.

Dornberger presented the idea to the German Navy. This was a way submarines could attack the sources of supply on the American coast. Hidden below the surface, U-boats could strike with bomb-tipped missiles at harbors, oil depots, shipyards, and cities.

The Navy, according to Dornberger, examined the reports and blueprints and then informed him that if there were to be submarine-launched missiles, the Navy would design them. In short, the Navy wouldn't accept something handed to them by the Army.

The mortars were removed from the U-boat, and it departed on war patrol. It never came back to Swinemünde.

Dornberger and Steinhoff returned to their main work—the A-4 missile, later to be known the world over as the terrifying V-2. The Navy stuffed the Peenemünde reports into a file and forgot them.

Rocket engineers do not discourage easily. They are bothered least of all by the disinterest of policy-making officials. Dornberger realized missiles launched from the sea held tremendous advantages. Unfortunately, there were many difficulties associated with developing such a weapon. However, solving these problems fascinated him and the other scientists on his team at Peenemünde. They continued to search for better methods. The mortars were not practical for combat because they acted like a brake, slowing the U-boat under water. Also much larger rockets would be needed to carry a bomb big enough to make the effort worth while.

Soon German rocketmen wangled another submarine and tried to launch bigger missiles attached to the conning tower. The attempt failed.

Meantime, the complexion of the war was changing. Hitler's *Wehrmacht* had bogged down at Moscow and Stalingrad in the invasion of Russia. The *Luftwaffe* had bloodied but failed to conquer Britain. The North African campaign was in doubt.

Hitler turned in desperation to Peenemünde and ordered the all-out development of the V-2. He also pushed into production the V-1 missile.

The two missiles differed radically. The V-1 had wings and was essentially a pilotless aircraft, its engine living on oxygen in the atmosphere. The V-2 was a rocket with an engine that hurled it out of the atmosphere. This was possible because inside its tanks it carried LOX—incredibly cold liquid oxygen— as an oxidizer to burn the fuel—alcohol. Where the V-1 could be shot down by antiaircraft guns and fighter planes, there was no defense against the bullet-like V-2. Soaring to an altitude of more than 100 miles, the V-2 plummeted down on its target at about 3,000 miles per hour.

Perfection of the V-2 proved extremely difficult. The first test model was launched successfully at Peenemünde on October 3, 1942. The missile traveled a distance of about 120 miles. However, it was not ready for mass production until a full year later, and by that time Allied bombers were inflicting severe damage upon V-2 manufacturing facilities. Peenemünde was struck by a Royal Air Force raid in August, 1943, which caused more than eight hundred casualties and wrecked testing stands and assembly hangars. British intelligence instigated the raid after vapor trails of test missiles had been observed across the Baltic from Sweden, and aerial photographs of missiles on the ground made the British realize something special was in progress there.

Because of crippling air raids, the Germans did not succeed in launching a production model of the V-2 until late in 1944. The first one crashed into Chiswick, England, at 6:43 P.M. on September 8, killing several people. It was fired by a German Army mobile unit across the English Channel, from near The Hague. The Missile Age was born.

About this time, Dornberger produced another idea for sea-launched missiles. In December he submitted 151 sketches of a submersible container the shape of a teardrop. It was designed to carry and launch a V-2.

Dornberger proposed that U-boats tow the missiles across the Atlantic to the American coast. It would take thirty days to get them into position. Once there, the waterproof capsules were to be opened. Then the missiles would be fueled and fired at New York, Washington, and other coastal cities. The idea captured the imagination of the half-demented Hitler as being a last desperate gamble to keep from losing the war. But he was never able to carry out the plan.

Time had run out on Peenemünde. Allied armies were rolling over Germany. Berlin had been reduced to rubble. Hitler entered the *Führer* bunker for the last time, and World War II ended. Hitler and his Third Reich died. But his rocket scientists and their revolutionary ideas lived on.

The Germans who launched the first small missiles from a submarine in 1942 had gazed far into the future. Long before the first V-2 smashed into metropolitan London, many of its inventors were convinced that missiles one day would be the ruling weapon on land and sea. The V-2 blitz on London was considerable proof.

If V-2 missiles carrying conventional explosives had been produced a year or two earlier, they might have drastically altered the outcome of the war. Submarine-launched missiles would have helped, by bringing the battle of the Atlantic into American ports.

Even as it was, the V-2s did strike a terrifying blow. Between September 8, 1944 and the time the blitz ended on March 27, 1945, the British calculated more than 1,340 V-2s fell on London and other targets in Britain. The toll: 2,724 people killed, more than 6,000 injured, and widespread, indiscriminate destruction.

The V-2 might have been more formidable, even at that late hour in the war, had it not been for Allied bombing of factories. German records seized by the United States Army show the Germans actually launched 3,300 V-2s against England. These captured documents reveal, however, that many of the missiles were defective because of poorly made parts attributable to the raids. Many V-2s tumbled to earth soon after take-off. Others exploded on the launching platform. After October, 1944, the Germans found that only 20 per cent of the missiles actually struck a specific target. The rest exploded in the air, damaging the target, but not with full effectiveness. The British apparently counted only those that did measurable damage.

For all its fearsomeness, the V-2 soon was all but forgotten by the American public, which had never felt its bite. The cataclysms wreaked upon Hiroshima and Nagasaki in 1945 by the atomic bombs obliterated the significance of the long-range missile.

The Free World entered the Nuclear Age without realizing the era of the missile had already begun. This was a tragic oversight of the Truman administration. The day was coming when the speed and destructive power of the missile and the nuclear bomb would be joined in one "ultimate" weapon.

German rocket development became one of the spoils of war, and Russia took the first helping.

Soviet troops in July, 1944, overran the city of Riga in Latvia and captured a V-2 assembly plant. The factory contained many missiles and skilled production workers. In February, 1945, the Russians seized Peenemünde. But there was little there to carry back to the U.S.S.R. The Germans had burned or carted off almost all their records and blueprints. The entire installation was a shambles from Allied bombing. What remained had been blown up by the retreating Germans. However, the Russians did take a missile research center pretty much intact in nearby Pomerania. And later on, the Soviets succeeded in rounding up a number of former engineers and scientists who had worked at Peenemünde. They were taken to Russia.

The United States was more fortunate, largely because the German scientists preferred to have Americans as captors. After evacuating Peenemünde in late January, the Germans moved south to the Harz Mountains and set up a V-2 production center in the little town of Bleicherode. Here they attempted in the waning months of the war to turn out more missiles, with about five thousand employees. American forces soon penetrated the town and took over the plant and laboratories.

Shortly before their arrival, however, five hundred of the top guided-missile scientists and technicians were seized by German SS troops (Hitler's elite storm troopers), who had orders to eliminate them. The collapse of Germany came before the executions could take place. The SS also directed the removal of all secret documents on missiles—three truckloads—to an abandoned mine nearby.

These documents were found by American Army units in April, 1945. The Army immediately shipped them back to the United States to its Aberdeen Proving Ground in Maryland for cataloguing and translation by a newly created Foreign Document Evaluation Branch. Meantime, it began collecting former Peenemünde scientists who had scattered into the Alps and who, after the war's end, indicated they wanted to team up with the Americans. This was Operation Paperclip.

Dr. von Braun was among the 150 top men screened and offered five-year contracts to go to the United States and work for the Army. Dornberger, who finished the war as a general, was convicted as a war criminal. After he was freed, he, too, came to America. He was hired as director of engineering for the Bell Aircraft Company, and became one of the leading exponents of an earth-orbiting space bomber called Dyna-Soar.

Transfer of von Braun and the others to Aberdeen began in September, 1945. They were set to work screening the thousands of papers stamped *Geheim* (Secret) that were exhumed from the Harz Mountains mine. Capt. Rudolph Nottrodt, an Army technical intelligence officer, has since said:

"It is impossible to estimate, in man-hours and dollars, the amount of time and money saved by our having had the German scientists and technicians available to assist us in segregating, cataloguing, evaluating, and translating over forty tons of documents. I assure you it was great, for often at a glance they could classify a document as important or trivial. Such speed was possible because often these men were working with documents that they themselves wrote or helped compile."

Operation Paperclip was a success—but never properly exploited. It produced a bonanza of rocket technology, which would have allowed the United States to pick up where the Germans had left off. All that was required was money. But precious little was forthcoming. No one in the Truman administration at war's end was interested in what many scoffers called "firecrackers." The Army could barely scrape together enough funds to begin a modest program of assembling captured V-2 parts and launching them as "high-altitude research rockets" at White Sands Proving Ground in New Mexico.

The other services fared no better.

However, German plans for a seagoing rocket quickly caught the attention of some young United States Naval officers. They had participated during the war in the development of short-range barrage rockets launched from racks and used successfully to support the landing of American troops on beachheads. The import of the designs drawn by Dornberger and his engineers was plain to them; the United States Navy should capitalize on them. In the late summer of 1945, they drew up a proposal for the Navy's Bureau of Ordnance, setting forth plans for a long-range missile that could be launched from surface ships as well as submarines.

The technical problems involved in such a venture loomed as large to them as they had to the Germans. But great advances had been made in rocketry during the war, and Navy engineers saw no reason why progress should stop.

The chief obstacles were the size of the missile and the means of propelling and guiding it to the target. A V-2, or anything like it, would be an unwieldy beast to handle aboard a ship.

It was 64 feet tall. Moreover, the two substances burned by its engine—liquid oxygen and alcohol—were both extremely dangerous, particularly in a ship or submarine, where they could easily explode if they spilled.

It was apparent, too, that something would have to be done to improve the so-called "kill" efficiency of the V-2, which was obviously too low for such an expensive weapon. It carried an explosive charge approximating that in a 2,000-pound bomb. Preferably, the warhead should contain an atom bomb. But this involved another problem. The rocket would have to be extremely powerful to lift an atom bomb any distance; the ones dropped on the Japanese each weighed about 10,000 pounds. Actually, a rocket five times the size of the V-2 would be needed to get this amount of weight off the ground.

The matter of directing a missile accurately to its target over hundreds of miles was another nasty headache left unsolved by the Germans. The best they could do was aim the V-2 on the ground toward the target, and once it was in flight, correct its course by radio. The results were not too good, even though they knew precisely the location of the site where the missile was launched in relation to the target. At sea, a ship's navigator was considered good if he could establish his position within several miles. Obtaining an absolutely accurate bearing on true north was also difficult. Thus, a way would have to be found to determine both position and direction of a ship with pin-point precision, or a sea-launched missile would go astray.

No attempt was made to minimize the magnitude of these problems. But the Navy missilemen stated their conviction that with sufficient effort—and money—the difficulties could be solved in research laboratories. In their opinion the undertaking would be well worth the expense to the nation.

A showdown came on a hot fall day at a lengthy meeting of high-ranking officers in the Bureau of Ordnance. Outside the conference room, all Washington was relaxing in the joy and relief of newly won peace. Inside, the missilemen fought a losing battle. Time and elusive memories have obscured the details of the secret meeting. But the result was unmistakable: the recommendation was rejected. There was too little money and even less vision.

This blow, dealt by the Navy itself, was the first of many that could have stopped development of a sea-borne ballistic missile permanently. For a decade the idea was kept alive—sometimes just barely—by the tenacity of a few engineers. With the end of the war, the best bone that the Army and the Navy could throw to the missilemen in their ranks was minor support for R&D—initials standing in Pentagon jargon for Research and Development, but also referred to on occasion as meaning "relax and deliberate."

The huge military machine that had won the war deteriorated rapidly in a great American hurry to return to latter-day normalcy. The divisions melted away; ships went into moth balls; planes and tanks were junked. Hardly anyone paused to notice that the Soviet Union wasn't disarming. In a world partly starving and partly in ruins, the United States adopted a schizophrenic military policy: It overtly relied on the newly formed United Nations to preserve the peace, while actually it depended upon its tenuous atomic monopoly should the UN fail.

By 1948, when the military threat of Communist Russia could no longer be ignored, America found itself all but disarmed, except for its atomic bombs and an insufficient number of long-range bombers to deliver them. Czechoslovakia fell. The Soviets isolated Berlin. The fall of Nationalist China became imminent. War with Russia appeared a concrete possibility. In the rearmament flurry that ensued, the Truman administration faced a fateful turning. It could have chosen to rebuild conventional United States military forces to hold the line for the Free World while it began the bold development of missile power for the future. Instead, it vacillated. It bolstered Army ground forces a little and continued to rely for the future on airplane-delivered atomic bombs.

This course was easier and cheaper. And the decision to follow it was made simpler for the Truman administration by the fact that few Americans even knew there was a choice. The fantastic possibilities raised by Germany's V-2 missiles were a secret in Pentagon vaults, safely locked away from the American public.

Despite everything, the dream of big missiles persisted—on the New Mexican desert at White Sands Proving Ground, in scattered industrial laboratories across the country, and in a few isolated Pentagon offices. Most of the dreamers were hard at work on small missiles to be fired in the air or against aircraft —the air-to-air, air-to-surface, and surface-to-air missiles. They also were occupied in the development of a few high-altitude research rockets.

On December 6, 1947, the Navy finally got a chance to launch a V-2 from the flight deck of the carrier *Midway* off the island of Bermuda. The test—first of its kind—was to determine whether so large a missile could be fueled and fired at an angle from shipboard while the ship was under way. The big "bird," as almost all missiles came to be called, swooped dangerously close to the carrier's bridge. Just after clearing it by inches, the missile blew up. The test was hardly gratifying.

The next year, the Navy ordered the development of Regulus I, the first sea-launched guided missile of any size. The 500-mile-range missile was tailored to be fired from both surface ships and surfaced submarines. It was not a space-soaring ballistic missile, but an air-breathing unmanned aircraft somewhat resembling the old German V-1. The winged craft was to be catapulted into the air with a pair of conventional solid-fueled rockets, which were powered by burning a dry chemical mixture packed in the rocket case much like powder in a skyrocket. Once a Regulus was in the air, a turbojet engine took over. The Regulus was big enough to carry a nuclear warhead, but it was vulnerable. It could only travel about 600 miles an hour, making it easy prey for a fighter plane or anti-aircraft missile.

Talk of rearmament faded with the upset presidential election of 1948 and the subsequent advent of Louis Johnson, President Truman's economy-minded new Secretary of Defense. Johnson began to "cut the fat" from the nation's rickety Armed Forces. But the Navy's ballistic missilemen managed to continue their almost bootlegged R&D program. Off Key West, Florida, they duplicated the German Peenemünde tests of six years earlier. Several small solid-propellant rockets were fired successfully from underwater launchers. And at White Sands the Navy played a grim joke on itself—Operation Pushover.

With carefully saved funds, the Navy built a mock-up of a steel warship deck on the sand and erected a tripod launching stand on it. Navy engineers lashed a V-2 to the launcher and loaded it with alcohol and liquid oxygen. Every step for a launching at sea was taken. The missile was ignited with a roar of flame. Then a leg of the tripod was yanked away, and the rocket crashed on the deck.

"It was like having a 2,000-pound bomb make a direct hit," one witness reported. "But that was only the beginning. The thermal shock of the LOX spilling across the deck cracked steel plates and even split the big supporting I-beams."

The object of the test had been to determine what damage an accident with a liquid-fueled missile might cause to a ship. The result was a blow to the whole shaky movement behind putting big ballistic missiles at sea.

"One look at that mess, and a shudder ran through every ship in the Navy," one high-ranking officer recalls.

However, still undismayed, Navy missilemen less than a year later, on May 11, 1950, launched a liquid-fueled Viking—an 11,000-pound research rocket—from the deck of the *Norton Sound* test ship at the intersection of the geographic and geomagnetic equators in the Pacific. The rocket reached an altitude of 105 miles. Developers of the Viking began talking of turning it into a weapon, but they got nowhere.

Work even more significant was in progress at the Navy's Inyokern, California, Ordnance Test Station. A group of engineers under the direction of a brilliant Navy commander, Levering Smith, was putting together a series of increasingly more advanced solid-fueled missiles. The propellants were more powerful and the motors were larger.

In late 1950 Smith's group constructed a relatively huge solid-propelled missile. It was called Big Stoop. This two-stage experimental missile was built specifically to determine whether it would be possible, with solid fuel, to deliver one of the heavy nuclear warheads of this period—a warhead weighing thousands of pounds.

Big Stoop successfully flew about 20 miles on each of three flights in 1951. Scientists connected with the project felt certain the 50-foot missile's range could be extended beyond 40 miles with little difficulty. But, in the end, the flights of Big Stoop and the promise they held were ignored by administration officials. The pattern of near-sightedness remained the same. And it was to remain the same for another four years despite the Korean War.

Russia took far more seriously the lessons of Peenemünde. After the war, the Russians aggressively set about exploiting the rocket work of the Germans while modernizing the entire Soviet military establishment. The Soviet leaders saw in missiles the means of furthering Communist expansion and began to work toward development of big ballistic missiles as well as small tactical types. The exact year that the Russians started an all-out effort to develop an intercontinental ballistic missile is uncertain. However, by 1950 the West had definite word that the Russians were testing large rockets. And United States military leaders have reported that as early as 1948—the year Russia broke the United States atomic monopoly—the Soviets had started work on ballistic missiles of at least 750- to 1,500-mile range, steppingstones to the intercontinental ballistic missile—

the dread ICBM. During this period the Russians also began work on their 3,000-mile-range TCBM—the transcontinental ballistic missile.

Russia had started a life-or-death missile race. Only the American public didn't know it was on. United States intelligence agencies were aware of the Soviet course, but the nation's leaders kept it a secret through Truman and into the Eisenhower era.

America's failure to meet the threat head on is evident in the early history of the Atlas ICBM program. Well into mid-1954, this first major United States rocket program was almost entirely made up of "feasibility studies," talk, and little financial backing. Then in June of that year the Air Force was allowed to proceed with the Atlas program on a high priority basis.

Thus in 1954—the year Russia matched the United States in the development of an H-bomb—the United States government made its first real decision to start running. Unlike Russia, the United States had waited until the size of nuclear weapons had been reduced before trying to put them on the business end of a missile. The United States developed its first H-bomb in 1952. The next year Atomic Energy Commission scientists knew that the weight and exterior dimensions could be reduced significantly. This meant that an ICBM carrying a multimegaton nuclear warhead could be much smaller than it had been previously believed possible.

However, even as late as 1954 there was still hesitation. Rather than move ahead swiftly with the development of a full arsenal of seagoing and land-based missiles, the administration ordered up a new survey of the East-West power balance. That winter, at President Eisenhower's direction, the National Security Council called in some of the best minds of the country to serve on a secret study committee. They came from industry, universities, and the armed services. Dr. James R. Killian, the highly respected president of Massachusetts Institute of Technology, became chairman.

The committee worked through the winter in the baroque, time-darkened Executive Office Building a few paces from the White House. Twice the committee asked the National Security Council for extensions of time, as week after week it assessed the minutest details of the nation's strategic position. All of the nation's top-secret files were opened. The committee had access to war plans, reports on the state of United States technology, intelligence estimates of Soviet rocket advances, and their imminent challenge to American air power.

However, the committee received no information that had not been previously available to the leaders of the administration. It was as if a man called in a group of other men and told them to go through his desk drawers and decide what he ought to do. Government committees and boards had gone over part or all of the same ground ever since the late 1940s. In the end, the Killian committee told the administration it ought to do precisely what a number of military men had been urging for years.

In a report never made public, but whose essence became known, the committee warned that the Soviet Union was rapidly overtaking the United States in over-all strategic power.

Three of the committee's principal recommendations called for immediate action to meet the oncoming missile threat:

The committee called for a further acceleration of work by the Air Force on the Atlas ICBM.

It called for development by the Army of a 1,500-mile intermediate-range ballistic missile—an IRBM.

It called for the parallel development of an IRBM that could be launched from ships at sea.

Under the circumstances, none of the recommendations was too surprising. But the President continued to delay.

The Killian committee handed its report to the President in the winter of 1955. The White House staff studied it and handed it along to the military services for consideration. Months passed.

The President left the country in midsummer for the first Big Four summit meeting. He returned with the syrupy "spirit of Geneva."

The immediate result of the Geneva meeting was a relaxation of international tension. But United States intelligence agencies continued to gather disquieting reports of Soviet missile progress. The Russian activity belied the bland smiles of Communist Party Boss Nikita Khrushchev and his stooge premier, Nikolai Bulganin. Finally, on September 13, 1955, the President decided to implement the Killian report. He directed the Pentagon to speed up the infant ICBM program and proceed with development of IRBMs that could be launched from land and sea.

# 2   Into the Wrong Bed

Navy missilemen were jubilant.

The reward  for years of grubbing, back-yard research had come. The Navy would be free to create a seagoing long-range missile—what it now called the fleet ballistic missile—on an equal footing with the big missile programs of the Air Force and Army. Or so the Navy thought.

Its thinking faced correction. In the weeks following the White House order of September 13, the victory dissolved. Rather than having coequal status with the other services, the Navy soon found that its big missile project was to be treated quite differently at the hands of Secretary of Defense Charles "Engine Charlie" Wilson. He regarded it more as a stepchild than a favored son. An agonizing battle lay ahead.

Circumstances rather than individuals were to blame for the frustration the fleet ballistic missile encountered in the next two months. Presiding over the Pentagon, Wilson was at the vortex of many forces—politics, ambition, fear—all aggravated by the stirrings of Moscow. Wilson himself, his advisers, and the many military men and civilian experts who had dedicated their lives to the defense effort, all suffered from the great stigma of the Eisenhower era—lack of national purpose and direction.

The administration, by its own vacillation, created in the Defense Department ultraconservatism and confusion. The administration was woefully late in waiting until 1955 to acknowledge that big missiles were the weapon of the immediate future; that Strategic Air Command bombers by themselves soon would no longer be able to preserve peace; that the United States, to survive, had to build missiles to counter those being built by Russia. When the administration reluctantly began putting money into missiles, chaos reigned in the Pentagon.

Hardly anyone on a decision-making level knew anything about missiles. The Russians had an eight-year head start. Now the Defense Department was forced to grope around blindly for a way to catch up. Officials like Wilson fell victim to their own ignorance. In a very real sense, their decisions were made for them by the small groups of rocketmen inside and outside the military, who did know or who could at least visualize what the United States must do to overtake the Russians. But the rocket experts couldn't always agree among themselves.

Great debates broke out over the size of the rocket required strategically. Should it be able to fly 1,500 nautical miles? Or 5,000? Or 10,000? Perhaps missiles with three different ranges were needed. Which one do you start developing first? Or do you work on all three at the same time? Who should operate these missiles? Where should they be deployed—on foreign soil or in the United States? How many are needed?

To all these major questions, and many more besides, there were scores of different answers. Ultimately, it was left to the services to resolve most of them. The Army, with its band of German rocket wizards from the beaches of Peenemünde, had been working the hardest and longest. It was well along with a 200-mile Redstone ballistic missile and was concentrating on one with a 1,500-mile range, called the Jupiter. The Army believed the Jupiter should be the initial step in long-range missilery.

The Air Force contended its program for a 5,000-mile intercontinental ballistic missile, the Atlas, was more suited to the nation's needs. For this missile, which was still largely on drawing boards, the Air Force was depending upon the Southern California aircraft industry for much of its technical know-how. Both the Army and the Air Force were funding these programs out of their own research money, and though neither one had been given major Defense Department status, contracts were being let to private companies for studies of the various problems; for experimental designs of rocket motors; for nose cones; for fueling systems and the like.

Though the detailed plans were changing all the time, both the Army and Air Force could tell Wilson generally what their missiles would be like. The Jupiter and the Atlas were to be liquid-fueled and land-based. Both were basically overgrown versions of the old German V-2. The Jupiter's warhead would carry the nuclear equivalent of about 500,000 tons of TNT; the Atlas' 2 million to 3 million tons. By comparison, the huge 20,000-ton blast of the first A-bomb dropped on Hiroshima would seem insignificant.

The Navy, on the other hand, had no such advanced missile under way. Its plans for one were still being hatched in laboratories under its modest research program.

During 1954, the argument started. Both the Army and the Air Force wanted to run the entire military ballistic missile program. Empire-building generals from both services sought to seize control of this brand-new type of weapon. The Army's brass claimed missiles were merely an extension of the art of artillery. For precedent they could point to the German "Big Bertha," an enormous cannon that hurled shells into Paris during World War I from 80 miles away. Missiles were like artillery also in that they were to be fired from fixed positions on land. Nonsense, retorted the Air Force. Ballistic missiles were strategic weapons, an extension of air power. They rightly belonged under the Strategic Air Command.

The President's September 13 decision to implement the Killian report landed on the Pentagon as the Army-Air Force missile row was reaching blast-furnace heat at the upper administrative levels. This decision put all three services in the ballistic missile business, but it didn't resolve the conflicts. The Army–Air Force battle continued, more furiously than ever. Under the decision, both Jupiter and Atlas were being given top national priority. This turned them into crash programs eligible for practically unlimited funds, so that both missiles might be obtained in the shortest possible time.

As for the fleet ballistic missile, it also received top national priority. However, what type of missile it was to be was not specified. That was Wilson's, and presumably the Navy's problem.

With the Army and Air Force, Wilson had merely to assign top national priority to already going programs. All the Navy had was an idea, radically different in approach from the Army and the Air Force missiles. Then the question of money came up.

What the Navy proposed to do was a massive undertaking. It would be expensive, there was no denying. Having investigated liquid-propelled large rockets thoroughly, the Navy knew it had to take another direction. Liquid fuels were simply too dangerous for surface ships or submarines. Liquid oxygen (LOX), used to burn the fuel inside the missile, would be extremely dangerous to carry aboard ship. If the LOX spilled, the slightest spark of static electricity would make it explode. One drop on an oily deck, if stepped on, would blow a man's foot off. The only sensible alternative was a solid-fueled missile, one that

Polaris!

could be easily and safely handled, completely eliminating the use of LOX. There was just one hitch: no solid fuel existed powerful enough to hurl a missile of the required size 1,500 miles. It would require a multimillion-dollar research program to get one.

And that was just the beginning. Millions more would be needed for the design of the missile and the thousands of individual parts that went into it, for the navigation and guidance "brain," for engineering a mechanism to launch it, for the ships and submarines themselves. The total could be only broadly estimated, but it was going to be in the billions.

Unfortunately, no one in the administration could see beyond the price tag.

Under the Eisenhower policy of "deterrency" the nation's survival depended, then as now, upon making the United States nuclear striking force knockout-proof. If Russia could wipe out most of SAC's bombers on the ground and sink the Navy's carriers in one swift blow, then Soviet leaders might be tempted to take the big gamble of nuclear war.

When the Russians had only bombers, this was a prohibitive gamble. The bombers of SAC were scattered at bases all over the world. There would be enough warning time that an attack was under way for them to take off and head for Soviet targets. This time could be measured in hours, virtually insuring Russia's destruction, if the Kremlin pulled the trigger first.

Long-range missiles threatened to eliminate even this small amount of time to react. An ICBM warhead takes about thirty minutes to travel 5,000 miles. The missile tosses the warhead like a fly ball to a peak altitude 600 miles above the earth. At this point, the warhead plunges in an arc down on the target at an incredible 15,000 miles per hour.

Theoretically it was possible to pick up incoming warheads on giant radar antennae while they were still fifteen minutes away, and intercept them with "antimissile missiles." But even optimists conceded this sort of warning and protection would not be available until long after Russia had hundreds of missiles ready to shoot.

Thus, the "reaction time" really was being reduced to zero. Some American strategists, pondering the grim meaning of Russia's missile development in 1955, knew that to preserve the invulnerability of United States missiles, then still largely on drawing boards, they must be protected somehow. They must be made to survive the first blow and be capable of making a retaliatory counterpunch.

The answer put forth by some Air Force planners was double-barreled: bury the ICBMs underground in so-called "hard" bases, and disperse them over wide areas of the American mid-continent. The Army's approach was to make the Jupiter IRBM mobile. By "mobile," it meant that the missile could be moved from one point to another by truck, set up on a portable launching pad, and fired. However, this could not be done very swiftly.

Both the ICBM and the IRBM, too, were as delicate as they were bulky beasts. Nothing would survive a direct hit. And no one could say for certain that even if placed deep in the ground in a reinforced-concrete "silo," actually a dry well, an ICBM would survive the earthquake-like shock following a nearby nuclear blast. There was no way to find out. The first Atlas went into SAC service in 1959 a year after nuclear tests were suspended in October, 1958, under an international agreement that included Russia.

Americans who breathed easier at the thought that there would be no further pollution of the atmosphere with strontium 90 probably never considered that suspension of tests at the same time weakened the missile defense system, which was designed to prevent war. Not only were experimental studies on missiles in silos precluded, but so were tests of the nuclear warheads the new United States missiles would carry.

Huge land-based ICBMs had other serious defects besides being fixed targets. A squadron of nine Atlas missiles required hundreds of men to tend the missiles around the clock day in and year out. Crew members would be prey to assassins trying to prevent them from reaching their launchers at the outbreak of war. One hit from a high-powered rifle bullet, moreover, could disable an ICBM as it was raised into firing position above the ground. Worst of all, these missiles would draw enemy fire to the United States homeland in any first all-out strike to wipe out SAC bases.

Jupiter had even more points against it. The major one: its 1,500-mile range. The range forced it to be based on foreign soil, subject to the jurisdiction of other nations, either North Atlantic Treaty Organization (NATO) countries in Europe or allies in the Far East. Would these allies accept such a weapon, knowing it would also draw fire in a Big War, and on what terms? Who would decide when it would be used? This missile was wide open to the same attack and sabotage, being a land-based weapon, as the ICBM.

How many of these deficiencies appeared significant in the minds of the members of the Killian committee during the long winter of 1954 can only be surmised. Perhaps not all of them could be seen then. But enough must have been apparent to attract them to what the Navy rocketmen had been proposing in one form or another ever since the end of World War II with little success.

Ocean covers almost three-fourths of the earth's surface of 192 million square miles. There are 350 million cubic miles of sea water—any one of which can hide a submarine. The ocean could become a perfect sanctuary for retaliatory missiles or, saying it the more optimistic way, deterrent strength. The enemy would never find them, except perhaps by chance.

In the secret depths of the sea, there would be no sticky entanglements with foreign governments, no need for agreements about bases.

The missiles in a very real sense would be intercontinental, even if their actual firing range was only 1,500 miles. Stationed at points ringing the perimeter of Russia, they could strike deep into the Soviet heartland with the same ease as a land-based ICBM.

Here, too, was the way to draw fire away from the American continent. If the enemy wanted to go after these missiles, it would have to attack them at sea.

The core of the Navy's plan was this:

Marry solid-fueled ballistic missiles to a submarine—a nuclear submarine. Nuclear-powered subs could stay submerged for months. They could hide under the polar icecap, camp at the bottom of the Barents Sea off Murmansk, in the Arabian Sea, or in the Pacific, ready to launch their hydrogen warhead missiles should Russia chance a nuclear war. The subs would be mobile missile-launching bases, silent, hidden, deadly—a gun pointed psychologically at the Kremlin and physically at a large number of strategic targets.

The idea was beautifully simple in conception, fantastically complicated in execution. The nuclear-powered submarine was in existence—the *Nautilus*. Perfection of the missile was yet to come. But there was more to it than that.

The Navy, by combining missiles and submarines, would be trying to bring off a revolution in sea power. Ever since February 17, 1864, when the Confederate-invented submarine *David* sank the *Housatonic* at Charleston, submarines had been one-purpose weapons. Even with nuclear power they were chained by their cruising element, restricted like other warships to combat at sea or against seacoasts. Only aircraft carriers gave the Navy a long-range punch—the ability to strike targets deep within enemy territory. But they were overshadowed by Air Force global bombers, both in nuclear-bomb-carrying capacity and in range. The giant flattops also were vulnerable to attack by aircraft and submarines. At best they could be relied upon by the strategists only to back up the Strategic Air Command in a big war, to serve as an insurance policy.

The perspective changed with the concept of big seagoing

missiles. So equipped, the submarine would become a variant of the strategic bomber. If surface vessels were similarly equipped, as the Navy also suggested, then the whole traditional idea of sea power would be upset. The Navy, with its much-desired mobility and secretiveness at sea, would be moving into the domain of air power—or "aerospace" power, as it came to be called by Air Force missilemen—as well. This fact was not lost upon Air Force generals.

Perhaps in deference to the Air Force, or out of sheer timidity at upsetting the traditional "roles and missions" of the three services, the Navy at first did not stress the strategic capabilities of its proposed missile. It kept trying to sell the weapon as a "tactical" missile to strike enemy submarine bases, which by some weird reasoning would fall under the Navy's destructive mission.

"That was eyewash," one Navy man involved in the fight has said. "But even when people in the Defense Department told us to come right out and say what the missile could do, the Navy still insisted for a long time in playing coy. It was a bad mistake."

Official secrecy still shrouds many of the details of the events following Wilson's receipt of the President's September 13 order. Like doctors, bureaucrats have a way of burying their mistakes—in vaults. This much is known:

Wilson hesitated until October 9—almost a full month—before doing anything. In the interim President Eisenhower had suffered a heart attack, throwing the administration into dazed confusion. There was a distinct possibility that he might not return to office. Against his complete incapacity, there was a great stirring and jockeying for position behind the scenes by those who thought their political fortunes should be tied more securely to Vice-president Richard M. Nixon, the man who would succeed Eisenhower.

Inescapably, perhaps, Wilson was caught up in the turmoil, and this may have seemed excuse enough to postpone the implementation of a sea-borne missile program. However, he had been ordered to proceed with one immediately, and on the highest priority. Therefore, it seems strange indeed that on October 9 Wilson took a step that would mean only further delay.

He appointed Assistant Secretary of Defense Frank D. Newbury to head a new committee to "survey" the entire guided-missile program. Newbury was to determine how the Navy's ballistic missile would fit in. That a "survey" should have been made at this late hour, when all the evidence was in and the decisions made, is difficult to justify now, though plausible excuses undoubtedly can be found. The Navy was dismayed. Further dalliance provided time for inertia to set in and for the Army and Air Force to whittle down the Navy.

In the Defense Department's budget for fiscal 1955, which began on July 1, 1954, only $40,900,000 was requested by Eisenhower for missiles. Before the year was out, the actual amount spent on missiles totalled $158,900,000—nearly four times what the administration thought was needed. But even 159 million dollars—large as it may seem to a taxpayer—is still not a great deal of money for financing the development of extremely complicated weapons. By fiscal 1960, the Eisenhower administration was making a budget request of $2,522,000,000 for missiles—and actually spending $3,303,000,000.

These figures, given to Congress by the Defense Department, throw a sharp light on the Eisenhower budget philosophy. They show a consistency in underestimating what actually had to be spent. If a housewife were to set aside $100 a month for food and then spent $150 on what her family actually ate, and this happened month after month, she would soon run into the red on paper if not at the bank. She could attempt to correct this fiscal contretemps by either increasing the amount set aside to $150 or cutting the amount spent to $100. If she did nothing, she could expect her sins to be exposed sooner or later by a bankrupt, and probably fuming, husband, who would accuse her of being not only stupid, but unrealistic as well.

Such was the missile householdry of Eisenhower's budgeters, consistently unrealistic, even as to what had to be spent on what it had figuratively ordered from the grocery store.

Estimating defense expenditures is admittedly an extremely complicated bit of business, with many variables—something like forecasting the amount of rainfall on Pittsburgh next year. But to be still underestimating the amount of money needed for missiles five years after starting to build them—and by more than 30 per cent—indicates an acute shortage of horse sense. All through this period the administration was being criticized for not moving fast enough on its missile programs. If it couldn't estimate reasonably what it should spend on the missiles it had ordered, how could anyone be sure the administration likewise wasn't underestimating the total missile and defense needs of the country? The evidence is that it did, and dangerously. There is no better example than what happened to the Navy's fleet ballistic missile program.

While the Newbury committee shuffled through papers, Wilson was doing some calculating that fall of 1955. He could see missile expenses starting to skyrocket, just at a time when he was preparing the defense budget estimates for the next fiscal year. These figures would be included in the budget to be presented to Congress in January of 1956—a presidential election year. There was a dark question-mark over Eisenhower. Would he recover, and if he did, would he run for re-election? No one knew. The defense budget was ballooning despite sharp cuts in manpower, and this looked bad for the Republicans. They were the party of "peace and prosperity" and the balanced budget. This was no year even to mention a tax increase to pay for rising defense costs. Quite the contrary, this was the time to think about tax reductions to woo the voters.

Wilson knew only too well the G.O.P. philosophy back home where the votes were. No ballots were won by spending money on weapons of war or sending it overseas in peacetime. New post offices and Federal housing projects were what kept a party in power, along with the benefits to farmers and veterans.

With the President lying near death in Denver, the "hard" decisions of how to hold the line on Federal spending in the new budget thus were largely Wilson's. He would have to help wield the ax over his own department. All the encouragement he would need was waiting in the offices of Secretary of the Treasury George Humphrey and the Bureau of the Budget.

Intricate weapons stuffed with electronic gear can bloat a defense budget quickly. Just a handful of transistorized switches for a single computer cost $500 off the production line. One gyro weighing a pound, used to help stabilize one missile guidance system, bears a $10,000 price tag—and these costs do not include the millions of dollars that must be paid out beforehand for research and materials and the designing of these delicate instruments.

Wilson did not have to be a prophet in 1955 to see where the Defense Department and the country were headed in the never-ending race with advancing technology. All the weapons of the services needed modernization. There were new B-52 bombers to buy for the Air Force (600 at 7 million dollars apiece); nuclear submarines for the Navy, of which the *Nautilus* was the prototype; more carriers and smaller craft to replace World War II models that were wearing out; better combat weapons for the Army. All this and missiles, too. This was not the year for expensive new gadgets such as the Navy desired.

As October dragged into November, the Newbury committee proved to be more than a delaying tactic; perhaps unexpectedly, it opened a way out for Wilson and his money problem. Its deliberations have not been revealed, but the special committee did apply a magnifying glass to the technical details of the Navy scheme.

"You can say there was not very much enthusiasm expressed by the Army and the Air Force for firing ballistic missiles from ships," a Pentagon Navy officer recalls, drily. "They told us we were out of our minds. They were having a hell of a time fueling up their birds and launching them from land where there was lots of room and nothing rocking under them. But the guidance problem really threw them.

"On land you have time to take a bearing on true north and line up your missile. If you want to hit a target 1,500 or 5,000 miles away, you have to know where true north is right on the button. The slightest error throws off the guidance system, and you miss the target. It is difficult enough on land, at a fixed launching site, to keep out error. At sea, aboard a continually moving ship or submarine, it looked impossible.

"Just for good measure, they told us our calculations for mixing a powerful-enough solid fuel for a 1,500-mile missile were much too optimistic. They said it would take years and years of more research to produce what we needed."

The Navy conceded all these difficulties existed. Then it proceeded to produce report after report of its exhaustive laboratory investigations—reports that indicated all the problems associated with launching long-range missiles at sea could be solved, and within a reasonable period of time.

Moreover, the Navy felt it had the answer to the most important question of all, the motor. A ballistic missile, in the jargon of rocketmen, is an "aerodynamically unstable vehicle." This means, simply, it has no wings. It will fall out of the sky like a stone, once its motor cuts off.

In a liquid-fueled rocket, there are two tanks in the fuselage. One holds RP-1, a hydrocarbon fuel closely resembling kerosene later substituted for alcohol, and the other liquid oxygen. By means of high-speed pumps, the fuel and LOX are injected simultaneously into the motor and ignited in a ball-shaped combustion chamber. The hot exhaust gases escape through nozzles at the end of the rocket like air escaping from a toy balloon, thrusting it forward.

For a long-range missile, the tanks are large—holding thousands of gallons of fuel and oxidizer. The Army's Jupiter in 1955 was to be 65 feet tall and 8 feet in diameter. The tank section in the middle took up nearly 50 feet, accounting for its tremendous size.

The motor in a solid-fueled rocket is the fuel itself. The fuel is encased in a metal shell or case, which is the outer shell of the rocket. Solid-fuel motors are of two types: they can be "cored," that is, have their centers hollowed out, usually in a star-shaped pattern so that more surface will be exposed and the whole interior of the motor can burn; or they can be "end-burning" so that the fuel is consumed in the same manner as a burning cigarette.

The hot gas, as in a liquid-fueled motor, escapes through nozzles at the rear of the rocket, providing the push or "thrust." Because no tanks are required, a solid-fueled missile can be much smaller—actually half the size of an equivalent liquid-fueled missile, if the fuel is powerful enough.

Such a missile—one about 30 feet long—would be far easier to put aboard a ship or a submarine than one 65 feet long.

The key to whether one could be built lay in the difference between liquid and solid fuels in their "specific impulse," which is the same thing to rockets as octane rating is to gasoline. The higher the octane, the more powerful the gasoline; the higher the specific impulse, the greater the thrust of a rocket fuel. Liquid fuels in 1955 were considerably more powerful than solid fuels.

However, Navy scientists took heart from the five-year-old memory of Big Stoop. Even more, they were greatly encouraged by a number of current studies in the field of solid-fueled rockets. Other missilemen, mostly from the Army, called in by the Newbury committee, said no, not with the present "state of the art"—present technology. The Navy's rejoinder was that it would advance the state of the art of the fuel while it was working on the rest of the missile system. This wasn't the customary approach.

Keith Rumbel and Charles Henderson, a pair of broad-shouldered scientists who might have been brothers with their sandy hair and horn-rimmed glasses, were engaged in a highly secret research project for the Navy's Bureau of Ordnance in the fall of 1955. At thirty-five, Rumbel already had a reputation as one of the country's most brilliant practitioners in the field of solid fuels for rockets. It was an art he started learning early. As a youngster of sixteen, he delighted his philatelist father and a group of friends in Mission, Texas, by putting together a rocket of his own invention, which was to make an "international rocket mail flight."

The rocket, only a few feet long, was assembled from cardboard and other odds and ends of material, and then loaded with a couple of pounds of powdered fuel young Keith had mixed himself. Mission's postmaster obliged the young rocketer by stamping several hundred letters as first-day covers. These were stuffed into the upper part of the rocket. Keith then touched off the fuse, and the rocket soared several hundred yards across the nearby Rio Grande into Mexico.

Henderson was a bright young chemical engineer, only twenty-six, who had graduated from Massachusetts Institute of Technology with no particular interest in rocketry. He wanted to devote his career to research rather than production.

Chance had brought the two together in the Atlantic Research Corporation, a small company in Alexandria, Virginia, just across the Potomac from Washington. Atlantic Research held a Navy contract, which had one objective: improve the specific impulse of solid fuels.

Working in a building that had been hastily converted from a supermarket, Rumbel and Henderson had begun theoretical studies on the problem in 1954. In these studies they became intrigued by the result of adding powdered metal to solid fuels. The fuel they were experimenting with was a mixture of arcite (plasticized polyvinyl chloride) and ammonium perchlorate, the latter containing the oxygen to make the arcite burn faster. Other scientists had succeeded in boosting the specific impulse of similar mixtures by adding powdered aluminum to them. But an unexplained phenomenon made them abandon their investigation. The specific impulse went up—to a point. The high point was reached at the addition of 5 per cent aluminum powder. If more were mixed in, the potency of the fuel decreased.

Unfazed by this strange behavior, Rumbel and Henderson tried very large amounts of powdered aluminum to see what would happen. The amounts they put in were greater than anyone else had tried. The specific impulse took a terrific jump upward. The two researchers had hit upon the key to high-powered solid fuels.

This breakthrough came while Defense Secretary Wilson and the Newbury committee were still considering the future of the fleet ballistic missile program. However, more study and experiments were needed to evaluate what Rumbel and Henderson had discovered. This took time. Working almost around the clock on into the winter, Rumbel and Henderson were not able to confirm their findings fully, by actual test firings, until January, 1956. By then, Wilson had rendered his decision on the Navy's missile.

Months preceding the decision, Garry Norton, a Pentagon consultant and later the Navy's Assistant Secretary for Air, became alarmed. Nothing was happening. The fleet ballistic missile was at a standstill. It did not exist even as a program, and it wouldn't until Wilson signed a piece of paper from SECDEF (Secretary of Defense) to SECNAV (Secretary of the Navy), authorizing one. One of Norton's former associates, reminded of this trying time, has said, "Garry kept running in and out of offices at the Pentagon, waving a copy of the Killian report. Every day he was demanding to know when in hell the Navy would get some action."

Still another high official has said, "The Navy was really in danger of being read out of its ballistic missile altogether. There just wasn't enough money in the defense budget."

The chief negotiator for the Navy at meetings to implement the Killian report was Rear Adm. John ("Savvy") Sides. All technical information on how the Navy could build a seagoing ballistic missile was funneled to Sides, who was the director of Navy research on guided missiles.

Sides and his former boss, Rear Adm. Daniel Gallery, had been studying the problem for several years before the Killian report was even issued. As early as 1953, they had laid down such a missile's range requirements by drawing circles on maps of Russia. They decided then that a minimum 1,200-mile missile was needed.

Norton, Sides, and other top Navy technical men pushed the fight unremittingly.

Largely through Norton's insistence, Wilson finally bestirred himself. A meeting was called on November 17 to decide the Navy's fate. This was a meeting of top Defense Department officials concerned with ballistic missiles. And, as in the case of many others that have charted the course of American defense policy, the details are secret. It is known, however, that right down to the end, Navy technical men fought bitterly for what they knew then to be the right course, a solid-fueled missile.

But no argument would avail. Wilson, in consummate disregard for the technical evidence, ordered the Navy to join the Army in the development of the Jupiter intermediate-range ballistic missile.

"We were shoved into bed with the Army against our will," an admiral said. "It was the wrong bed and everyone knew it."

Against the better judgment of its technical men, the Navy thus was forced to embrace liquid oxygen, the volatile, extremely dangerous oxidizer used by the Army's Jupiter. There was no escape. If there was to be a fleet ballistic missile, it had to be liquid-fueled.

This wasn't the only nasty surprise Wilson handed out that day. The Secretary of Defense also informed the Navy that if it wanted the seagoing missile so badly, it must fund the program entirely out of the regular Navy budget. There would be no extra money. The program would receive a top national priority, but only as a label.

The meaning of Wilson's decision was clear: other highly

important Navy programs would have to be starved if the fleet ballistic missile program were to live.

The Navy accepted the new burden with all its drawbacks. Any mobile, seagoing ballistic missile was better than none.

The Navy's next step was the most important single decision to be made involving the fleet ballistic missile—selection of a man to create it. A boss.

Ever since the Killian report had come out in the early winter, two Navy agencies, the Bureau of Ordnance (BuOrd) and the Bureau of Aeronautics (BuAer), had been scrapping over who would get the job on the new missile. Both bureaus had submitted competing plans on how they would undertake the assignment.

In September, the Navy decided that if and when the program was started, development of the new weapon would be done by a small "task force." Another squabble immediately started over who would have jurisdiction over the task force. Navy officials settled this argument by creating an organization completely independent of any Navy bureau. They named it the Special Projects Office.

The director of BuOrd's planning was Comdr. Bill Hasler, chief of the bureau's missile research branch. Now Hasler was ordered to begin setting up the new organization on paper.

The man who was to head SP, as the Special Projects Office quickly became known inside the Navy, would be given extraordinary authority. He would have the power to call upon any individual in the Navy and upon any of its bureaus with their large technical resources either to join the program or render immediate assistance. He would report to only one man—the Secretary of the Navy.

An extraordinary man was needed for this most extraordinary job.

Admiral Arleigh ("31 Knot") Burke, Chief of Naval Operations, and others of his top command studied the records of a number of possibilities. Among them was Rear Adm. William F. Raborn, Jr., Admiral Sides' former deputy director of guided missiles.

"Red" Raborn, a square-jawed, newly made rear admiral, had always been a fighter. Six years after graduation from Annapolis, he became one of the Navy's early carrier pilots. He was a seasoned veteran of the carrier war against the Japanese. He had helped the Navy lead the world in the development of small, tactical air-launched missiles. He was tough. He was smart. He could excite intense loyalty. He could lead. He could see ahead.

Sides personally recommended him.

The Navy concurred: Raborn was the man.

The first that he heard of it was a phone call from Sides. On this Thursday afternoon, Raborn was in his office at Norfolk. Not much later Admiral Burke called. Both men congratulated Raborn and told him that he held the future of the Navy in his hands—perhaps the future of the Free World.

That night Rear Adm. Elton W. Grenfell, special deputy to Admiral Burke, called Raborn at home. He told him to wind up his affairs so that he could be in Washington the next afternoon. Grenfell told him not to plan to go back to Norfolk; his orders were in the mail. Also awaiting him was a letter from the Secretary of the Navy and Burke, granting Raborn extraordinary authority—a grant that became known as Raborn's "hunting license." The letter said, bluntly: "If Rear Admiral Raborn runs into any difficulty with which I can help, I will want to know about it at once, along with his recommended course of action. . . . If he needs more people, those people will be ordered in. If there is anything that slows this project up beyond the capacity of the Navy and the department, we will immediately take it to the highest level and not work our way up through several days."

The next day Raborn was in Washington and Burke personally added the small print: "Anytime it looks as though you're batting your head against a technological wall—if you see the job isn't technically feasible—it will be cut off dead."

# 3    Red Builds a House

The time: 8 A.M. The day: Monday, December 5, 1955.

Commander Hasler met Admiral Raborn at the door. They were in a grubby, prefabricated Navy annex known only as the "W" Building. The occasion: the opening of the new Special Projects Office.

Workaday Washington ignored the event.

The morning papers headlined the merger of the nation's two huge labor organizations, the AFL and CIO. Fans talked about the Washington Redskins pro football team losing to the New York Giants the day before. Some newspaper readers noted that Soviet Boss Nikita Khrushchev had called the British imperialists while making a stop during a trouble-rousing tour of Asia.

Washington and the Republic felt at peace. The temperature hovered pleasantly in the fifties. Christmas was almost at hand. The President had all but recovered from his heart attack.

Just south of the White House in the old Presidential Park, a dozen workmen were erecting the stand for the national Christmas tree. Along F and G Streets store windows displayed expensive clothes, shiny pop-up toasters, and wide-screen television sets decorated with holly. The classic white buildings of the Federal government shone in the winter sunshine. Three seemingly endless lines of automobiles crept across the Potomac River bridges. A hundred thousand civil servants were headed for their round of reports, letters, and forms in triplicate. A few early tourists wandered about the brooding statue in the Lincoln Memorial, which rose like an island in the stream of cars.

Not far from the Lincoln Memorial, the "W" Building stood

hidden just off Constitution Avenue in the concrete back yard of the old Main Navy Building. It was one of the so-called temporary buildings with which Washington abounds. Built during some forgotten emergency for some forgotten reason, it lived on—like many others squatting drably in the Federal City's parks and open areas—another architectural untouchable of the overexpanding bureaucracy.

Like all temporary government buildings, the "W" Building was ugly. It was uncomfortable; it was grimy; it probably was condemnable. But every time someone moved out, someone else who needed office space moved in.

At the time Raborn and Hasler took up residence at the "W" Building, the principal occupant was Rear Adm. Hyman Rickover, developer of the world's first atomic-powered submarine. Six years earlier, as an irascible but brilliant captain, Rickover had begun cultivating atomic power in a former ladies' powder room. Since then his Nuclear Power Division had spread throughout much of the building.

Rickover made it the birthplace of the mighty submarine *Nautilus,* first of the Navy's nuclear-powered fleet of ships. This slight, sad-eyed man had created over the years an engineering elite. Brilliance was enshrined.

Now the man who would unite Rickover's submarine with the long-range ballistic missile had quietly arrived: Raborn—a man with methods and personality very different from Rickover's. Raborn used masterful persuasion. But in the end both would be able to make the same claim: they had done what other men said was impossible.

Raborn was not relegated to a former ladies' rest room that first morning when he stepped into the steamy warmth of the "W" Building. But he didn't fare much better. He drew two cramped rooms near the building's storeroom. From these two rooms Raborn's organization was eventually to move across a parking lot for its headquarters—and across a continent for its operations.

Except for Hasler and some part-time assistants, Raborn had no staff. He had no money. He had no facilities. He had no detailed plans. He was committed to developing a seagoing Jupiter that many in the Navy regarded as the worst fire hazard since sailors stopped cooking over open fires on the decks of wooden sailing ships.

These were only some of the obstacles that first confronted Raborn in the old "W" Building.

The Navy believed that with Jupiter Raborn would be spending millions of dollars at the most—certainly not billions. The total Navy budget was getting smaller and smaller in relation to what it had to do. If anyone had seriously said this new program would absorb from other Navy activities the sums that it eventually did, the program probably would have been killed that December.

The Navy thought the new program could be adequately handled by a staff of a dozen or so officers—a figure that some considered outrageously high. Raborn always sought to keep his organization small, and—compared to other programs of equivalent scope—he succeeded. But the notion that a dozen men could do the job was dismissed within six weeks.

The Navy, with Raborn's agreement, thought the missile could be at sea in about ten years. This was the schedule submitted earlier to the Defense Department and later officially adhered to by the Special Projects Office. But Raborn felt from the day he arrived that he could and had to do the job sooner —much sooner.

Public interest in the program was zero. No one knew it existed.

In the beginning, there was extreme secrecy. The name "Special Projects Office" was chosen as a cover-up. Few officials outside the Navy knew what Raborn was doing. Many in high places in the Navy were equally unaware.

When, in a few months, the Navy did disclose that the Special Projects Office had only one project—the development of a fleet ballistic missile system—there was little stir. Everyone was too busy watching the Army and the Air Force struggle over which would operate the nation's land-based IRBMs. The Navy program was only a sideshow.

As Raborn put it several years later, "You might say we had a small sweet voice singing lightly on one side and two anvil choruses going on the other." He smiled when he said it. But by then he could afford to. In December, 1955, there was little for him to smile about. At least superficially, the future of the fleet ballistic missile program did not appear to be particularly promising.

However, "Red" Raborn had two tremendous advantages. One was his "hunting license." The other was himself.

Raborn talked to Hasler about an hour that first morning in the "W" Building. Then he left for the Pentagon; this was to be his routine for months.

"I want to impress upon everyone what I need and why I need it," he told Hasler when he left. "It's much better to do it this way, to get them enthused about the program, than to go around saying, 'Now, Admiral, under the authority granted me by the Secretary of the Navy and the Chief of Naval Operations, do this.' "

Raborn knew what he was about. The Secretary's letter might be a short cut. But it could be fatal, too. Few things can be more deadly to a program in the Pentagon than unenthusiastic 100 per cent compliance.

And so, like a supersalesman, Raborn began to spin a magic spell along the Pentagon's corridors. He obtained a second office near the Secretary of the Navy's in the Pentagon. Day after day he would stop by the "W" Building and then hurry across the river to pay calls on admirals who could do things for his program.

He always carried the Secretary's letter in his pocket. It became worn and dog-eared. But he seldom had to show it to anyone. Instead, he talked. He persuaded. He charmed. He explained. He was patient.

In the end, he generally got what he wanted and won an ally as well. He would need allies in the years ahead.

"There was a lot of skepticism," he recalled later. "This was a new idea in many ways. Everyone wanted to know how much money it was going to cost. They knew it was going to have to come out of their hides. They wanted to make damn sure I needed every penny."

Scattered around the earth the Navy had a great wealth of technical talent. This is what Naval officers proudly refer to as "in-house capability." Raborn systematically ransacked the Navy's house for the most capable people he could find.

Technical brains were not enough. If he was to succeed, he also needed managers, agile experts at getting things done in Washington. No program, no matter how good, could survive if its directors were strangled by the bureaucratic noose. Raborn proved himself to be a wizard in this treacherous area. But even wizards need help.

For his technical staff, Raborn already had Hasler. Raborn turned over to him the direction of developing the sea-borne Jupiter itself. In less than a month, Hasler was on his way to Huntsville to work with the "Paperclip" rocket experts who were directed by von Braun. Hasler and the former Germans who had first launched rockets from a submarine fourteen years before would now work side by side.

The second man to join Raborn was a civilian financial expert and civil servant of many parts named Edward J. Mernone. The two had met several years before while Raborn was assistant director of guided missiles. At the time he was impressed. Hasler had temporarily borrowed Mernone from the Bureau of Ordnance where Mernone was budget officer of the Research and Development Division. In a matter of weeks, Raborn and Mernone agreed that the loan would be permanent.

By title, Mernone was to become Raborn's director of administration. By occupation, he almost immediately became Raborn's chief trouble-shooter.

Mernone was particularly adept at unwinding red tape. He had been in government service for almost twenty years, first in the Agriculture Department, later in the budget office of the Bureau of Ordnance. He had worked for W. A. Jump, often called "father of the Federal budget." He could steer through the reefs and shoals of the Federal government with the skill of a master navigator.

Raborn next selected Capt. John B. Colwell as his deputy. This was the man that Raborn turned to for help in putting together the rest of his staff. Colwell had served widely in the Navy: at sea, in the Bureau of Ordnance, in the Pentagon. He was particularly gifted in tracking down the best men. At the same time, he served as Raborn's chief of staff and administrative organizer.

These three—Halser, Mernone, and Colwell—became the nucleus of Raborn's organization. Around them he was to create a Navy-Industry team that spread across the continent.

Time was the scarce commodity from the beginning. Raborn knew it, felt it in his heart. If he was going to do what he believed must be done for the security of the country, he somehow had to find a way to do more things in a shorter time than had ever been done before in the development of a modern weapon system.

By the mid-twentieth century, modern weapons had become so complicated that men received medals for developing a new weapon in seven or eight years. Then, if sufficient funds were made available, the new weapon might be produced in quantity and placed in the hands of the troops within another three years. Usually by this time the weapon bordered on being obsolescent. In some almost scandalous cases, it was already obsolete.

A number of American leaders saw the threat posed by this

lengthening time lag. It was a sickness that in the Cold War between Russia and the United States could prove fatal. Russia could develop, in five years, the same weapon that took the United States eight. The Russian secret was autocratic control of industry. The cure for a free society that wished to remain that way seemed elusive.

Raborn faced the problem from the day he walked into the "W" Building. He knew that 1965 was the date set for delivery of sea-borne Jupiters because that was the normal development period for a major weapon. He was determined not only to beat it but to beat it by a lot. In order to do so, he put himself and everyone around him on a wartime footing.

Within weeks the Special Projects Office officially increased its work week from five to five and a half days. Unofficially the work week already was six and seven days plus nights. There were no coffee breaks. There were no idle chats. Each day began at eight o'clock in the morning. Many ended the following morning.

"None of this five-day-week stuff," Raborn said. "None of this 'we'll get it done after we have our golf game.' With that kind of effort you can drag out any program."

He set the pace. He also told everyone around him why he was setting it. He had a fighter's acute sense of the Soviet threat. He let no man forget it.

"Put your hand on the back of your neck," he began telling skeptics. "All right. You feel it? That's your neck. Well, that's what we're trying to save. That's what this program is all about."

The Special Projects Office never became a place where people went to work in the morning to pass the hours until supper. From the start it was an engulfing vocation, a force, a labor of patriotism and love into which each addition to the staff hurled himself, caring for little else.

They came to Raborn from around the earth. Raborn and Colwell surveyed the Navy. They studied the Navy Register.

They made lists, circled names, crossed out others. Raborn knew many missilemen from his days as Sides' deputy. Colwell, although no missileman himself, also knew many and knew how to find more. If he didn't know whom to get, he and Raborn knew whom to ask. The problem was to make the right choices the first time. There was no time for error. The Special Projects Office couldn't afford dead wood.

As soon as Raborn approved a name, Colwell asked the Navy to reassign the officer immediately. The orders chattered on teletypes around the world from the Pentagon. No arguments from angry admirals losing their best men had any effect. All protests were silenced by the Secretary's letter. What Raborn wanted, he got.

Levering Smith, the expert in solid propellants and the builder of Big Stoop and other missiles, was now a captain in charge of Navy missile test programs in the New Mexican desert at the White Sands test range. He was detached. Raborn needed him to head the Special Projects propulsion branch.

Capt. Frank B. Herold, an electronics expert, had been ordered to report to a new post at the Naval Research Laboratory. The order was canceled. Raborn wanted him to head the Special Projects fire control and guidance branch.

Comdr. Roderick Middleton, a missile expert, was commander of the destroyer *Benham*. He was detached. Raborn wanted him to assist Hasler at Huntsville.

Comdr. Dennett "Deke" Ela, an expert marine engineer, was deputy chief of the development division at one of the nation's secret nuclear warhead centers. He was detached. Raborn wanted him to head the Special Projects launching branch.

One officer was ordered to halt his studies at the Industrial War College because Raborn wanted him. Such a transfer was previously considered inconceivable.

Other officers came from Pearl Harbor, from ships at sea. Raborn had only to ask.

Obtaining the civilians he wanted and getting them quickly

was not as easy. The red tape of the Civil Service Act stood in Raborn's way.

The Navy can take a Navy man from the other side of the earth and put him in a new job in a new organization in Washington in the time that it takes a plane to cover the distance. Not so the Civil Service. For the Civil Service, such a transfer would be impossible even in the unlikely event that everyone favored it.

John Jones, civil servant, may want to transfer from his present post to another that has been offered him in a new agency. His present agency may raise no objection. The transfer may be most desirable for the national welfare. But, under the law, first comes paper work; and then, usually months later, comes action.

The Civil Service Act forbids the hiring of a man for a government post until the job has been described in detail on an official form and classified in relation to the Federal pay scale. Every job must fit into a slot somewhere on the Civil Service ladder. Each slot pays so much. Not just anyone can do this classifying of what other people are expected to do. This work is done by professionals from the Civil Service Commission. They are called job description writers. Speed is not something for which they are noted.

Since the Special Projects Office was a new organization, all its civilian posts had to be properly described and classified. Normally this process would take months. A half-year delay in completing the staff loomed ahead. Scientists, secretaries, file clerks, dozens of people Raborn needed immediately could not be hired immediately.

Mernone solved the problem. He obtained two job description writers from their natural habitat at the Departmental Civilian Personnel Division and brought them into the electric atmosphere of the Special Projects Office. He gave them desks. He told them precisely what Raborn wanted done. Other

Special Projects officials provided the description writers with additional information. Veteran government administrators gasped at the results. The job was completed in two weeks.

"They turned out a job description every two hours," Mernone reported, grinning. "Absolutely unheard-of."

"Nothing like a full day's work," Raborn said.

With the job descriptions in hand, he recruited the civilians he needed. Most were veteran civil servants from the Bureau of Ordnance and other Navy agencies. A few came from outside the government.

Some ten weeks after he arrived, Raborn had his basic staff. It included more than fifty people.

Even as the staff assembled, Raborn and his growing team of top assistants swiftly began to outline the major problems that would have to be solved to adapt Jupiter to the sea. This process could easily have taken a year under normal circumstances. And if it had, few in the government would have raised an objection. But it didn't take a year, it took only weeks. The reason again was Raborn.

His staff laid before him what had to be done, what the alternatives were, what was possible and barely possible. He, in turn, showed a remarkable facility for absorbing this information and finding the critical obstacles that had to be overcome. He showed an even more remarkable facility for being able to make up his mind rapidly and announce decisions that proved to be good ones.

Raborn gave his staff enormous responsibility and the authority to exercise it. Junior officers—as Raborn put it, "some of my kids"—had more authority than they would have had anywhere else in the Navy. At the same time, Raborn put great trust not only in the capabilities of his staff to cope with the problems confronting them but also to report the truth about them no matter how painful it might be. Failure to report the truth was the most heinous crime that could be committed.

As a result, Raborn felt that he could almost always act immediately on the information given him. There was no need for more studies, outside expert opinions, or the many other temporizations of the uncertain. Raborn could and did make the decisions needed without delay. As the clock ticked on, he felt he could do nothing else.

Raborn's attitude energized everyone. All were aware that if the problems they faced were to be overcome with any speed, the customary way of doing things would have to go. Originality and initiative were needed. Every short cut that could be found had to be taken.

Communications—telling each other what is being done and what help is needed—is the bane of organizations. In the Pentagon, weeks can go by while the simplest memo requesting information is passed from desk to desk and then occasionally lost.

In the early days of the Special Projects Office, memos within the organization were unnecessary. All a man had to do was raise his voice. Important communications to other parts of the government were "hot handed"—a messenger or the sender himself would deliver the communication in person and bring back the answer. Later, when the Special Projects Office had expanded beyond a few rooms, communications were "hot handed" inside the organization as well.

Raborn worked closely with his staff. Colwell and Mernone spent hours with him in his office during the first months. And each Saturday, Raborn met with all his top staff members to review what had been done during the week and discuss what would be done during the next.

The Special Projects Office quickly found that its pace was too fast for the other offices in the Navy on which it had to call for assistance. Legal services, contract negotiators, budget people, and other experts were needed intermittently. But every time Raborn sought outside help, he lost time. People a block away couldn't be used without a bottleneck's developing.

The experiment with the job description writers was repeated. The needed experts were physically removed from their agencies and brought into the Special Projects Office. The result was dramatic. They quickly began to think like the rest of the staff. They felt that they were part of a vital program. Papers that normally would not be processed for weeks now were processed in days.

In one area alone—the processing of plans for the construction of facilities such as test stands and laboratories—months were saved.

The whole business of building facilities is a very touchy one in Washington. Everyone is interested. Few matters are closer to a congressman's heart than the building of anything anywhere. If it is being built in his district, that means votes. If it is being built in someone else's district, that means he'd better have something coming. For similar reasons, the administration is just as interested as Congress. The result is that plans to build any kind of facility must be seen by many people. In Washington the construction of a doghouse can get more attention than the assassination of a premier.

Of course, all this attention takes time—lots of time. But the Special Projects Office didn't have that kind of time. Therefore, a small group of Navy facility experts was brought into the office, thoroughly indoctrinated, and put to work. As usual, the results were amazing. They performed bureaucratic miracles.

The group's carefully but rapidly prepared proposals were "hot handed" along the tortuous route that they had to follow. From the Bureau of Yards and Docks they went to the Office of Naval Materiel. From the Office of Naval Materiel they went to the Office of the Secretary of the Navy. Each office knew in advance what was coming. At each office a representative from Raborn stood by to answer any questions immediately. No memos were needed.

The Special Projects Office engineered approval of two of its largest facilities in one day by this method. Normally, it would have taken three months.

In the spring of 1956, the Special Projects Office faced two internal problems. The first involved management. Something or someone was needed to give Raborn the means of keeping his increasingly complex program from bogging down. The second involved housing. The staff had grown too large for the few additional rooms that were available in the "W" Building.

Mernone proposed that the first problem be solved by bringing in a brilliant management expert under whom he had worked several years before in the Bureau of Ordnance. The man was Gordon O. Pehrson, then deputy director of financial operations for Army logistics in the Pentagon.

"He is outstanding," Mernone said. "A really top guy."

"Okay. Get him," Raborn said.

"Well, it won't be easy. He is presently a super grade. We'll have to get a special job-description paper written. It may be complicated."

"Get him anyway."

Mernone called Pehrson at home that night. Pehrson expressed interest in the job and called on Raborn. Six weeks later he moved into the Special Projects Office as Raborn's director of plans and programs.

Meantime, Mernone busied himself with arrangements for moving Raborn's organization into larger quarters. A considerable amount of space had been allotted to Raborn on the third floor of the crumbling old Munitions Building that flanks Main Navy on Constitution Avenue. Much of the area during World War I had been occupied by Yeomanettes—forerunners of the Waves. But now, except for a few isolated offices of the Veterans Administration, the area was an unoccupied, dirt-caked cavern.

Mernone directed the planning of the new headquarters.

Unlike the "W" Building and offices in the Bureau of Ordnance, the rooms were designed to be as comfortable and psychologically appealing as possible. Rugs were laid on most of the floors. Walls were painted soft colors. Pictures were hung. By contrast, the offices at the Bureau of Ordnance looked like a nineteenth-century sweatshop.

The center of Mernone's plan was a large suite of rooms. This was to be Raborn's Management Center. Here charts showing the status and future plans of the fleet ballistic missile system could be kept on display. Here Raborn could hold his Saturday meetings and direct his program. Pehrson called it "a work room—not an ivory-tower board room where people come out once a month with long faces and big decisions." Raborn regarded it as a room where his staff and industry representatives could see at any time how their efforts fitted into the over-all plan.

This relationship of men to the program was always one of Raborn's pet themes. Men ran the program. Men always worked better if they understood how their efforts contributed to large goals. Raborn's Management Center was designed to keep those goals always in sight.

"Some like to call it the program countdown room," Pehrson said.

Mernone took particular care in designing the Center. He visited staff centers set up by the Army at Huntsville and the Air Force at the Ballistic Missile Division in Inglewood, California. He felt both were more like board rooms; neither was what Raborn wanted.

The Management Center that finally was built was a room within a room. A heavy steel door with a combination lock led from the hall into a reception room guarded by a noncommissioned officer. The reception area surrounded the actual Management Center on two sides, giving the noncommissioned officer access to a projection booth for showing films and slides to people inside the Center. The entrance to the Center itself was through a second steel door that also had a combination lock.

Inside was a long, narrow room with ninety chairs in fifteen rows, divided by a center aisle. Raborn's chair, the only one bearing a name, was in the front row on the right side of the aisle. The walls were soundproofed and partly paneled in plywood that had been stained a light brown. A thick beige rug covered the floor.

At the front, a four-foot-square glass movie screen partly covered the wall. Below it hung a green chalk-board. A lectern stood to the left.

All around the room on the other three walls hung large charts stamped "Secret." They showed the progress of the program as of any particular day. Here was some of the nation's most closely guarded military information.

This was the room that became Raborn's attack center.

The new offices were ready that June. On a hot Friday afternoon at the "W" Building the staff packed for the move, locked the safes, and made last-minute checks. Then Raborn declared a holiday. The job of transferring everything from one building to the other was left to movers and a staff member appointed by Mernone.

Mernone himself spent his first Saturday off in six months yacht-racing on Chesapeake Bay. Raborn spent the holiday working at his office in the Pentagon.

On Monday the staff reported to the new headquarters, and the push for the fleet ballistic missile continued unabated.

# 4    Life with a Monster

"I don't care how big and ornery it is, we're going to take the bastard to sea."

Raborn's words still ricocheted through Bill Hasler's mind as he drove his '46 Chevvy into the dreary town of Huntsville. The long drive down from Washington through the flat tobacco country had given the forty-year-old missile engineer an opportunity to reflect on how he had been catapulted into this new turning and what lay ahead. The last thing Hasler had thought he would be doing, even two months ago, was heading for Alabama and teaming up with the Army. The ways of the Navy were often inexplicable.

It was a relief, though, to get away from Washington. The past two months had been a wild series of crises, most of which were dumped into his lap.

Raborn had moved like a man possessed, firing off orders for men to join Special Projects, and frequently neglecting—until too late—to tell Hasler about what he had done. The first Hasler would learn that Raborn had "kidnaped" another expert for his staff would be when he answered the telephone and there was a sputtering-mad admiral on the other end of the line.

It got so that Hasler hated to pick up the phone. Raborn was off roaming the Pentagon. It was left to Hasler, only a senior commander, which is pretty far down in the Navy hierarchy, to explain why one of the caller's best men had been transferred on forty-eight-hour notice. Most of the time Hasler didn't know who the man was, or why Raborn wanted him. What made these conversations even more trying was that practically no one had heard of SP or knew what it was about.

Hasler was greatly relieved when Colwell "came aboard." He was much better at arguing with admirals—he had the rank.

Although Hasler had been instrumental in drawing up the plans for the Special Projects Office, working under Adm. "Savvy" Sides, Hasler had no idea he was to be its first employee. As Defense Secretary Wilson moved ponderously closer to a decision on the Navy's ballistic missile, Hasler was dreaming of leaving Washington for Spain. One prospective assignment at the Navy shipyard in San Francisco, the city where his wife had been raised, disappointingly was no longer possible because he was about to be made captain, a rank too high for the job. Next the chance presented itself for him to open some ordnance bases in Spain. He had the job and was ready to go. Then he was abruptly ordered into SP.

Bill Hasler, who like Raborn had red hair, but whose pate was beginning to show, began learning the art of missilery in 1947 at the Navy's experimental station at Inyokern, California. In those days, he became engaged in research on high-speed propulsion systems, including rocket motors, for torpedoes. Later he moved to a new testing site on San Clemente Island, 65 miles off San Diego in the Pacific, and worked on air-launched torpedoes, air-to-water rockets, and underwater rockets.

Hasler was a bright star. The Navy's Bureau of Ordnance moved him in 1952 to Washington and put him in the missile branch of its research division. There Hasler devoted his energies to the new Talos and Terrier anti-aircraft missiles and to the fearsome little Sidewinder, the missile that destroys fighter planes by flying up their jet tailpipes.

Then came the fleet ballistic missile. . . .

Hasler's destination in the Deep South was the Army's Redstone Arsenal in the low hills outside Huntsville. The arsenal had been hurriedly constructed during World War II to manufacture artillery shells. Now it was the thriving center of all Army missile activity.

The arsenal had been left to decay after the war. But it surged back to life in 1950 when the Army decided to bring its former German rocket scientists there to staff the Army Ballistic Missile Agency. Redstone's large factory buildings were ideal for all the laboratories, the offices, machine shops, and the fantastic assortment of electronic testing gear that had become the necessary accouterment of the new missile technology. Rockets could be assembled here. Their giant motors could be fired on special stands in the hills.

New buildings were being erected and others enlarged among the rows of temporary barracks still standing from the war, when Hasler arrived. Experts and officials bustled everywhere. Off in the hills, rocket motors thundered and whined, their flames splashing red reflections in the night sky.

For the Navy, the journey to Huntsville was full of irony. At the arsenal were the same men who so many years before had fired the first ballistic missiles from a submarine off Peenemünde. Now they were still land-bound, devoting their skills to providing the Army's ground troops with combat missiles. It would be Hasler and his fellow officers who would carry forward the early German work on a seagoing missile. Most ironic of all, Hasler was supposed to use the former German scientists' creation—the Jupiter—to do it.

The Jupiter in early 1956 still existed only on paper. This big missile was a grown-up version of the Redstone missile, which in turn was a direct descendant of the old V-2. The Redstone was then almost fully developed. It was "hardware," in existence. Much to the joy of Army missilemen, it was already flying distances up to 200 miles.

Officially—and purposely—the Army was vague as to the mission for Jupiter. There were pronouncements to the effect that it was to be a long-range tactical weapon to support the operations of ground troops. Air Force officers, however, needed only one glance at its 1,500-mile range to know that it was a challenge to SAC's strategic bombing mission.

While circumspect about what it would do with Jupiter once it was built, the Army also had something else in mind. Dr. Wernher von Braun regarded the Jupiter as a vehicle for thrusting satellites into orbit around the earth as well as a weapon.

Army missilemen and leaders were infected by von Braun's ideas and his awesome determination to conquer space. They had already suffered one bitter disappointment. Two years before, von Braun had provided much of the inspiration and knowledge for a serious plan to place a satellite in orbit. In 1954 it became known as Project Orbiter. Von Braun conceived a multistage vehicle with a Redstone as the first-stage booster. The other stages were clusters of small solid-fueled rockets, which would achieve orbital velocity—18,000 miles an hour—for a tiny satellite carried on top.

Orbiter would have been scheduled to make its first flight in the summer of 1957. But the indifferent Eisenhower administration ignored it. Then Orbiter was shoved aside permanently the following year, when Eisenhower approved a "civilian" satellite program proposed by the National Science Foundation and supported by the Navy. This was the ill-fated Project Vanguard.

Von Braun's own frustrated ambitions enabled him to sympathize with the Navy in its painful pursuit of a seagoing ballistic missile. The handsome, stern-faced scientist had made space exploration a goal as a student in Germany, when he had enthusiastically joined the *Verein für Raumschiffahrt* (Society for Space Travel) in 1930. No one was interested in spacemen in those days, either. But the German Army had a place for a brilliant young rocket scientist.

The Treaty of Versailles after World War I stripped the German Army to a skeleton force and prohibited it from developing specific weapons such as long-range artillery and warplanes. However, the treaty made no mention of rockets. Von

Braun was taken into Army service as a civilian scientist and put to work under Capt. Walter Dornberger, before he became commander of the Peenemünde rocket development center.

In those days, and later as he worked on the V-2 during World War II, von Braun had continued to study and investigate scientific requirements for space travel. Brought to the United States under Operation Paperclip after surrendering to the American Army in 1945, von Braun found himself still working on missiles, but with more latitude for his astronautical interests. He published several papers on space travel, among them a 1952 technical treatise detailing an expedition to Mars.

Hasler's appearance at Huntsville posed a threat to the Army's ambitious plans for the Jupiter. The Navy wanted to make the missile shorter. Such a reduction—necessitating a slowdown—jeopardized the Army's position in the race with the Air Force for control of the military missile program. The Army's strategy for winning out over the Air Force was based upon producing a 1,500-mile-range Jupiter in 1958—well before the Air Force could perfect its intercontinental Atlas. A successful Jupiter IRBM then could be increased in size to become a 5,000-mile—or more—ICBM.

Many missilemen in and out of the Army were convinced the Air Force would fail, anyway. Without much substantial experience with missiles, the Air Force was attempting to start by building a missile more than twice the size of the Jupiter. This was a mistake in the opinion of more conservative experts. They believed missile sizes should increase in relatively modest jumps, with every increment predicated upon known technology; there should be a logical progression of the "art." Von Braun became, rather than an exponent, a captive of this philosophy—mostly because there was no one in the Army in 1955 who could sell the administration on a reason why the Army should start building a huge rocket with one million pounds of thrust—a project von Braun thought possible.

All the people in the various services actually working on missile projects were approaching the problem of constructing large missiles as scientists and engineers. They were feeling their way. Their viewpoints differed, for a variety of reasons—mostly in their approaches. But all were based upon honest convictions. The Army sincerely believed its step-by-step approach, engineered by the former German rocket team at Huntsville, would benefit the country most. The Air Force, with possibly a more unfettered way of thinking, was equally convinced that the big leap directly to an ICBM was best to counter Russia's missile lead in the shortest possible time. The Navy's concern over a seagoing ballistic missile sprang from a similar basic conviction.

The missilemen from each service regarded what they were doing—and the way they were doing it—as being of the utmost importance to their country. However, in widely publicized "interservice rivalries," which broke out later over missiles, this point was largely obscured. Rivalries existed, certainly, but at a level far removed from the men at drawing boards and those who got their hands dirty. Most of the battles the public heard about exploded at high levels and resulted to a great extent from the shortage of money and from indecision upon the part of policy makers.

The scarcity of knowledge in these early days of the nation's struggle to arm itself with missiles established a common bond among all missilemen. Never was this demonstrated better than at Huntsville. Much as they may have hated Wilson's pushing the Navy into their bed, the Army and the former German scientific team displayed no rancor toward Hasler and the members of the small team that joined him a few weeks later. On the contrary, they opened up their laboratories, their secrets, and their minds to the Navy's problems. Hasler and his men worked shoulder to shoulder with the von Braun group.

"I know it's hard to believe," Hasler later told a friend in Special Projects, "but the Army men and the Germans really accepted us as members of their team.

"Von Braun looked at the Jupiter as strictly an engineering evolution, a bigger Redstone. Now, what the Navy wanted was something really different. It became a real challenge to him and his team. They got so interested, they began spending more time on the Navy problems than their own."

Hasler found this enthusiasm a little difficult to cope with at times. On arriving at Huntsville on February 1, 1956, he was assigned an office next to Maj. Gen. John B. Medaris, commander of the Army Ballistic Missile Agency for which the von Braun team worked. Medaris, while all for co-operation, had to get a land-based Jupiter built, too. He took a dark view of having the attention of his engineering force pre-empted.

But von Braun's men were not easily contained. If some problem of underwater launching of missiles was brought up in casual conversation, the next day Hasler would find a dozen people working on various solutions. It was a two-way street, however. Though they were delaying the Jupiter program by forcing changes in its dimensions, the Navy men felt some of their ideas also helped the Army.

The Jupiter was to be mobile on land. The Navy wanted to shorten the missile from 65 feet to 55 feet, so that it could be put on a ship. This made it easier to load the big bird aboard a truck trailer and to erect it for firing. The Jupiter, to compensate for the loss in height, was also to be made fatter, expanding in diameter from 95 to 105 inches. The Navy wanted the missile free of fins on the outside. This led the Army into the design of engine nozzles that swiveled to control the missile in flight. This type of control later was deemed preferable to the original fin controls, which were useless once the missile left the atmosphere for the part of its flight that passed through airless space.

Summer descended, laying a steaming dishrag over the dusty hills. It was evening, and a baby whined with discomfort. Barbara Hasler lay on a couch in her tiny house, exhausted by the

stifling heat, listening to her son's cries. She had tried everything to make him comfortable, but he would not stop. She
waited resignedly for sleep to silence him.

The crying rasped into the thoughts of Bill Hasler, trying to
do some work at his desk. He got up, noticed unhappily that
the thermometer registered 105° in the house, and walked outside. The temperature had been over 100° for days. Hasler
ambled across the street to another tiny house just like his and
found Rod Middleton, his thirty-seven-year-old deputy, slouched
in a deck chair on the lawn, sipping a can of beer.

Middleton offered his boss a beer. Then the two fell into a
quiet discussion of a fuel tankage problem that had come up
during the day.

A half hour later their conversation was interrupted by the
headlights of a car coming down the street. The car, a flaming-
red Jaguar coupé, slowed and came to a halt in front of Hasler's house. An impeccably dressed officer clambered out. A carefully clipped mustache was discernible in the fading light.
Stars glinted on the shoulders of the starched summer uniform.

"Damn," muttered Hasler. "It's Medaris. He's paying a call—
on me!"

Glancing down at his own rumpled off-duty clothes, Hasler
almost took a walk around the block. Then he thought of his
wife—and what she might say to him later. He walked across
the street and shook Medaris's hand instead, with the air of a
man wearing evening clothes.

The next day he organized an alert system. From then on,
whenever the red Jaguar was sighted, phones rang all over the
Redstone area.

"If we can build a missile, we can lick this," Hasler told his
fellow officers.

Holding the same kind of open "hunting license" as Raborn,
Hasler built up a staff of twenty at Redstone. It included eleven
civilian engineers. One problem that soon became apparent was

a complete lack of training facilities for enlisted technicians who would be needed to maintain and fire the Jupiter from aboard ship.

Hasler succeeded in talking von Braun into allowing some technicians into the labs, although there was much debate over whether they would get in the way. The Navy contingent grew larger.

Everyone quickly fell into a routine revolving entirely around work. There was a clock running in Huntsville, too. Raborn and Hasler didn't let anyone forget it.

Every inch of progress was reported to Special Projects. Daily Raborn was on the telephone, inquiring, advising, complimenting. There was a continual procession of visitors from the Pentagon's special Army-Navy Ballistic Missile Committee, which was watching over the change in Jupiter's dimensions.

Gradually the big warbird took on a shorter and fatter shape. SP was moving.

Reports of the successful test firings of the high-powered solid fuel developed by Rumbel and Henderson of Atlantic Research reached Raborn's desk in Washington in late January. The firings were conducted in the Civil War skirmishing country at Gainesville, Virginia, where the company had a 500-acre reservation. Simultaneously, the findings were dispatched to the Sacramento, California, plant of Aerojet-General Corporation and into the hands of Aerojet's Dr. Werner Kirchner, a World War II Polish aviator turned research scientist.

Raborn realized immediately what this breakthrough could mean to the Navy's dying hopes for a solid-fueled fleet ballistic missile. This was what everyone had been looking for—proof; confirmation of what Navy scientists had expected would come from intensive research. There was one step more to be taken before the Navy could sue for divorce from the Army's Jupiter. Rumbel's and Henderson's new fuel had been tested in only small quantities. Now it must be produced in large quantities and made to burn with the same efficiency. This was Kirschner's job at Aerojet.

Meanwhile, with considerable prescience, the Navy quietly placed a contract with Lockheed Aircraft to study the problem of thrust termination—how to make a solid-fuel rocket stop moving at the exact moment it is desired.

Cutting off thrust was one of the nagging technical questions that had helped make it easier for Defense Secretary Wilson to divert the Navy into the Jupiter program. Duration of thrust must be controlled precisely if a ballistic missile is to hit a target. With a liquid-fueled rocket, the problem is easily solved. A timing· device merely closes valves, shutting off the flow of LOX and fuel. But a solid-fuel motor is a single piece of combustible material that can't be doused even if dropped in a lake. There had to be an entirely different approach. And in early 1956, no satisfactory one had yet been found. This obstacle had to be cleared before Raborn could move to a solid-fuel missile.

Conversion of the Jupiter proceeded grimly. To help his engineers grapple with the realities of the job, Raborn ordered more tests similar to Operation Pushover. Valuable new data were obtained, which could be used in determining ways to deal with the dangers of liquid oxygen aboard ship. More than anything else, however, these tests provided fresh evidence of the horrifying risks involved in launching liquid-fueled rockets at sea. Raborn put it bluntly:

"We are taking our chances with disaster—one little accident or spillage and the whole ship goes."

Almost complete responsibility for minimizing the catastrophic dangers rested with "Deke" Ela, Raborn's quick-witted branch head in charge of launching, and Ela's deputy, Comdr. George Halverson. Captain Ela, working at Special Projects in Washington, and his group of engineers looked at the launch problem from every conceivable angle. They made drawings. Built models. At endless conferences and meetings in Ela's corner office in the back of the Munitions Building, they stood in front of a large chalk-board on the wall, arguing, debating, scratching diagrams. Every hour was haunted with one thought: safety.

Ela could only envy the relatively simple safety problem involved in a rocket launch on land. There is no danger whatever until fueling commences. This elaborate ritual, performed by specialists garbed in weird rubber suits with special devices to eliminate static electricity, takes place shortly before the final countdown. Only the fueling crew is present on the launch pad when the trucks of liquid oxygen and fuel are driven up to the missile. Everyone else connected with the launch is in an air-conditioned blockhouse a quarter of a mile away, protected by fifteen feet of concrete, steel, and earth. Once the missile's tanks are full, the fueling crew also retires from the scene.

Such safety in distance was impossible aboard a ship. The farthest one could get from the missile at sea would be 200 feet.

One by one the approaches were considered and then discarded by Ela and his men.

The most intriguing idea involved catapulting the Jupiter off a ship like a plane. Here was a way of getting distance. But there was one characteristic of the missile that limited this virtue. The engine in the first stage of the Jupiter needed a few seconds to work up enough thrust to lift the missile into the air. While this was happening, the Army planned on keeping the missile locked to the launch stand. If for some reason the engine failed to generate enough power in these few critical moments, it could still be shut down and the missile saved.

Ela's catapult idea entailed the ignition of the missile after it had cleared the ship. "If there were a failure in ignition," he said, "then we'll just have a big splash." But the idea still seemed attractive. And the Naval Air Engineering Facility at Philadelphia, which specialized in catapult work, was asked to look into it further.

"We didn't like the idea of starting the thing burning aboard ship," the pipe-smoking former mountain boy has commented in retrospect, and with casual understatement. "If for some reason we had to hold fire, or the launch failed, then we would be sitting there with a fairly hot object clamped to the deck. Yes, sir, fairly hot."

Ultimately, however, they had to contend with a hot launch from shipboard. Studies of the catapult scheme showed it to be too unreliable and to contain too many engineering problems to perfect even in the ten-year time period allowed. Similar studies also showed the old idea of Walter Dornberger's—to fire the missiles from special capsules towed by submarines—to be impractical.

Jupiter had another failing. It could be fueled only in an upright position. The delicacy of its complex insides—the valves, piping, and other fittings—could not withstand the stresses created in raising the missile while its tanks were loaded.

Vertical fueling was unquestionably the most desirable procedure on land. But rigged on the deck of a wave-tossed ship it presented an enormous safety problem. Even if the missile were reduced in size to a 55-foot length, it still would wave frantically back and forth with every pitch and roll of the vessel like a giant wand.

One answer was to find a way to stabilize the ship. Ela's engineers came up with two paddle-shaped pieces of steel plate, which would be attached to either side of the missile ship just below the waterline. The British had used these fins previously on channel steamers. Called "fin stabilizers," they would minimize the roll from side to side in much the same way a fish balances itself. To counteract the pitching motion from end to end of the vessel, they proposed welding a V-shaped steel cup around the bow, well below the water line.

In the summer of 1956, Special Projects acquired two merchant ships of the 17,600-ton Mariner class. Fin stabilizers were added to the hulls of both of them, and to one—renamed the *Compass Island*—the antipitch device was attached. The fin stabilizers worked well. But the big steel cup created so much turbulence that it shook the ship, and in a rough sea some thought the ship was about to break in half.

Stuck as they were with a launching from an open deck, Ela and his crew realized that it would be senseless to design a system that involved fueling the missile while it was "sitting on its tail waving in the breeze." There was no recourse but to store the missile in an upright position below decks and to fuel it there. This meant they would have to design and build an extremely complicated elevator to raise the missile to top-deck level for launching. It also meant more problems in handling liquid oxygen.

There was one factor running in their favor. The Navy knew a great deal about elevators, as well as catapults. There had been elevators aboard aircraft carriers for decades, to move planes between the flight deck and the hangar deck below.

The elevator system had the decided advantage of leaving the missile above decks the shortest possible time before launching. Even so, veteran seafarers shook their heads at the thought of what might happen if a launching were attempted in a moderately rough sea or gale winds. They could visualize the thing toppling over. The tanks would crack, spilling liquid oxygen down into the hold. The ship would turn into a floating bomb and explode the instant the LOX evaporated into gas and came into contact with a spark or open flame.

Elaborate safety precautions were dreamed up by Ela's engineers. Their major concern, however, was loading the LOX aboard the missile while it was below decks. The LOX was to be kept in a huge Dewar vessel, which is akin to a vacuum thermos bottle. The vessel would hold 30,000 gallons of the supercold liquid gas at a temperature of nearly $-300°$ Fahrenheit.

In itself, the storage vessel was not too dangerous, unless it were broken accidentally. The hazard lay in the actual pumping of the LOX into the missile. There was a danger of spillage. Moreover, if a stoppage or break occurred somewhere inside the missile, it might be necessary to exhaust the LOX from its tanks while the missile was still in the hold.

Operation Pushover had proved all too vividly that LOX could crack thick steel plate like a cooky. Unless there were something protecting the bottom, a stream of LOX would cut right through it, sinking the ship.

Ela's hard-working group thought of a solution to this problem, too. The bottom of the ship under the missile section could be tiled like a shower stall. The LOX would not affect the ceramic tile, and huge exhaust fans in the bulkheads would suck out the fumes in seconds, to keep them from gathering in explosive concentrations.

"It won't be the safest thing afloat. We know that," Ela said. "But we're pretty damn sure it will work—and that's all that counts."

No one in the Navy would have been surprised if it had taken Ela and SP a year or two to conjure up this scheme. For one thing, there was no "hardware" to design from. The Jupiter was still on the drawing boards. In that day it still would have been "normal procedure" to wait, for example, until an airplane had been delivered to the Navy, before setting about designing a catapult for it. Ela himself had been involved, just before coming to SP, in converting cruisers to carry the Navy's Terrier and Talos antiaircraft missiles. The conversions had been ordered *after* the missiles were almost completed. However, now Ela and everyone else in SP were working at top speed simultaneously.

Raborn's timetable depended largely on when a seagoing launch system could be devised. This was a most important part of the entire project, and the responsibility rested wholly upon Ela's muscular shoulders. There were so many unknowns he was working with—the size of the missile, the exact procedure for fueling it, testing it aboard ship, and many others—it can only be called an engineering miracle that Ela and his men produced a launching design in less than three months.

The plans were speedily approved by Raborn, and a contract

was let immediately to the Westinghouse Electric Corporation's elevator division to build it. And with the launching system on paper, the entire scheme for putting Jupiter to sea took shape. Raborn's team decided to install three Jupiters to a ship. The first was to be the Mariner-class merchant vessel, the *Observation Island*. Again because of the limitation on funds, there were to be just three fleet ballistic missile ships outfitted initially. But this was only the beginning.

The decision to start with surface ships first was influenced by time as well as money. It would be much faster and simpler to convert existing vessels than to build them specially. These missile ships would be slow and vulnerable to enemy submarines, but at least they were a start, and something to bolster the spirits of the SP team when they looked at the job of marrying Jupiter to a submarine.

The world's first nuclear-powered submarine, the *Nautilus,* had been at sea for nearly a year when Raborn organized Special Projects. Since steaming away from the Electric Boat Division dock at Groton, Connecticut, on January 17, 1955, for the first time under nuclear power, the *Nautilus* had demonstrated her great speed and, more important, an ability to stay submerged for long periods of time. Her atomic-reactor-driven steam turbine needed no air. She had no large batteries, which forced conventional submarines to surface for recharging; she did not need a snorkel. The nuclear-powered submarine would be an ideal missile base.

However, size was a problem. The *Nautilus* was 320 feet long and 28 feet in diameter and weighed 3,300 tons—large for a submarine, but not when a shortened 55-foot Jupiter IRBM was stood up alongside. She was much too small.

Obviously the submarine had to be made bigger. Ela's launching branch, shaving every corner possible, designed what it felt would be a minimum-sized sub that would hold a total of four Jupiters. The missile sub would weigh more than 8,000 tons—the displacement of a cruiser.

A still larger sub would be needed for what was planned next. Toward the end of 1956 the SP team at Huntsville collaborated in the design of a solid-fueled Jupiter. It was a cluster of rockets that, because of the low power of the fuel, turned out to be an even bigger monster. If it had been built, the Jupiter-S would have weighed around 160,000 pounds. The liquid-fueled version was bad enough, weighing 110,000 pounds.

One Special Projects officer, looking at the Jupiter-S design, shook his head, saying, "It looks like it might be easier to leave the missile and launch the submarine."

The submarine had one other drawback. It still would have to surface to launch its missiles.

Taken as a piece, the seagoing Jupiter was a fantastic series of compromises. But it was a system all the same. A workable system. And by the fall of 1956 Hasler and his team at Huntsville already saw the end of the line.

In two years—1959, not 1965—they felt the first Jupiters would be sent to sea. America would have a new first line of defense.

# 5   Birth of a Missile

Fall, 1956 . . .

Soviet tanks rumbled over the Hungarian countryside toward Budapest. The shadows of British bombers skimmed across the Egyptian desert. Units of the American Sixth Fleet in the Mediterranean deployed for battle. The Russians spoke of loosing a rain of missiles on London and Paris. The rattle of arms could be heard around the earth. World War III again seemed near.

At the height of the crisis, President Eisenhower, ailing but as popular a military hero as ever, rode back into the White House for a second term on one of the greatest outpourings of votes in history. Worried Americans turned again to the conqueror of Hitler to save the peace. By Christmas, the crisis began to disappear. The Anglo-French expedition to the Middle East failed for lack of American support. Hungary's "Freedom Fighters," for lack of American support, lay crushed beneath the tank treads of the Red Army.

The stores on F Street in Washington and Market Street in San Francisco sparkled anew with tinsel and American abundance. Most Americans, as they decorated their Christmas trees, had already turned to the more immediate concerns of their personal lives. If the Soviet talk of missiles was remembered at all, it was generally discounted as typical Russian boasting. Few Americans believed the Russians could have ballistic missiles armed with nuclear warheads with which they could obliterate London and Paris. The United States didn't. And what American know-how—the same American know-how that had won World War II—hadn't done, no one could do, certainly not the backward Russians.

However, not all Americans brushed aside the early Soviet missile threat. One of those whose sleep it troubled was Raborn. There was good reason for it to bother him particularly at this time. He faced one of the biggest decisions of his life.

Since March, Navy and Lockheed scientists and engineers had been conducting studies exploring the possibility of developing a solid-fuel-propelled IRBM that would be much smaller than the huge Jupiter. At the same time, the team at Aerojet had been developing the new solid propellant for the even bigger Jupiter-S.

Nor was this all.

Capt. Levering Smith, the solid-propellant expert, had directed NOTS—the Navy Ordnance Test Station at Inyokern, California—to make another study, a study that eventually proved to be crucial. Originally the NOTS group was directed to investigate development of an improved missile that would be used in the Jupiter submarines in place of the first Jupiter-S. However, the study group kept returning to Smith with the same answer: Throw away the Jupiter submarines and develop a small solid-fuel-propelled missile.

During the summer of 1956, the NOTS group joined forces with a study group that originally had been set up by the National Academy of Sciences for studying antisubmarine warfare. The group of scientists met for weeks at Woods Hole, Massachusetts. Their conclusions were issued that fall in a report sponsored by the National Academy. In effect, the report said the Navy should begin the development of a small solid-fuel-propelled ballistic missile immediately.

The report also contained a piece of very interesting news: The scientific grapevine had heard that the Atomic Energy Commission—supplier of warheads for all missiles—believed another big reduction in the size of nuclear warheads appeared possible. Raborn immediately wrote to the AEC, asking if the report were true. The AEC, which had sat on the news until then, replied that it was. The solid-fuel-propelled missile that was being proposed would be able to carry a warhead of much greater destructive power.

Sitting at his desk, Raborn read and reread the studies on possible solid-fuel-propelled missiles. He looked again at the AEC letter. Occasionally he would glance up and gaze out the window. Traffic moved swiftly along Constitution Avenue. Across the street stood the broad facade of AEC headquarters.

For days he had met with his principal staff members. They had talked out the situation from every point of view. Taken together, their advice was to go ahead with the new missile. Drop Jupiter altogether, if necessary. But go ahead with the new missile.

However, this decision was Raborn's alone. He had to call this shot. Win or lose, the responsibility rested on him.

*Polaris!*

Certainly, he saw the drawbacks of the Jupiter.

The converted merchant ships that would carry the big liquid-fuel-propelled missiles were vulnerable to attack by enemy submarines and aircraft. The submarines that would carry them were almost as vulnerable because they had to surface to launch them.

Also, because of the Jupiter's bulk, neither the converted merchantmen nor the submarines would be able to carry many missiles. Therefore, a large number of ships would be needed in order to send a sizable force of missiles to sea.

The greatest drawback of all was the very nature of the Jupiter. The idea of taking liquid propellant to sea was enough to make any insurance underwriter shudder despite the precautions that were being taken.

The old Pushover test at White Sands and the more recent test at Huntsville still haunted Raborn. They haunted the Navy.

"You only have to have one of these birds go, and you lose your ship," Raborn told one staff member. "Kapowie, one goes. Pow, the others go. Gum-by! Jump over upwind because the breeze will take the stuff the other way."

The still formative plans for the solid-fuel-propelled Jupiter-S weren't much comfort either. This monster of a missile would need a monster of a submarine to launch it. Designs on SP drawing boards called for subs approaching the size of cruisers.

On the other hand, the new missile would be much smaller than the Jupiter. Many of them could be put inside a nuclear-powered submarine. They would be safe to handle. And they probably could be launched by submarines from beneath the surface of the sea.

There was no reason why these submarines could not be nuclear-powered. The *Nautilus* had been sailing the seas of the world for nearly two years. Given the ability to launch long-range missiles, nuclear-powered submarines could checkmate Russia.

Such ships could prowl for months beneath the sea, unde-
tected by the Soviet Union. At any time, they could strike into
the heart of Russia. Yet, unlike ICBMs deployed on land, they
would not attract war to the American soil but to the vast oceans.
Still Raborn had good reason to pause.

So far, this new missile was only made of pieces of paper.
The Jupiter program was much further along, and despite the
missile's obvious faults, the program appeared to be assured of
success. Raborn had little hope that the administration would
relax its tight budget enough to permit the developing of both
the seagoing Jupiter and this new missile. Therefore, if Raborn
chose the new missile, the seagoing Jupiter missile most certainly
had to be dropped.

Except for the experience and knowledge gained, a year would
be lost. In place of operational Jupiters in hand within a year
or two, he would have at best better missiles on the drawing
boards and test stands. At worst, he would have nothing.

Moreover, precedent was against him. For the military to
throw away a going program when not forced to is a rare event
indeed in Washington. It takes boldness and courage—and the
intelligence to make sure that the new course is the right one.
It is always easier—and safer—to do nothing.

Therefore, as Raborn looked out on Constitution Avenue,
he stood at a turning point in history. Whatever he decided
could be fatal. His country, his service, his career were at stake.
He chose the bold course. He chose the new missile.

Once Raborn made the decision, there was no stopping him.
His staff worked from morning to morning, providing him with
material to win over the Pentagon. Within a matter of weeks,
he carried the new plan to the Secretary of the Navy and
obtained his approval.

That was the easy part. The tough part was convincing the
Secretary of Defense.

"Engine Charlie" sat looking like a sulky Buddha while

*Polaris!*

Raborn talked. High-ranking officers and military secretaries crowded the room just off the Pentagon's E Wing. Raborn used all his charm, all his enthusiasm and drive, to describe the benefits of the new missile.

Dozens of colored slides were flashed on a projection screen as Raborn pressed point after point. Some slides depicted the ideas for the missile, showing how it could be made. Some showed proposals for the submarine. Some showed how much of Russia could be hit by 1,500-mile-range missiles launched from the sea.

Then, toward the end, Raborn flashed on the screen a slide showing that ships for the new program would cost considerably less than ships for the old one. Moreover, fewer ships would be needed, because each could hold more missiles. In all, about a half-billion dollars could be saved.

Wilson leaned forward eagerly. He appeared fascinated as he stared at the graph showing the possible savings. Light from the projector reflected from his silky white hair.

"You've shown me a lot of sexy slides, young man," he told Raborn. "But that's the sexiest, that half-billion-dollar saving."

The new program was sold. Wilson even agreed to accept Raborn's proposal to take three or four months to determine precisely what the new missile system would look like.

In a secret directive December 8, 1956, Wilson ordered the Navy to stop work on Jupiter and begin work on the new missile.

Raborn named the new missile Polaris.

From the beginning of the fleet ballistic missile program, he had liked the name. Polaris, the North Star, was the ancient guide of sailors. It was their friend and protector from danger. This new Polaris would do the same for the nation.

Raborn had been unable to convince the Army that Polaris was a good name for the missile that was being born at Huntsville. The Army preferred Jupiter, and the Army got its way.

But now Raborn had his own missile. He christened it even as his staff began to work on what it would look like.

Throughout the rest of that winter, the men of Special Projects attempted what was widely believed to be impossible. They decided to build a weapon, not out of what they could do in January, 1957, but out of what they thought they would be able to do by 1963.

Their guide was not what the "state of the art" of missilery was then, but what the "state of the art" could be expected to become. They would push the knowledge of rocketry to its limit and beyond.

This was Raborn's answer to the deadly eight- to ten-year cycle for development of modern weapons. By staking everything on the future instead of the present, Raborn would break the cycle and produce a weapon system that would be the most advanced of its time for years to come.

Fortunately, there was much from the Jupiter program that could be salvaged.

The two test ships were being outfitted. The *Compass Island* would still be used to test the highly accurate navigation system needed. The other ship, the *Observation Island,* could still launch test missiles from the surface of the sea. Only the method of launching would have to be changed.

Little other equipment was being made. The only things that would be thrown away were, for the most part, pieces of paper and plans.

The change-over had a sharper effect on contractors. Chrysler, the prime contractor for Jupiter, was dropped by the Navy. Lockheed was about to assume the role.

That January, Raborn called into his offices top representatives of his principal contractors and government agencies concerned with the Polaris program. There were representatives from the Atomic Energy Commission, the Bureau of Ships, the Naval Ordnance Laboratory, and the Chief of Naval Operations. Officials from Massachusetts Institute of Technology, which was working on the navigation system, were present. So were company officials of Lockheed, Aerojet-General, General Electric, Westinghouse, and Sperry. These people became known as the Steering Task Group.

Raborn told them at that first meeting that his command was attempting to do what many said it couldn't. He said he expected to be successful. He said he had no doubt about it. He said the security of the country depended on it, upon them all.

The Steering Task Group then broke up into a series of committees, each responsible for deciding what a particular part of the Polaris system would be like. Their decisions were to be based on predicted technical improvements over the next six years. They met almost continually for three months. Capt. Levering Smith—the man Raborn came to call "the best scientist in uniform"—acted as grand co-ordinator.

Each committee first determined what would be the best missile or best launching system or best navigation system that could be developed on the basis of what probably could be invented or improved by 1965. Then the proposed pieces were put together. If, for example, the launching system was not good enough to fire the missiles fast enough, the committees sought to see whether an even better launching system could be developed. If the experts felt that what they had already proposed was the furthest that the art of building launching systems could be pushed by 1963, then some compromise was sought elsewhere.

In the middle of the committees' meetings, the Defense Department struck the Polaris program a backhand blow. Raborn's top national priority was withdrawn.

The Polaris program remained a top priority program within the Navy. But in competing with any programs outside the Navy, it would be hobbled.

Raborn ignored the move. It had no immediate effect since the new missile was still being planned. However, he made a point of mentioning it frequently in his sales trips to the Pentagon. He would have to get back his top national priority later in the year, or face seeing his schedules seriously delayed.

The committees sped ahead with their work.

During the three months that they met, there were hundreds of adjustments. Some involved pushing development of an element even further than many at first thought wise. Others involved a step backward from a very advanced design, in order to accommodate another element of the system that it would be foolhardy to expect to advance further in the given time period.

In the end, the Steering Task Group delivered to Raborn a blueprint for the Polaris system that was a weapon system for the mid-1960s, not the late 1950s. Each part was the best that these men believed could be conceived tomorrow. When the first Polaris submarine went to sea, it was designed to be not only the most modern weapon of its time but the most modern for many years.

The Polaris missile would be only 28 feet long and weigh about 28,000 pounds. It would look like a fat champagne bottle. Sixteen missiles would be carried inside a nuclear-powered submarine that would be almost twice the size of the *Nautilus*. The missiles also could easily be placed in quantity aboard cruisers and other surface ships.

The first Polarises would have a range of 1,500 miles—enough to hit all but a small area in Kazakh in Soviet Central Asia.

The system would be perfected by 1963.

But this was only the blueprint for developing Polaris. Raborn didn't stop here. With the master blueprint in hand, he and his staff then proposed to go the impossible one better. They would do everything at once. They would not build the missile first, see how it might have to be changed, and then build a submarine for it. They would not hedge their bets on the size of the fire control equipment or the launchers. They would simultaneously create the entire system as it had been conceived on the blueprint, so that it would be operational by

1963. If they had erred and therefore lost, they would lose everything: money, time, possibly the program itself. But if they were right and won, they believed they could contribute immeasurably to preserving a precarious peace.

Raborn shoved all the chips into the middle of the table and said, "Let's go to work."

# 6    Birth of a Leader

Most people who came to work for Red Raborn at Special Projects would agree on one thing about him. He was lucky.

Somehow he spread a special brand of luck over Polaris. Things went wrong many times. But never very far wrong.

"Every time we'd get into a real tight spot," said one SP officer, "we'd luck out. This program got hot right from the start and stayed hot. There's only one reason. It's Raborn. The man has incredible luck."

Many of the engineers in the program found it difficult to explain otherwise how Raborn made so many "right" decisions in the early days, when the whole system for a submarine-launched solid-fueled missile was just beginning to jell. Day after day, for each part of the system, alternate approaches were offered to him. Over and over again he was asked to make decisions on some of the most intricate machines ever conceived by man; machines that were to run a missile that had not yet been built. These were decisions that had to be made quickly, surely. For many of the major ones, there was no turning back. A decision could not be unmade without drastically revising the whole system.

How Raborn could coolly pass judgment on a particular part of the missile and commit millions of dollars for it amazed the technical people who themselves had sweated over various conceptual designs and were not absolutely certain which one was best. There was amazement because invariably it turned out that Raborn did pick the best approach—and he was not an engineer.

"Red's an old pilot. He flies by the seat of his pants," one of his associates once remarked to a friend in an attempt to explain the Raborn phenomenon. Some individuals, particularly those representing contractors, said he must be equipped with built-in radar capable of sensing not only right courses, but even their own hidden thoughts. When called into his private office to explain some deficiency on their part, they claimed they could almost hear it click on. After a particularly trying session with Raborn one day, an Aerojet engineer exclaimed to one of the men in his company, "I tell you, he takes you apart into little pieces. He doesn't yell. He doesn't snap at you. He just smiles and asks you one damn question after another about things you thought he knew nothing about."

Raborn the administrator, as this engineer and others who became embroiled in the Polaris program soon learned, was a far different person than Raborn the salesman. As a salesman, he exuded geniality, graciousness; he was a fancier of salty stories that evoked laughter. He was a rather short squarely-built man with a cocky roll to his gait, and had a warm smile and a friendly word for everyone. As an administrator, if the occasion warranted it, he could be tough. The blue eyes flecked with brown could turn icy cold; the smile could flatten into a thin scar; his voice could harden, and he could drive words at his listener as if they were belaying pins. In tense moments, Raborn even seemed to change physically, to grow in stature. His head, closely shaven at the sides where it was turning gray, would rise attentively like that of an Irish setter getting a scent.

When he listened to a conversation, or a verbal report given by one of his team members, he never missed a word or an inflection. The spoken word was the yardstick by which Raborn measured those with whom he dealt. "If you can't explain it to me," he told some men bluntly, "then you really don't know what you are talking about or what you are doing." The written word, the reams of paper work associated with bringing forth a new missile, he regarded as so much batting to inhibit personal communication, which he felt was far more important because it was faster. And speed was what he wanted. Almost entirely through his own scrupulous attention to honesty and fairness, and his insistence that personnel in SP follow his example, Raborn very quickly wove a remarkable relationship with the men he was depending upon in industry. He felt he could trust them implicitly, as they could trust him. So it was that in a single telephone conversation with Lockheed in California, or perhaps with some other contractor, he could set in motion a whole new phase of the program, involving millions of dollars, without wasting a moment. Other military programs at this very time were bogging down by the copious written reports entailed in continual justification and evaluation of the work that had been done, while Raborn's program sailed on, unobstructed—by paper.

Nothing ever stood still for long in the Polaris program. The reason again was Raborn. Abounding with energy, he prodded everyone and everything as fast as they could go. His own pace was a killing one; yet he appeared to thrive on it. In the office at 8 A.M., Raborn usually did not get home until late at night. Two or three days a week he traveled, visiting plants to talk to company presidents and production workers, addressing a big crowd in a convention hall, speaking at Kiwanis Club luncheons. He was on the telephone incessantly. No week went by without a personal call to the top executive in each of the major contractor companies. Raborn would place a call to one of these men, with orders to trace him wherever he might be. On one occasion the company president had left the East Coast to make several stops across the country. Everyone in his company was told Raborn was looking for him, and they assumed, quite naturally, that there was a big emergency. When the call finally caught up to the contractor in San Francisco a day later, he came on the line, worried, saying, "What's happened, Admiral? Is something wrong?" Raborn said, "No, nothing. I just wondered how you were doing, how you are coming along." And he launched into a pleasant fifteen-minute cross-examination, interspersed with frequent references to the urgency of the program.

It didn't take long for every company president to begin to think as Raborn did. Polaris was the most important thing any one of them had ever done.

The first encounter of William Francis Raborn, Jr., with the Navy had occurred when he met two midshipmen, home on leave from Annapolis, showing off their tightly cut white summer uniforms to the farm boys in Marlow, Oklahoma.

"Those fellows made a real impression on all us dusty dry kids with sand in our hair," Red Raborn was to recall later with a laugh. "They had all of us wanting to join up in no time."

The thought of water, ships, and glamorous uniforms intrigued not only the youthful Raborn but two of his classmates as well. All three were admitted to the Naval Academy in 1924.

The trip East 2,000 miles across the country was the farthest Raborn, then nineteen years old, had traveled in his entire life. He was born in Decatur, Texas, about 100 miles south of Marlowe, and during his early life his travels were confined to a succession of small Oklahoma towns where his father, a strict Baptist and operator of a cotton gin, took the family of six boys and two girls. They finally settled in Marlow about the time Red entered high school. For a boy burning with energy and possessing a quick perceptive mind, life in southern Oklahoma had been pretty humdrum. His spirit thirsted for adventure.

There were things to do in life besides feed sacks of cotton into a gin.

Adventure, in Raborn's mind at that time, was synonymous with flying. As soon as he arrived in Annapolis, he began the pursuit of a pair of aviator's wings. But for a boy who even then liked to get things done in a hurry, it was to be a painfully long time before he would win them.

Sending airplanes to sea was considered just as harebrained an idea in 1924 as sticking a ballistic missile in a submarine was thirty years later. The battleship admirals harumped against it. Sea power meant battlewagons, destroyers, minesweepers. There were those who still looked warily at the Johnny-come-lately submarine, which had been introduced in 1900, only twenty-four years before. It wasn't much of a weapon yet, but it might have possibilities later on.

There was a lot of talk about the new airships Germany was building, and young Navy men wondered if they held a future. Shortly after Raborn arrived at the Academy, the dirigible ZR-3 made a three-day crossing of the Atlantic from Friedrichshafen, arriving at Lakehurst, New Jersey, on October 15, 1924. The feat swung the public's mind to the skies and intensified Raborn's desire to fly.

Masking the serious side of his nature with an engaging grin and a ready quip, Red Raborn dug into his studies. He was a fair student in the standard Academy courses designed to turn him into a salt-water Navy officer. Opponents on the class boxing team found him a tough, aggressive welterweight. Red toyed with the idea of going out for the varsity boxing team, but decided it would take too much time away from his consuming interest.

Weekends, the young midshipman usually headed straight for an airfield called Anacostia, which the Navy had just built near Washington. The friendly redhead got to know the young aviators, and they taught him all they could. Occasionally, they let him squeeze aboard and take a flight.

On two such occasions the plane's engines conked out coming in for a landing. Both times Raborn barely missed death in the Anacostia River. But it didn't discourage him. What nearly did so, however, was the realization that upon his graduation he had to spend at least two years at sea before he could ask for flight training. But there was no escaping it; the rule was firm.

For a man burning to get his feet in a cockpit, it was a long time to wait. Then came Charles Lindbergh. The mail pilot's solo flight across the Atlantic on May 20, 1927, blazed a warning that even the battleship admirals found difficult to ignore; six years before, they had tried to ignore the sinking of the captured German battleship *Ostfriesland* by Brig. Gen. Billy Mitchell's bombers. But, if airplanes could cross oceans, they could bomb battleships. Naval aircraft would be needed to protect the warships. Suddenly, Navy men took on a new respect for the pilot training station at Pensacola, Florida. Naval aviation was on its way; the future lay aboard aircraft carriers.

A streetcar whanged and rattled down Fourteenth Street, stopping with a steel wheeze.

In a hotel room looking over the car stop, Red Raborn lay wide awake, staring at the ceiling. Hours dragged by. Every time he started to doze off, another streetcar would go by, jangling his senses completely awake. All night his mind, as it had done for days past, raced over what lay ahead. A three-year tour on the battleship *Texas* was behind him. He would be heading for Pensacola soon. This was the last lap. All he had to do was take a physical examination in the morning and he would be set.

But dawn came over Washington, and Raborn still had not slept. Two hours later, he presented himself at the Navy Building for the examination. His eyes were bleary. He was exhausted. When he came to the eye test, he flunked.

None of his friends on the *Texas* would believe him. They all accused him of spending the night on the town. "Imagine me, booting the eye test," growled Raborn, "when I've got the best goddam eyes in the Navy."

Unbeaten, he immediately reapplied for flight training. Another year passed aboard the *Texas,* and he was back in Washington again. This time he passed the physical. It was now Christmas, 1932. But there was no stocking for him with a ticket in it to Pensacola. The school was filled.

Raborn was reassigned to a destroyer. Three years later he finally got his orders to depart for Florida. Flight training took almost another year. And on April 16, 1934—more than ten years after leaving Marlow—Red Raborn proudly pinned a pair of Naval aviator's wings on his tunic. He was ready to start his career again.

Many men bridle under the peacetime leisure of the Navy. It takes a long time to get promoted, often years to effect a change in career status.

For all its faults, inherent in any military system, the Navy believes benefits still may be gained by moving an officer along gradually. He gets seasoned. He learns a job thoroughly. Above all, he learns how to lead. Patience is as much a prerequisite of leadership as imagination and daring. An imaginative man in a dull job may learn a lot about himself, as well as about the people he may have to take into battle some day. He may learn how to make a dull job rewarding.

The officer must learn to endure as well as act. Wars, even a nuclear-balancing cold war, are fought and won by men who can still function in battle amid wholesale death and privation when they are called upon.

Red Raborn was tempered thus for seven long years. Then he faced the black maw of war.

Noise from the antiaircraft bursts caught Raborn's ears almost as soon as the guns started firing.

He was in a beach house on Kaneohe Bay, spending his first

Sunday in months with his wife and young son and daughter, who had arrived in Hawaii the previous week from the States. There was no gunnery practice scheduled that morning at the Kaneohe Naval Air Station. Raborn knew, because he was the gunnery officer.

Telling his wife to remain in the house, the newly made lieutenant got in his car and drove off for the airfield five miles away. On the radio, just before he left, a strangled voice had announced, "Japanese planes are attacking Pearl Harbor," and the station went off the air.

As he approached the airbase, which was on the opposite side of the Koolau Range and 40 miles from Pearl Harbor, Raborn could see planes wheeling over the airstrip, strafing and bombing. It was going to be difficult for him to reach his post on the field. A row of palm trees paralleling the highway offered some concealment, so he drove off the road, keeping the trees between his car and the planes. Then the line of trees stopped. Nearly a mile away the row began again. Raborn stopped and prepared to make a dash for it. As he waited for a lull, he looked behind him and found a whole line of cars, which had been following him under the palms, bound for the air station.

The air looked clear, and Raborn stepped on the gas and rocketed out into the open. Halfway across open ground, he saw a Japanese Zero bearing down on him. Just as the Japanese pilot brought his plane's nose down to fire, Raborn hit the gas pedal. The bullets sailed over his head and struck a car behind him, killing the man driving it and setting it on fire.

A few minutes later Raborn gained the relative safety of one of the hangars, only to find there was nothing he could do.

Some Navy planes from the station had been able to take off before the Japanese hit. They were still in the air. The remainder were caught on the ground and were burning. One hangar that had not been touched was full of planes. But it would have been suicide to attempt to bring them out.

Raborn, who was also squadron intelligence officer, grabbed

an "action report" form and walked over to an open doorway to get a better view of the dogfight going on overhead.

He was proud that his "boys" were up there. The only reason they were up was that they had bullets in their guns. Raborn foresightedly had insisted to his commanding officer that all planes in the squadron be kept loaded with live ammunition. There was a reason for his insistence. Two years before, in battle exercises aboard the carrier *Lexington,* Raborn had participated in a raid on Pearl Harbor and found it unprotected against an air attack. When assuming his new job at Kaneohe, he looked at the war plans and found them unchanged. The island was still unprotected. Only battle units at sea were provided with air cover.

"Hey, Red! Duck!" a voice yelled at Raborn, who was scribbling some notes on his report. Raborn looked up to see a Zero diving straight at him. An instant after he had dived to one side, a splatter of bullets hit the place he had been standing.

It was an ignominious way for a Naval aviator to begin a war—on the ground. For Raborn it proved to be an omen. At thirty-five years of age, his days as a fighter pilot were over as of then. A more important job lay ahead.

Though several Kaneohe planes battled the Japanese, their pilots were shamefaced. Not one of them had shot down a single attacker. While the fires from Japanese bombs still flamed over Oahu, Raborn was handed a new job: training air gunners. It was a task he accomplished with considerable success. In a matter of days he set up at Kaneohe what became the Aviation Free Gunnery School, the "free" as in "free-shooting." Gun turrets were removed from wrecked planes and mounted on the backs of trucks so the trainees could learn how to hit a target from a moving vehicle. Raborn also adopted the practice of shooting from a stationary gun mounted on the beach at targets towed by a plane.

Soon the school was open to Marine and Army Air Corps gunners as well, and hundreds of gunners were pouring through it every month. Raborn's methods were so effective that he was given a medal and brought to Washington in mid-1943 to take charge of the Navy's entire aviation gunnery training program. A new talent was recognized.

The war in the Pacific howled on.

Bitter land and sea fighting slowly pushed back the Japanese. Island after island was retaken from the Oriental conquerors. Carriers had stopped the Japanese in the Coral Sea and in the South Pacific at Midway. The tide had turned, and the final drive was on for the Philippines.

In the fall of 1944 Raborn returned to the war aboard the carrier *"Fightin' Hannah,"* the U.S.S. *Hancock*. Off the Philippine Islands, he got his first taste of combat since Pearl Harbor.

The *Hannah* was the brawler of the carrier fleet. Her men boasted of the wounds she'd taken that would have killed another ship. They were a proud and tough crew. Raborn, as the *Hannah*'s executive officer, second in command, became one of them.

Tragedy struck shortly after he came aboard. One of the *Hannah*'s torpedo bombers returned from a strike, its pilot unaware that a bomb was loose in its bomb bay. The plane came in and landed on the flattop. As her wings were being folded up, the bomb bay opened and the bomb dropped out and exploded. Fifty men were killed. A gaping hole was torn in the flight deck.

Raborn committed the *Hannah*'s dead to the sea with full military honors. The great ship repaired herself and went on fighting.

Three months later, while supporting the Iwo Jima invasion, the *Hancock* was hit again. A Japanese Zeke carrying a 2,000-pound bomb skimmed in low over the water into the middle of a task force. The plane was so low, the ships could not fire at it for fear of hitting each other. Approaching the *Hannah* at close to 500 miles per hour, the Zeke dropped a bomb on the forward flight deck. Instead of exploding there, the bomb hit, bounced into the air, sailed down half the length of the ship, and landed on four parked airplanes. The Zeke, which was overhead, was blown into a million pieces. Flying shrapnel riddled the *Hannah*. Fire broke out, quickly spreading over most of the ship. Wounded men lay everywhere. The bomb had gashed a 20- by 30-foot hole in the deck and set fire to four more planes below on the hangar deck.

To the other ships in the task force, it looked as if the *Hannah* were finished. Aboard her, however, the indomitable crew recovered quickly. Working like demons, they beat out the flames and had patched the hole in the flight deck just 2 hours and 41 minutes after the explosion. Less than twenty men had been killed. The *Hannah* triumphantly had bandaged her wound in time to land her air group, which had been out on a mission.

The sight of those planes coming aboard that day remained always in Raborn's mind. They landed in routine fashion, as if nothing had happened in their absence. The men of the *Hannah* had saved her—not only by heroics, but by know-how; every man had known what to do and had done it. They had been prepared, by their familiarity with everything from emergency fire-fighting gear to the steel plates and the supporting I-beams, to fill the gap in the flight deck. Men—leaders like Raborn—had thought ahead.

"You can't fight a war without getting hit," Raborn reflected long afterward in his matter-of-fact manner. "The big thing is to come out smelling like a rose. Men will work harder for a leader who can bring them out looking real good—and if he can make them proud of what they're doing."

Plenty of medals were passed out aboard the *Hancock* after she took the Zeke bomb on April 7, 1945. Raborn himself received a Silver Star with a citation which read in part: "for conspicuous gallantry and intrepidity . . . when an enemy bomb exploded on the flight deck of his ship (he) actively supervised the fire fighting and damage control units despite the blinding smoke and large fires that were threatening ammunition on and around the flight deck . . . rendered invaluable assistance to his commanding officer . . . and contributed in large measure to the saving of his ship from further damage. . . ."

The war ended with Raborn, a full commander about to be promoted to captain, picked to control part of the air operations for the invasion of Japan. When that job became unnecessary, he became chief of staff to the commander of a Navy task force and later chief of staff of a carrier division, spending two more years in the Western Pacific. He then returned to Washington for a tour of duty in the Bureau of Ordnance. He was put in charge of guided missiles and air weapons. With the outbreak of the Korean War, Raborn returned to the sea in command of a task group patrolling Far East waters for Russian submarines that might have tried to interfere with the United Nations military action in Korea.

As a captain two years later, Raborn once again anticipated the times, when he became assistant director of the Navy's Guided Missiles Division in Washington under Rear Adm. "Savvy" Sides. It was a new challenge, and he became absorbed in the science of making missiles. He helped the Navy bring forth the Regulus, a whole family of antiaircraft missiles, and the deadly air-to-air Sidewinder. He thus gained the knowledge of how to produce complex new weapons and learned what missiles would mean to the future.

Though he may have appeared to some to be an extremely lucky man, troubles continued to dog Red Raborn.

The strain of being a Navy wife had finally told on the Texas girl Raborn married a year after his graduation from the Naval Academy. She divorced him in 1953. A year later Raborn got ready to go to sea again, this time to qualify as a flag-rank officer. He was given command of the *Bennington,* a huge aircraft carrier built in the latter days of the war.

Raborn had been aboard only two weeks when explosions and fire shattered the ship 100 miles off Rhode Island. A giant pressure vessel containing hydraulic fluid for an airplane catapult inexplicably blew up at dawn. Fumes spewed into the carrier's ventilating system. The gas permeated compartments, setting off more blasts. The explosions went off like a string of bombs through the officers' quarters and down into the hangar deck, crumpling thick bulkheads like tin cans.

One hundred and three officers and men were killed, many as they lay in their bunks. Fire raced through the ship.

The flames licked around the great bombs and other weapons loaded with high explosives. For several minutes it seemed as if the *Bennington* were doomed. But Raborn, who was standing on the bridge at the time, found he had a crew equal to the one aboard the *Fightin' Hannah.* Like veterans, the officers and men battled the raging fires. It took hours to put them out. Men descended repeatedly into the smoke-filled, smashed compartments and carried their shipmates to safety up ladders that were so hot the skin was burned from their hands.

Fortunately the engine rooms were not damaged. Raborn pointed the ship for Quonset Point, Rhode Island, and radioed ahead for help. By the time he entered Narragansett Bay, a large group of helicopters had been mobilized and began taking off the badly injured while the *Bennington* steamed into port.

Raborn met newsmen in a smoky wardroom. He took no credit. He said the previous skipper had done the job; he was the one who had imbued the fighting spirit. But again his men had come out "smelling like a rose."

The *Bennington* was being repaired and overhauled at the Brooklyn Navy Yard when Raborn got the idea for holding dances.

Many of the *Bennington*'s officers and men were new to the Navy. Raborn feared they would get into trouble during nine months on the beach in New York. Raborn felt he ought to do something about their social life.

Over the objections of older seamen and chiefs, Raborn succeeded in getting the ship's service fund to put up money to rent a hall on Saturday nights near the Navy Yard. He also persuaded the USO to provide dates for his men. Saturday night dances became the social event of the week.

However, Raborn felt he had to do something along the same lines for his young officers. One day during this period he dropped by the Naval Hospital at St. Albans, Long Island, and told his problem to the commanding officer.

"Do you think your head nurse might arrange for some of the new Navy nurses coming through to attend dances here with some of my young fellows?" Raborn asked. "Maybe I could talk to her."

"Have you met our head nurse?" the C.O. asked.

"No," Raborn said.

"Well, let me do the honors. You have a treat in store."

A few minutes later Red Raborn was introduced to Comdr. Mildred Terrill of Texas.

"The cutest little brunette you ever saw," Raborn said later. "I guess I must have looked at her a moment too long, because she tucked her ankles underneath her chair."

Commander Terrill wasn't overly impressed with the idea of the dances, but she agreed to arrange them. Raborn thanked her and suggested that she might accompany him to the first one. She accepted.

When Captain Raborn and Commander Terrill arrived at the dance, they found the atmosphere was less than festive. About twenty-five nurses were lined up on one side of the room, and twenty-five officers from the *Bennington* were lined up on the other.

Turning aside to his date, Raborn said, "You'll have to excuse my officers. Most of them didn't go to the Academy. I guess civilians lead more sheltered lives."

Then, walking to the front of the room and looking over the group, he said as if he were standing on a carrier deck:

"All right. The only reason all of you are here is to meet each other. So I want the gentlemen to form a line and walk past these lovely young ladies and introduce themselves, and when everyone has been introduced, you're all on your own."

The dance was a tremendous success. It eventually resulted in two weddings—one of them Raborn's. The bride traded her three stripes for an apron string.

One final bit of polishing remained before Raborn was to embark on his greatest adventure. He left the *Bennington* in February, 1955, and became the assistant chief of staff for operations, under the commander of the Atlantic Fleet at Norfolk, Virginia. It was a key job, demanding an intimate knowledge of the Navy's ships, some of which were converting to missiles, and afforded him an opportunity to acquire considerable managerial skill. In July, the President approved his appointment as rear admiral. Six months later Raborn and ex-Commander Mildred were on the road to Washington. Special Projects was under way.

The Navy's choice of Raborn was an interesting one. He was essentially a combat sailor, uncomplicated by nature and simple in his tastes, a man accustomed to direct action. Yet the people he would command in Special Projects and industry would, by and large, be his direct opposites. They were all highly trained specialists in electronics, chemistry, physics, and mathematics. Many of the men in industry were highly ranked scientists.

It would be a real test of Raborn's many-faceted character to get these people to work for him and to produce a weapon. If this problem troubled him, the new admiral never let on.

The Raborns bought a new split-level house that had been

built in a grove of trees on a hillside overlooking the Potomac from the Virginia shore. It was only ten minutes away from his new office. Raborn gave up golf and became a Sunday gardener, so he could spend the few hours away from his job at home. He planted 135 rosebushes and cultivated the grounds like a Japanese garden. Later he bought an electric organ, and taught himself how to play. It was on the first level of the house, near a second kitchen that he claimed as his personal galley, where he planned to indulge in another hobby—cooking. He didn't get many chances to use it.

# 7   Sputnik Nudges the Sleepers

The schedule at the International Rocket and Satellite Conference said: U.S.S.R. Ground-Based Experimental Satellite Programs (40 minutes).

About fifty scientists from a dozen nations waited eagerly in a paneled lecture room at the National Academy of Sciences. The question in the mind of everyone in the room was whether Russia would for the first time disclose some details of its endlessly announced plan to attempt launching a man-made satellite similar to the one America was preparing. The date was October 3, 1957.

The Russians were late. Other scientists spoke. Thin snakes of cigarette smoke floated in the warm room. Through the window, traffic could be seen moving toward the Lincoln Memorial.

A few more scientists entered the room. Several conversations were under way in corners. Most of the scientists were skeptical of Russian boasts that the Soviet Union was ready to put a satellite in orbit. They considered Russia a backward country technically. Launching a satellite was a fantastically difficult feat that only the most advanced technology could achieve.

The door opened and two of the Russians entered: A. A. Blaganravov and K. M. Kasatskin. They sat down in the front row. Blaganravov was a short man with a thatch of white hair. He looked like a worried college professor. Kasatskin's head was shaved. He had blue eyes and a pointed nose and smiled nervously.

Sergei M. Poloskov of the Soviet Academy of Science arrived last, carrying an orange leather briefcase under his arm. He wore a boxlike black suit over his big body, and square-toed shoes. An enormous shock of black hair kept falling over his eyeglasses.

Poloskov showed the other two Russians a paper, and they bent their heads together. He puffed on a cigarette and listened, hunched over in his seat as the other two spoke to him. At one point, he took a comb from his breast pocket and ran it through his long hair.

Finally his name was called. The room became very quiet. He began talking in Russian. He talked rapidly but distinctly, as if everyone in the room were taking in each word. His brow creased several times. He held out his hands to show how long something was, how long something else was, how high. His hair kept falling over his glasses, and he kept brushing it back impatiently.

Then he suddenly stopped talking and looked expectantly at the audience. There was an awkward pause. Apparently he had finished. The audience clapped.

Dr. N. T. Brobronikoff of Ohio State University translated the address. Poloskov had said that a satellite in flight could reveal much information. He urged the nations of the world—especially the United States—to help track the radio signals of the Russian satellite while it was in flight.

Shortly afterward, the scientists adjourned for lunch and the first innings of the World Series. The Western scientists were still skeptical.

"Oh, yes, yes, the Russians were interesting," Brobronikoff said later. "But they didn't say whether they have anything." Several people around him laughed smugly.

The next day—October 4—there was a late-afternoon cocktail party at the Soviet Embassy. Scientists, officials, newsmen crowded into the baroque former town house of the millionaire Pullman family. Here in the high-ceilinged, gilded rooms the Communists had centered their activities in the United States since the 1930s.

The three Russian scientists who were attending the satellite conference smiled and mingled with the guests. The normal chatter of a Washington cocktail party swelled and filled the elaborately decorated rooms. Vodka, Scotch, and bourbon flowed into hundreds of glasses. The few plates of caviar were soon empty.

In one of the many rooms someone was saying something in a loud voice, but it was impossible to hear him. There were some cheers. People were shaking hands. The word rapidly spread. The Union of Soviet Socialist Republics, the workers' paradise, had launched the world's first man-made satellite into orbit.

Blaganravov, who later turned out to be a leading figure in the Soviet missile program and a lieutenant general of artillery in the Red Army, smiled his professorial smile and drank a toast.

The Polaris program had been moving along since the spring of 1957, for the most part close to the schedule that would put the first Polaris submarine on station in 1963.

Contracts had been let. Tests were under way. Raborn and his staff were full of confidence.

Hasler, who had taken charge of the SP office on the West Coast, felt the same way. Detailed designs were being completed on components. The launching system had already been worked out. Problems were there, plenty of them; but they were being overcome. Hasler could look back and almost smile at conversations he had had during his last days at Huntsville.

The former German scientists had been openly scornful about Polaris.

"A goose chase," one told Hasler. *"Ja,* sure, it's a good idea, but you can't do it. If you could do it, we would be doing it here."

"Believe me, my friend," another said, "stay in Huntsville. Don't waste your time."

When Sputnik I soared into orbit, the chill of panic ran through Washington. Lights burned late at night in the Pentagon and the White House. Congressmen, newspaper editors, prominent citizens demanded that something be done. If only for a moment, the great, fat, prosperous country was aroused.

The President—apparently still trying to shield the public from awareness of the dawning Missile Age—tried to calm the uproar. He told a news conference that Sputnik I had "no military significance." He said the Soviet satellite made not "one iota" of difference to the security of the Free World.

Many scientists and military men disagreed. The Russians had had to use a big military rocket of ICBM proportions to launch Sputnik I. This was positive proof of Russian advances in missilery. Moreover, Sputnik I gave the Russians another sinister gain that was never made public. The satellite's radio beacon enabled the Russians to measure the distance within feet between United States cities and Soviet ICBM bases. Until this time, maps had been far less accurate. Russia had not only long-range rockets, but the means of finding their targets.

The administration thrashed about desperately in an effort to answer the demands that it do something. It turned to the three military services for help. Meantime, the President and other administration leaders continued to issue a stream of soothing statements.

When the Navy turned to the Polaris program Raborn already had an answer waiting. Immediately after Sputnik I was launched, he and his staff had begun to consider whether the Polaris program might be accelerated. The answer that they arrived at was: Yes. By three years.

It would mean some compromises.

Rather than have a 1,500-mile range for the missile, it would have to be shaved to 1,200. The test navigation system and fire control system designed for the *Observation Island* would have to be used in the submarines too, rather than the smaller, more advanced systems that had been planned. A somewhat less powerful propellant, originally designed for the now-defunct solid-fuel Jupiter project, would have to be used instead of a more powerful one, because materials that could withstand the resulting higher temperatures would not be fully developed.

Finally, the latest of the Atomic Energy Commission's lighter big-punch warheads would have to be used, because they could not wait for a still better one expected in the early 1960s at the latest. As it happened, even the warhead that Polaris adopted was put through its final tests just as the moratorium on testing went into effect a year later.

By accepting these compromises, Raborn could put a Polaris submarine on station in December of 1960 rather than in 1963. It wouldn't be easy. A lot would have to be done very fast. A lot of sacrifices would have to be made by a lot of people. A lot of chances would have to be taken. But if the acceleration succeeded, Raborn felt it would be worth whatever the cost.

Raborn called in his principal contractors to tell them about the plan and ask what they thought. They crowded into the Management Center, the representatives of Lockheed, of General Electric, of Aerojet, of Westinghouse, of Sperry. Something big obviously was about to be unfolded. The air was tense.

Capt. Levering Smith, now Raborn's technical director, outlined the new proposal. He spoke in his slow, exact style. Each step was gone over thoroughly. Each job that would have to be done was spelled out. When he finished, he asked if there were any questions.

Frank Bednarz, Lockheed's technical director for the Polaris program, rose to his feet. Bednarz was big, heavy-chested, and wore black-framed glasses.

"Do we have any choice?" he asked.

Smith laughed. Everyone in the room laughed.

"No," Smith said.

The contractors and Raborn's staff then came to terms. The contractors agreed that the acceleration could be executed, but only with certain stipulations.

The Special Projects Office had to promise that there would be no radical changes in the Polaris system. It had to promise that much red tape would be cut. It had to promise that there would be adequate funding for overtime, and that there would be no bottlenecks in funding.

Raborn agreed.

He went to the Navy with the plan. The Navy went to the Secretary of Defense. The Secretary of Defense went to the White House. The President approved.

The Polaris program would be accelerated, so that the first submarine could go on station by December, 1960. Later, even this early date was trimmed to fall.

No one who attended the meetings between Raborn and his staff and between Raborn and his contractors doubted that once more this tough, gregarious admiral would "come up smelling like a rose."

"These contractors don't dare fail him," Pehrson told some of his associates. "They can't. The wives of the presidents of these companies won't let their husbands let Red Raborn down."

Benjamin Parrin, GE manager of Polaris fire control and guidance, put it another way.

"One of the reasons why so many people want this program to succeed so much is they want to prove that a guy like Raborn can run one," he said. "You don't *have* to have a son of a bitch."

# 8 Puzzles, Parts, and Red Tape

Fortunately for the Polaris program and the United States, Gordon Pehrson was a very special kind of genius. This small, neat man in a tweed suit had a passion for order that affected everything he touched. The polished shoes in his closet at his home in suburban Arlington lay in as precise a row as the top-secret papers in his office files at the Munitions Building. He approached his personal household budget and the affairs of a local Cub Scout pack with the same exactitude with which he handled billions of taxpayers' dollars.

But Pehrson's genius was not to be confused with the mere finicky liking for order of a minor bookkeeper. The order that he pursued with the care of an artist is found only in the higher reaches of human thought. He sought the mental orderliness of the chess player: the orderliness that must precede and follow the precisely right choices when a multitude of choices is offered: the orderliness that can come only from correct analysis.

Because of his specific brand of genius Pehrson, as director of plans and programs for the Special Projects Office, was invaluable to Raborn.

The problem of making perfect choices for the Polaris program presented difficulties of staggering proportions. The chessboard that confronted Raborn was the size of a football field. The number of pieces was legion. And time, which had been wasted for more than a decade, now was ebbing quickly. For Raborn to win the race against the calendar, correct choices had to be made almost every time. There was almost no room at all for error.

Raborn clearly recognized this from the beginning. All the early management machinery set up during the year of the seagoing Jupiter had this problem in mind. But this machinery was no longer good enough; with the birth of the new Polaris program, the problems had multiplied in complexity and the Russians had gained another year. Much better management machinery was needed. Raborn turned to Pehrson to build it.

Gordon Pehrson was well equipped for the job he was called on to do. Since his days at the University of Minnesota in the late 1930s, he had developed and sharpened a mental ability to organize a group of complicated facts, toss out the unessential, and come up with the essence of any matter. At the same time, he had developed an ability to present the essence in a style both colorful and concise. These qualities had made him a particularly potent debater first in college and later at government conference tables. One close associate has described him as "a man who can make the dullest subject interesting." Another has called him "a man who sees farther than most and who can convince you that what he sees is right."

Pehrson began his climb to recognition as a government management expert after he ended a three-year hitch as a Navy supply officer during World War II. Before the war he had held a variety of government jobs. He was a personnel clerk in the Labor Department. He was a supervisor of WPA records. He was a bank examiner. He was an investigator for the Civil Service Commission. Shortly after his return to civilian life in 1946, he became first the planning officer and later administrative officer of the Veterans Administration office at Dallas, Texas. It was from here that he arrived in Washington in 1949 to become a budget examiner for the Bureau of the Budget.

The move to Washington was a critical one. Previously he had been a minor Federal official operating at a provincial outpost. As a budget examiner, he attracted enough favorable attention in little more than a year to be appointed chief of the budget branch of the multi-billion-dollar Navy Bureau of Ordnance. He immediately began to demonstrate his talents.

First as chief budget officer, and later as the first civilian comptroller of the Bureau, Pehrson completely reorganized the old Bureau's entangled money operations. At the same time, he so brilliantly handled the fiscal arrangements for maintaining a flow of ammunition to United States forces in Korea that his activities were officially recognized in a Presidential citation as "a masterpiece of planning and scheduling."

Pehrson left the Navy in 1954 to establish and head an Army Business and Industrial Management Office. Again Pehrson introduced new methods of management. These specifically involved control of the Army's world-wide supply organization. Later he produced a brilliant advance analysis of what manpower and spare parts the Army would need for its nationwide network of Nike antiaircraft missiles. The analysis was so good that months were cut from the time needed to deploy the missiles.

But if Pehrson's past prepared him for what lay ahead, none of it even approached the challenge of the Polaris program. Somehow in an unbelievably short span of time the millions of individual parts in the Polaris system had to be designed or invented, produced, assembled, and tested. Crews had to be trained. Supporting facilities had to be built. And, finally, all of it had to be put together and sent to sea. The work of the growing number of companies that eventually totaled more than two thousand major conractors and six thousand subcontractors had to be supervised—so that all the jobs would be done correctly and completed by thousands of different deadlines.

If Raborn were to succeed, he had to have a way to make sure that everyone was doing what he should be doing, precisely when it should be done. Raborn and his staff had to have the information so that they could try to make up for any failure if it occurred. Just as important, they had to have the information so that they could try to capitalize on an unexpected success.

Moreover, Pehrson saw that in order to be usable, this information must be kept as brief and as uncluttered as possible.

*Polaris!*

"Since everything is so complicated, our planning and control system must be simple," he told his staff. "But we need a system, an important word which I keep emphasizing: system. It must keep us informed of what we need to know to make decisions. But it must provide us only with the information we need and nothing more. We are not going to build huge statistical sandpiles."

On January 24, 1957—six weeks after the Defense Department had put its official blessing on Polaris—Raborn issued to his staff a basic memorandum on how the new program would be managed. The memo said bluntly:

*The management structure established for direction of the Fleet Ballistic Missile Program is special and unique. . . . The decision to obtain a FBM capability was made in terms of a complete "program package." This total decision could be carried out only by making an assignment of responsibility and a delegation of authority in the same complete terms. This means that the "buck stops at my desk" for decisions made in carrying out this program.*

Raborn said if the "small select group" that made up his command was to succeed, it must develop "a completely integrated management control system." The memo added:

*I must be able to reach down to any level of Special Projects Office activity and find a plan and a performance report that logically and clearly can be related to the total job we have to do.*

Raborn's objective was clear. Achieving it was another matter. Pehrson and his staff surveyed the management control systems currently in use throughout American industry. None was adaptable. No existing system would do the job that Raborn and Pehrson knew had to be done if they were to beat the clock that was running on Moscow time.

"No one had any management technique which had to do with actually scheduling research and development," Raborn said later. "One distinguished laboratory man told us, 'I've got a group of people sitting over here thinking about a problem. If they come up with something this year, that's fine. If I have to wait two years, well, I'll just wait two years.' Obviously we couldn't do that. We had to schedule the research that we had to do. We had to have production on top of that. We had to build facilities. We had to build plants. Most of the equipment never had been built before. To do all of this on time, we had to get up a system of our own."

Pehrson devised one in June of 1957 as the Polaris program finally got under way. Basically it involved reporting when day-to-day milestones were met. There were thousands of them. But the system was so simple that almost anyone could play.

The lifeblood of the control system was communication. The means of communicating was a simple chart called a management plan. This was divided into four main sections that told Raborn and his staff at a glance precisely where the Polaris program stood and precisely why.

The charts formed a pyramid of eight layers. The top layer had one chart covering the entire Polaris system. The next layer had five charts: one for each of the five major parts. The next layer had about fifty charts, the next nearly one hundred. In all there were more than five hundred. Each had exactly the same format.

The top left-hand section of each chart stated in precise terms the product or task that it covered. For example: propulsion.

The top right-hand section listed the major parts of the product or task. In the case of propulsion: motor cases, fuel, and support programs. A simple bar graph for each part gave the dates when it should reach various stages toward completion.

The bottom half of each chart stated up to twenty-five specific milestones that must be met in order to complete the job covered. It also stated who was responsible for seeing that each milestone was reached, and a black descending line on a graph showed when each should be reached. Various colored markers beside the milestones told the rest of the story. A blue star meant the milestone was reached ahead of schedule. A red triangle designated a delay. A green circle meant the work was exactly on schedule. An orange square signified uncertainty; it still might be possible to complete the job on time, if something were done quickly.

By glancing at the colored markers, Raborn and his staff knew the exact place to look in the pyramid of charts to find what had to be done to resolve trouble or to exploit a gain. They always had updated copies of the charts on hand. All were reproduced on 8- by 10-inch sheets of paper, which cost about a penny apiece and were used like scratch-paper. At the same time, a special staff kept master charts up to date in the Management Center. Pehrson deliberately kept the number of large charts as low as possible.

"The small charts can be turned out by unskilled clerks in less than two hours," he would say proudly. "Too many organizations are swallowed up in cardboard and paste pots."

The system was a tremendous success. But soon Pehrson found it was not good enough. Companies still could fall down on jobs and the Special Projects Office wouldn't know about it until too late. The holes had to be plugged. By that October, Pehrson put a second potent management tool in Raborn's hands: so-called "line of balance" reporting.

This system originally was aimed at contractors who were producing items for the Polaris system, but later it was adopted for such projects as testing. Under it, a contractor had to specify the precise things that had to happen—and the precise time they had to happen—in order for him to deliver a finished product or complete a task on a specific date. In effect, Raborn was saying to a contractor, "Tell us what you have to do in order to meet a specific milestone." Then this information was presented on a simple graph, which also showed whether these things were done or *not done* on time.

"We are taking the guesswork out of it," Pehrson said. "A fellow no longer can get by saying, 'I'll have it there on June so-and-so,' and then say at the last moment that he can't. The line-of-balance graph shows us whether he is making it or not from the day he starts."

The controls remained simple. But more and more Raborn knew where all the pieces were on the vast board. Because of this, he could reach in at any time, at any place, and make the adjustments necessary to keep the program surging forward.

There was nothing arbitrary about either system. Milestones and schedules were worked out in conferences between contractors and Raborn's staff. But once agreed on, the pattern was put together and watched day by day for deviations. Schedules had to be met in some cases within hours. Those who failed faced Raborn. The cracking of whips could be heard from Washington to Los Angeles.

Meantime, Pehrson turned his organizing attention to what Raborn's staff was doing with the carefully groomed reports that the new systems were producing. The need for further simplification was apparent to him. Somehow the information transmitted to the Special Projects Office by contractors had to be translated into some simplified form that told busy men where each major phase of the program stood in general terms.

Pehrson's answer was a simple bar chart for each work area. Each branch of the Special Projects Office kept one that was displayed at the weekly staff meetings, which were now held in the Management Center Monday mornings, instead of Saturdays. Raborn, in turn, used a similar chart for the entire Polaris program when he reported to the Secretary of the Navy.

The bars on the charts rose and fell like barometers. Each of the four possible readings had an unequivocal meaning. A bar at the highest point meant that this particular phase of the project was "in good shape." The branch head making the report was saying, "Everything is fine. I'm on schedule where I should be." If the bar dropped one level, it signaled "minor difficulty." The branch head was saying, "I have trouble, but I can fix it." The next lower level meant "Boss, I need your help." The lowest level meant "critical difficulty." The branch head was saying, "Boss, you need help."

Pehrson, of course, felt he could do even better. He regarded both milestones and line-of-balance reporting as "pretty crude stuff." Compared to what was to come, he was right. But for the time, they served well.

Pehrson leaned on the lectern in the Management Center and talked about his handiwork.

"We recognize that our plans should be like gyros on a surfboard," he said. "You get a breakthrough in a fourth-stage plan. You swiftly recognize its significance all the way up. You hit a snag. You see instantly what the effect will be—what must be done."

He paused and smiled thinly.

"Engineers don't like to take their problems out of their pockets. If we are to succeed, they must. Managers must have blueprints, too. They must know what is going on. We have all the authority in the world to ask for information. But we must resist indulging in asking. We only want the information we need to know. We do not need to know a hell of a lot about how they are doing, building a million-dollar hangar at Cape Canaveral; that is straightforward construction work. But we may need to know a lot about a ten-thousand-dollar research project on which a whole area of progress may depend."

Pehrson silently signaled the projection man, and a vuegraph showing a colored map of the United States flashed on the screen. Thousands of black dots were scattered across it from coast to coast.

"Here are just some of our more important contractors," he said. "The members of our industry team. I get kind of excited when I see a map like this. This is just a single program—the Polaris program. This gives you an idea of what it takes to produce a weapon system. You must understand this: This is what we are dealing with: hundreds of companies throughout the country, every branch of the Navy, millions of dollars. Our job is to keep in mind the parts in relation to the whole and in relation to the clock.

"And this is another thing: People want to know what is expected of them, and they want to know their importance in relation to the whole. The guy who does the stupid thing does it because he doesn't know what he is supposed to do; he thinks he's doing what he is supposed to do. He isn't stupid. He is ignorant. We must tell him what he is supposed to do and show him its over-all importance. This is the subtle flavoring of our particular soup—getting the man into the whole picture. He must understand our high purpose. We are helping to save the country. As far as we're concerned, we are at war."

Comdr. Robert Gardemal and Ed Mernone sat in the sound booth of a Hollywood studio. They were listening to the script of the latest Polaris documentary film, designed to keep contractors and government officials informed of progress in the program. This was another of Pehrson's means of communication.

Through the booth's window Gardemal and Mernone watched George Fenneman, Groucho Marx's radio and television announcer, whose voice had become identified with the Polaris program in a dozen such films. As usual, Fenneman was having trouble with some of the terms.

"The G-load on the missile at time of ejection . . ." Fenneman said. "Aw, come on, what the hell is this? I don't know what I'm talking about."

"Just read it," Gardemal said. "You don't have to know. You're just supposed to sound as if you know."

"Westinghouse engineers faced the problem of G-load early," Fenneman read dramatically. "They also faced the problem of shoving a hydrodynamically unstable object . . ."

He made a face and looked up again.

"What's a hydrodynamically unstable object?"

"Just read," Mernone said.

"You want me to sound intelligent, don't you? How can I sound convincingly intelligent if I don't know what I'm talking about?"

"Don't worry about it," Mernone said. "You sound wonderful. Read."

# 9    Launching:
# Soapsuds and Redwood Logs

One of the engineers said, "Maybe we could fool it by putting in some detergent."

"How about pulling it out with a parachute?" offered another.

"As I see the problem," said the first engineer, "we have to kid this bird and make it think it's in the air and not in the water. That way it won't do any handsprings."

No one laughed. The conversation was deadly serious to every one of the men in the motel room. They had worked all day in the plant at Sunnyvale, and now they were still at it, proposing, questioning, and debating. The conversation was helped along by a bottle of bourbon thoughtfully provided by their boss, Dr. W. H. (Butch) Brandt, who wanted to make these nightly sessions relaxed. Brandt felt they could accomplish more if everyone loosened up away from the office.

"Maybe the best approach would be to let the missile go through the water in a big air bubble, or in a plastic bag filled with air," continued the first engineer.

"The trouble is we don't know enough about air bubbles, and we don't have the time to find out," interposed another engineer, lounging on the bed. He absently tapped a pocket slide rule against his glass.

"I know that, and that's why I think this idea of putting detergent in to create some foam—lighten the water around the missile—might do the trick."

The speaker looked inquiringly around the room. There was silence while everyone considered the idea, mentally picturing a Polaris missile rising from a submarine in a column of soapsuds.

Brandt, looking professorial with his steel-rimmed glasses and sparse gray hair, took a couple of puffs on his pipe and said dryly:

"What'll we use, Dash or Rinso?"

This time everyone chuckled.

Butch Brandt and his men were tussling with one of the most difficult problems of the new Polaris system—the launcher. The month was May, 1957, just a few weeks after the over-all blueprint for the sea-launched missile had been drawn up in final form by Special Projects. They worked for Westinghouse, which had been awarded the prime contract for developing the launcher. Some of them had been in on the design of the elevator launcher for the seagoing Jupiter. That seemed relatively simple, compared to what they were now up against.

For one thing, they knew virtually nothing about the missile except its dimensions and its shape, which was much like a champagne bottle. They were supposed to find a way to fire it from a submerged submarine, before either the missile or the submarine was built. They did know, however, that the missile could not be ignited in the submarine. The resulting danger would be too great. A "hot launch" might blow up the missile while it was still in the sub.

The key question then was how to get the missile out of the sub to some place where it could be ignited safely and sent on its way. Ideally, it should ignite above the surface of the ocean, for an explosion in the water even some distance away would hit the sub like a depth charge.

A thousand years ago the Chinese used tubes to fire rockets. When Lockheed engineers began studying the design for submarine-launched solid-fueled missiles in 1956, they decided on the ancient tube for a launcher—with an improvement. They developed an idea for expelling Polaris from the tube with compressed air while the submarine was submerged. This was the same principle as that involved in the use of the catapult for launching an airplane from a ship.

Just what sort of tube and equipment were needed to pop out the missile was Westinghouse's problem.

Brandt knew the missile would have extremely delicate instruments inside it; just how delicate no one could say. There would be nozzles on the base end, and other equipment to help steer the missile. No one knew how much of a "shot in the tail" they could stand.

This was the reason behind the serious proposal to create a column of soapsuds in the water to make it easier to get the missile to the surface. The air in the suds would make the water less dense. Therefore less push would be needed.

Dozens of ideas were considered and rejected by Brandt's group. Then it was decided that the missile didn't have to be treated so terribly gently. It would be able to withstand a pretty strong kick by compressed air. This helped narrow down the problem—they could forget about suds and air bubbles.

But the engineers immediately ran into a new batch of unknowns. No one had ever tried to eject from a submarine, through many feet of water and up into the air, a missile weighing several tons. How would this big bottle behave in the water, they wondered. It was important to find out. For if it was ejected too slowly, it might tip over. There were currents under water that might complicate matters.

They roamed the country, looking for helpful information. They found practically none. They even consulted an ichthyologist in one laboratory about how a porpoise is able to leap from the water.

They asked Navy torpedo experts for data on acceleration and velocity of torpedoes through the water. "Hell!" was the reply. "We never bothered to find out. Torpedoes have never had that problem."

In June, 1957, Ela laid down a deadline.

The first shot from a prototype launcher would be made in six months—January. This launch of a dummy missile, moreover, would be from underwater.

The Westinghouse crew began pushing night sessions well past midnight. By the end of summer, they produced a conceptual design of the tube and how it would work. The design was okayed, and following the drawing of detailed blueprints, production was begun.

Then the Westinghouse team suffered a serious loss. Brandt, who was forty-seven, died of a heart attack on September 17. Leaderless, the engineering group pushed on.

They had already turned out a test launch tube, a rather crude but effective means of gathering badly needed information.

The tube looked like a misplaced factory smokestack when it was set up on the end of a pier in the San Francisco Navy Yard. Dummy Polarises made out of redwood logs were fired from it into the water in a series of tests someone called Operation Peashooter.

The dummies popped out of the tube with a noise that

sounded like a jet plane breaking the sound barrier. Some people thought it was an earthquake.

Later on, more sophisticated tubes were built, and ingenious ways were devised to prevent recording instruments inside the dummy missiles from being damaged. At the San Francisco Navy Yard, the tube was placed on the ground under a high steel crane used to build ships. Cables were attached to the top of the missile, and when it flew up, they caught it in mid-air. This became known as Operation Skycatch. A similar technique was employed later to catch dummies popped up from underwater tubes, and this was called Operation Fishhook.

At the same time they were trying to develop the all-important underwater launcher, Ela and his Special Projects crew tackled the design of a machine that would duplicate the effect on a missile tube of the movements of a surface vessel carrying it. This became the "ship-motion simulator" which eventually was put into position at Cape Canaveral. The Navy intended to launch Polaris from both underwater and the surface of the sea, requiring the building of this latter machine.

Peashooter, plus considerably more study by underwater research laboratories at Stevens Institute, Penn State, Lockheed, the Naval Ordnance Test Station at Inyokern, California, Aerojet-General, and the Navy's David Taylor Model Basin in Washington, produced enough data to warrant building a prototype launcher. This was to be set up in the water off San Clemente Island, which lies in the Pacific about 60 miles from San Diego, for the shot in January.

But the launcher proved more difficult than anyone expected. The bars on Ela's charts in the Management Center edged downward in the fall as Sputnik rocketed into orbit. Most of the trouble lay in the special equipment that had to be sunk in the harbor with the tube to fire the missile.

The launcher's outer design was now set. There was no turning back. Across the country, men were getting ready to build the first Polaris submarine. Naval architects in the Bureau of Ships were designing the sub around the missile tubes.

Several engineers were called in to meet their new boss in his office. The slender physicist Dr. George F. Mechlin had been brought in from Westinghouse headquarters in Pittsburgh to replace Brandt.

He began to discuss the launcher while leaning back against a long table. As he talked, and went deeply into his subject, he pushed himself backward on the table, pulling up his feet, and sat with arms wrapped around his knees. Soon he leaned back on one elbow. The engineers, fascinated, watched him uncoil. As Mechlin became more engrossed, he eased himself farther down on the table. By the time the conference ended, he lay stretched out flat on his back.

"This is our new director?" one of the engineers said to another on the way out the door.

They soon discovered, however, that Mechlin was a brilliant man. And they grew accustomed to his habit of becoming totally unconscious of his physical attitude while deep in an engineering problem.

The storm hit in February, and it lasted for days. White-capped waves rolled over San Clemente harbor.

The launcher test, which was scheduled in January, still had not taken place. Men cursed the weather and had nightmares, worrying whether the thing would work. Toward the end of the month, the storm let up intermittently. Several attempts were made to anchor the launch tube on the bottom with its com-compressed air and firing equipment. Just at the critical moment gale winds sprang up capriciously, and the equipment was almost lost two or three times.

Weeks sped by before everything was in place. The whole Polaris program was now moving at an accelerated pace, and Ela's group was more than a month behind.

The final step was to rig some steel nets in the water above the launcher to catch the dummy missile. The missile was to be fired through a hole in the nets, and as soon as it cleared the water, the hole was to close, catching the missile when it fell back. The nets would keep it from dropping upon the tube, which was not too far below the surface, and which contained instruments to measure how the launch went.

Rough seas thrashed at the thick hawsers of the nets. Every time they succeeded in getting one of the nets moored, a line would part and they would have to start over again. There were one hundred tons of steel in the nets. The waves chafed steel hawsers against each other, cutting them like string.

Ela cursed. The days dragged on. Tension rose among the engineers and technicians. They'd never get the damn thing rigged.

The weather continued viciously sullen on into March. Raborn was on the phone almost daily. And Ela had nothing good to report. They were making practically no progress. As time wore on, the success of this first underwater shot grew increasingly important to Ela and everyone at San Clemente. What if the thing didn't work after all this trouble? They hated to think about it. It had to work.

Finally, the weather cleared a little, and things started to improve. All the instruments were now in place on the bottom. The nets were moored. The last task was to cock the opening in the nets so the dummy missile could pass through. Hours passed. The hole refused to stay open. Night fell and they had to quit.

The next day, they started again at dawn. Everyone was near exhaustion. Engineers snarled at the men in the boats hauling on the cables. By midafternoon, they got the opening cocked.

Ela stood on a barge nearby, wearing earphones and talking into a microphone hung around his neck. One by one, men at various posts indicated all was clear. The launcher was ready for its first test.

Sea gulls clawed the air overhead and everyone said a silent prayer. Ela pushed the button.

The dummy missile weighing about fourteen tons jumped

through the surface on a geyser of water. It shot up into the air about 50 feet. The nets snapped shut behind it, precisely as they should, and caught the missile when it fell back. It was all over in five seconds. Everything had worked perfectly.

Ela gave a hoarse shout of triumph. The other men on the barge and in the boats yelled and thumped each other on the back.

They had done it. The damn thing really worked.

Ela didn't wait for any celebration. He was on a plane two hours later, heading back to Washington.

# 10   Propulsion:
# Two Foes and a Friend

The power that enables a Polaris missile to travel 1,200 miles and farther was developed in the gold fields of the Sierra foothills, near Sacramento, California.

There at the Aerojet-General plant, scientists and engineers did what no man had done before. They designed and built the world's first large solid-fuel-propelled rocket.

The Chinese had used a solid propellant in their rockets. It was a form of gunpowder. Similar rockets had been used on and off in war ever since. But these were always small.

Then, in the early 1950s, the size of solid-fuel-propelled rockets began to grow. The propellant was no longer simple gunpowder, but various mixtures of chemicals that, once ignited, would burn rapidly with great heat, but would not explode. The diameters of solid-fuel rockets went to 10 inches, to 15, to 20. Then they stopped.

*Polaris!*

The problem was to make large quantities of a propellant that, when poured into big motor cases exceeding 20 inches in diameter, would solidify without cracking in the cases. If cracks developed, the motors were worthless. Cracked motors will explode.

This was Aerojet's problem. They had to find a way to cast large motors made of a sufficiently powerful propellant. This they did.

Two former foes and a friend pooled their talents on the West Coast of the United States to give Polaris its power.

One was Karl Klager, an Austrian chemist who had worked for Hitler's war machine. Another was Werner Kirchner, a Polish engineer who fought Hitler's Germany as a member of a Free Polish fighter squadron. Both men worked on the Polaris program at Aerojet: Klager as manager of the company's solid propellant development division, Kirchner as chief Polaris project engineer. The third man was Willie Fiedler, a brilliant German-born rocket expert who worked for Lockheed.

During World War II, Klager was a chemist for I.G. Farben at Ludwigshafen in Germany. One of the projects he worked on was the development of liquid rocket fuels that were used in German test rockets. After the war, he continued to work for I.G. Farben for three years; then he emigrated to the United States as an Operation Paperclip scientist.

First he worked for the Office of Naval Research at Pasadena, California. In 1950 he moved to Aerojet. Four months after he joined the company, he was accompanied by a Naval officer to San Ysidro on the Mexican border. He walked across the line, remained twenty seconds, and returned as a full-fledged immigrant. Five years later he became an American citizen.

Klager became involved with the Special Projects Office, the same year he became a citizen. Raborn, General Medaris, and Wernher von Braun arrived at Azusa, California, site of Aerojet's headquarters, to discuss the possible use of large solid-fuel-propelled motors for the seagoing Jupiter.

"Raborn not only listened well, he seemed able to think while he was listening," Klager recalled later. "I think we won him over to solid fuels on that day."

By 1956, Klager was head of a new Aerojet department established to work on the development of solid propellants for possible use in Jupiter. This department switched to Polaris a year later when Raborn dropped out of the Jupiter program. Klager and Kirchner, incorporating the early work of Atlantic Research, proceeded to try to make large rockets weighing thousands of pounds. It was during this period that Aerojet had its first bad accident involving Polaris solid propellants. A small plant for mixing propellant blew up. The entire solid-propellant operation was thereupon transferred from Azusa to the old Sierra gold fields.

The move reduced the risk, but it didn't end the explosions. Two more propellant mixers blew up in the summer of 1957. The first killed a man. The second killed nothing except Klager's spirits. Hasler felt even worse.

"You might say this was one of our lowest points," Hasler recalled later. "If a mix station blows up, what happens when you put the stuff on a submarine? Ponder that."

Klager did. He and his men worked almost around the clock. Lights burned at the Sacramento plant throughout the night. By the end of the year he had solved the problem, and corrections were made in the propellant.

"I always knew the propellant was no problem," he told people airily. "The Polaris motors are on firm ground."

Werner Kirchner escaped from Poland as the Nazi armies marched on Warsaw. Fleeing through the Balkans, he managed to reach the Middle East and double back to France. He had had pilot's training, and offered to fly a fighter for the French, but there were no planes. So, he joined the infantry. Six months later Hitler was in Paris and Kirchner had fled to England.

"Having lost the war in Poland and France, I offered my services to the R.A.F.," he has recollected.

Kirchner was accepted and flew in a Polish squadron throughout the war. One of his principal joys in life was knocking down V-1 guided missiles as they came across the English Channel.

"We weren't supposed to, of course," he said. "That wasn't our job, and they put cameras on our guns to make sure we only shot at what we were supposed to shoot at. So we would sneak under the V-1s' wings and give our plane a flip, and the V-1s would go over too far for their gyros and spin into the channel. Of course, you weren't supposed to stay around and watch. I had a friend who watched, and the V-1 came around and caught him on his bottom. Messy."

After the war, Kirchner left England with his English bride and emigrated to the United States. He studied at the Massachusetts Institute of Technology before moving to the West Coast and joining Aerojet.

His approach to Polaris always was frank.

"Sure we had trouble. Want to see the scars?" he has said. "We had it early. That's when it's best. You have a lot of early successes and then have trouble and you have very, very bad trouble. That we didn't have."

However, Aerojet did have a free-flying Polaris motor one day. The motor was being tested on a stand in the mountains when it broke loose. A young engineer, who was considered to be something of a dreamer, rushed into his boss's office and shouted, "There's a Polaris motor flying over the plant."

His boss said, "You're fired."

"It landed on some property we were renting to another company," Kirchner said. "It was the first interplant ballistic missile."

Polaris's two motors are basically quite simple in design. The rubbery propellant is mixed in huge vats, poured into the rocket cases, and allowed to harden. Down the center of the case is the mold, which is pulled out to form an open star-shaped core. At the end of each motor are the nozzles through which hot gas from burning fuel escapes.

The link between the two big motors and Polaris's brain is the jetavator—a metallic ring that cuts into the jet streams from the nozzles and directs their flow, steering the missile.

The inventor of the jetavator was Willie Fiedler.

During World War II, Fiedler had worked at Peenemünde and had become particularly concerned with controlling the flight of missiles. In fact, he had become so interested in the problem that he voluntarily became a test pilot on one of the early V-1s—the missiles that Kirchner later fought over the English Channel.

After the war, Fiedler emigrated to the United States and moved to the West Coast. But he was unhappy, and by the mid-1950s he planned to return to West Germany. He had already arranged for his passage when he received a personal phone call from Raborn.

The admiral had been told that Fiedler was the world's leading expert on jetavators and that his services would be most valuable to the Polaris program. That was all Raborn needed to know. He talked Fiedler out of leaving.

Two foes and a friend were the principal contributors to the motors that make Polaris go. The three had found a common cause.

# 11   Navigation and Guidance: This Way to Moscow

The meeting was something very special.

Security, always tight, was drawn tighter. Anyone whose credentials were not in perfect order was turned away. Security men carefully compared each man's signature with one on a master list, as he signed for his red Top Secret badge. No opportunity could be allowed for a Soviet spy to slip into the Management Center today. Too much was at stake.

Those invited to the meeting were a select group of contractors. The purpose: to reveal the plans for the master "brain" of the entire Polaris system—both submarine and missile.

Secrecy was essential. If enemy agents had even an inkling of how it would work, they could lay plans for sabotage in factories. They could try to find a way to jam the system at the critical moment when the missiles would be launched in anger. This latter possibility was remote, for the "brain," as conceived by SP engineers, was considered impervious to counter measures. However, there was a real danger that development, as well as production, of the fantastically complicated mass of electronic equipment needed could be sabotaged. For this reason there was to be absolutely no disclosure of the nature of contracts then in existence or to be awarded later. Raborn wanted no delays.

The long, narrow room filled and the presentation began. In clear, concise language the men in the audience, for the most part young and intense engineers who rarely smiled, were told that success or failure of the whole seagoing-missile program rested upon them and their companies. They had the responsibility of making the parts and putting them together. They

# The Men

(*Right*) Rear Admiral William F. Raborn, Jr.

(*Below*) This cartoon hung outside the office of Admiral Raborn in Washington. Admiral Arleigh Burke, Chief of Naval Operations, later wrote across the top: "Now will be better than tomorrow—and your excellent efforts have made it possible *now*."

Captain Levering Smith,
technical director

Captain John F. Refo,
testing director

Captain Monroe Hart, in charge
of ship construction

Gordon Pehrson, director of planning

Edward J. Mernone,
director of administration

Captain Dennett K. ("Deke") Ela,
director of launching

Raborn waiting to testify
at a Congressional hearing

(*Above*) Raborn arrives on
the pier at Electric Boat
for the commissioning ceremony of the *Patrick
Henry*

(*Left*) Vice-Admiral Hy-
man G. Rickover talks to
members of the Joint Con-
gressional Atomic Energy
Committee at the cere-
mony

# The Missiles

Early Polaris test missiles launched from Cape Canaveral
(*Left*) The X-17 carries an experimental nose cone
(*Center and right*) FTV's with and without stabilizing
tail fins

One of the AX series, when Polaris assumed its final shape

Launching-tube tests with dummy Polaris missiles
(*Top left*) Dummy missile leaving launcher in a test of the launching system
at San Francisco Naval Shipyard
(*Top right*) Launching a dummy missile in an assembly
that catches it in mid-air
(*Bottom left*) An underwater "pop-up" launching off San Clemente Island
(*Bottom right*) Firing a slug from a tube in the test ship *Observation Island*

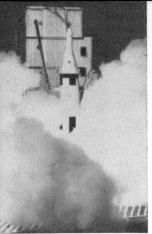

The first nearly operational Polaris soaring from
Cape Canaveral on March 9, 1960. It impacted in the ocean
about 1,000 miles down the Atlantic Missile Range

A nearly operational Polaris rips from the tube of the Ship Motion
Simulator at Cape Canaveral in a night launching

# The Ships

(*Right*) The Polaris submarine *Patrick Henry* under construction

(*Above*) The *George Washington*—first Polaris submarine—slides down the ways into the Thames River at Groton, Connecticut

(*Right*) Commander James Osborn, skipper of the *George Washington,* and Admiral Rickover standing in the *George Washington*'s sail

A Polaris submarine heads toward the North Atlantic

would create the intricate systems that, on a moment's notice, must be capable of sending a covey of sixteen nuclear-tipped missiles unerringly to their targets.

First Capt. Lew Schock, then Capt. Frank Herold, took the lectern at the front of the room. They spoke about navigation, fire control, guidance. They spoke of current theories of what was known and what had to be invented. They pointed to carefully prepared charts. Diagrams and slides were flashed on the glass screen in the front wall. The presentation was complete. Every detail had been thought through down to the delivery dates, precisely as called for by the Steering Task Group in its master blueprint.

The display of competence was dazzling. Most of the lean and brainy electronic engineers were having a new experience. They were men accustomed to having the roles reversed. Ordinarily, they would do the talking, the planning, not the man in uniform. It was disconcerting. The men running SP were pushing them beyond the limit of what they knew technically and what their companies were capable of producing.

The presentation came to an end. There was the customary "Any questions, gentlemen?" It was intended to open a discussion period. Instead, no one spoke. A heavy silence fell over the room.

Red Raborn, standing now at the front of the room, had already informed the group that he expected them to voice their candid opinions and reactions. He did not want anyone on his team to harbor a private resentment or notion as to the wisdom of the undertaking. They were all working together, or would be from now on. Either they agreed this massive brain for Polaris could be created, or they could get off the team.

He waited. But no one spoke.

Tension rose in the silent room. In another minute Raborn would be forced to break off the meeting prematurely on a bad note. These men would walk out diffidently, not as an enthusiastic team. Raborn wanted criticism, interest, ideas, to bring the job alive. There was no time for anyone to retire to a cubbyhole and mull things over. Some of the reluctance to speak up certainly could be attributed to the unfamiliarity of the group with the plan and each other. They were practically all strangers. Several of their companies were competitors. Bright as they were, some of these men were now on thin ice. The one who said something first might betray himself and appear stupid. The whole task looked positively frightening.

Raborn surveyed the room coolly, patiently. There had been moments like this one before. He would not let them go until he absolutely had to.

Finally, a man wearing a dark suit and steel-rimmed glasses rose slowly to his feet. He spoke a little hesitantly and without expression, his voice carrying clearly.

"As I understand it," he said, "you want us to take the submarine down, leave it down, and launch missiles under there if and when the time comes. Well, that's not so hard. We can invent inertial navigation to guide the submarine. We can develop a computer capable of cross-checking it. We can get side position readings from star fixes taken through the periscope. We can use radio aids, electrologs, any of twelve or so different instruments."

He paused, looking squarely at Raborn.

"That leaves us only one problem. In my opinion, the whole thing's impossible!"

Laughter exploded through the soundproofed room. Everyone joined in. A grin split Raborn's freckled face.

The laughter cleared the air. Everyone began to talk. They enthusiastically attacked the problem.

It was impossible. But it would be done. As every man in the Navy knows, the impossible is only supposed "to take a little longer."

The master brain for the Polaris system was conceived as having three distinct parts, all with separate functions and all integrated with each other. They were designated as navigation, fire control, and missile guidance.

Navigation unquestionably was singularly important. An error of one degree in determining the direction of the submarine from true north at the time of launch would mean, over a 1,500-mile distance, the missile would miss the target by 30 miles. Hence, the submarine had to know its position almost to the yard—and its direction from north to a very small fraction of a degree—at all times, an incredibly difficult feat. The stand-bys of navigation—the sextant and magnetic compass—could never achieve this degree of accuracy, no matter how skilled the navigator. Most ships' captains consider their vessels on course if their calculated position is within a few miles of the actual position at sea. That is all that is needed to get from one port to another.

The SP men who looked at the circles "Savvy" Sides and Dan Gallery had drawn on the globe around Russian targets also realized something else. Even if the sextant and magnetic compass could be made to pin-point a position accurately, they would be useless in a Polaris submarine. The subs would be operating under the polar icecap and in waters where it would be impossible many times to raise a periscope for a star "fix," the classic means of accurately determining the position of a ship. Furthermore, above the Arctic Circle, magnetic compasses go askew. They are then too close to the northern terminal of the earth's magnetic field to hold any one position.

The only answer to the problem was *inertial* navigation. Inertial navigation gets its name from a physical characteristic of the gyroscope; once set in motion, a gyro will remain in a fixed position or course by its own momentum or *inertia*. This is the principle that makes it possible to ride a bicycle "no hands." The wheels of the bike are gyros. Unless the rider touches the handle bars, the bike will follow a straight course down a street of its own momentum.

An inertial navigator could work independently of the stars

or the earth's magnetism—in theory. What bedeviled the contractors was translating this theory into a piece of equipment. There would have to be electronic devices to sense every new direction of the submarine, using the gyro as the reference point. And all this information would have to be accumulated in and processed through a computer to indicate the sub's position continuously. It would be one of the most complex electronic computation systems ever created.

Compounding the problem was the fact that somehow it all had to be squeezed into the relatively narrow confines of a submarine. Many computers of the day, which might be adaptable, were so large they filled an entire building.

The men working on the navigation system were told they had to "miniaturize" the computer and the other sensing devices at a time when "miniaturization" of electronic equipment was still relatively in its infancy. The tiny transistor that made it possible, by eliminating the bulky vacuum tube, was still a fairly untried device. However, there was no question that transistors had to be used in the Polaris system. This was a risk—one of the many calculated advances in the "state of the art" necessary to the achievement of the fantastic goal Raborn had set.

Fortunately, the Navy already had a running start.

When the Navy reluctantly awakened after the war to the possibilities of nuclear propulsion, a few men in the Bureau of Ships began casting around for a better system of navigation. They knew it would be needed in a nuclear-driven sub that could stay submerged for many days and weeks. The sub would not be able to take advantage of its release from surface recharging of batteries if it had to come up repeatedly to establish its position.

A small navigation study group was set up in 1948. But, like the rest of the Navy, it was starved for funds. Several times, the exponents of inertial navigation—they called it SINS (ships inertial navigation system)—were nearly budgeted out of existence.

The foremost expert in the nation on navigation was Dr. Charles Draper of the Massachusetts Institute of Technology, and the Navy went to him with the problem. Dr. Draper headed a laboratory that had developed the ultraprecise bombsights used late in the war by the Air Force. He also had developed and built inertial navigation equipment for aircraft.

But not much of a practical nature was known about gyros, the key instrument in any inertial system. The German rocketmen had used them to stabilize the V-1 and V-2 missiles on course. For ballistic missiles, however, gyros did not have to work very long; only a few minutes or a half-hour at the most. Gyros for a shipboard system would have to operate for months and years. This was a major problem. Scientists had discovered that a gyro, even if perfectly balanced, had a tendency to "drift" off course after a period of time. Some way had to be found to measure drift and compensate for it.

Draper and the other experts in his laboratory went to work. They struggled with the problem for five years. Finally, late in 1953, they delivered the first experimental model SINS to the Navy.

The inertial navigator made its historic first run on land. The strange new device was put in a truck trailer and hauled over highways on a route running from Boston to New York and then south to Washington. Technicians checked its readings against known reference points and mileage figures throughout the trip. The debut performance wasn't bad. Over the nineteen-hour run, the first inertial navigator ended up only sixteen miles off course.

Much encouraged, the SINS group installed the navigator aboard an oiler, the *Canesteo,* and tested it for six weeks at sea. Later it was put aboard the auxiliary vessel *Alcor,* where it successfully navigated a course across the Atlantic to the Mediterranean, thence to the Caribbean, and back to Norfolk, Virginia.

Convinced that they now had achieved the first major advance in naval navigation in a century, the SINS group proudly arranged a demonstration of their new gadget in Washington during the summer of 1954. Invitations were extended to high officials throughout the Navy. But, on the appointed day, only one man appeared: Rear Admiral Rickover, the waspish "father" of the nuclear submarine.

"Everybody apparently figured," a Navy officer said wryly, "that a 150-pound ensign with a sextant and compass could do everything that SINS could."

Rickover's interest was sufficient, however. SINS was kept alive for him and the nuclear submarine. Although the M.I.T. equipment worked fairly well, it needed considerable improvement. There were many "bugs" to be worked out, and it had a questionable reliability, particularly in compensating for gyro drift.

Special Projects began looking at SINS almost from the beginning. It would have been invaluable in the launching of Jupiters from surface ships, since the same problem of pin-pointing their position at the time the missile was fired existed for them, too. By this time, late in 1955, the SINS division was under the command of Lew Schock, an extremely intelligent and articulate Naval officer who, according to one of his associates, "came out of shipbuilding and learned everything there was to know about SINS in six months."

Raborn obtained the transfer of Schock from the Bureau of Ships to SP in February, 1956, while the Jupiter was undergoing its metamorphosis. Later on in the year, the entire inertial navigation division was made SP's responsibility. Refinement of the system continued doggedly ashore and aboard the *Compass Island* after she was commissioned late in 1956. Gradually the moratorium on money lifted, and Schock was able to let seventy contracts to various companies and universities, each to improve some part of the navigation system. The gyro problem persisted, nevertheless.

SINS still was not considered good enough in 1957 to put aboard the *Nautilus* when the nuclear-propelled submarine made her first probe under the Arctic ice to within 200 miles of the North Pole. This trip proved that inertial navigation was going to be absolutely essential for Polaris submarines. The *Nautilus'* skipper, Comdr. William R. Anderson, later reported that after turning around near the Pole, the submarine became lost and almost ran into the coast of Greenland. The magnetic compass and a new gyrocompass, which had been installed aboard the submarine, failed, the latter after it had blown a fuse.

A solution to SINS' difficulty was still evading SP as winter approached in 1957, when a chance encounter in Boston introduced new hope. One of the SP navigation experts fell into a conversation with John Moore of the Autonetics Division of North American Aviation during a meeting of electronic engineers at M.I.T. Moore was bemoaning the cancellation by the Air Force of a big missile project known as the Navaho. As general manager of the division, Moore had been forced to lay off 1,500 engineers who had been working on the missile's guidance system. The Navaho was a winged 5,000-mile-range missile powered by air-breathing ramjet engines. Because it would take at least four hours to reach a target, Autonetics had invented what basically was an inertial navigator to guide it. The system, different from the one Dr. Draper had conceived, had already shown a high degree of accuracy.

The SP man lost no time in bringing Moore to Washington. He had a lead worth looking into. Schock agreed, and Moore went back to California with a contract to deliver, by September, 1958, one Navaho navigator modified for submarine use. Moore moved quickly. His company produced a navigator, which was installed in the *Nautilus* in April, almost two months before the *Nautilus* was to set out upon her epic transpolar voyage. The *Nautilus'* successful trip from the Pacific to the Atlantic across the top of the world opened a northwest passage. It also opened the era of the shipboard inertial navigator.

Thanks to all the early work that had been done, one SINS unit alone did not present too imposing a production problem. But its auxiliary equipment—the gadgets to check gadgets that were checking other gadgets—became an enormous headache. SP was determined to leave nothing to chance. Every possibility for error had to be eliminated. This meant duplication—so-called "backup" instrumentation.

A submarine like the *Nautilus* could sail a course with one inertial navigator. One was sufficient to show the way, particularly for short point-to-point voyages. Polaris submarines, however, would have to stay submerged on station for sixty days, lying quietly in the water, or perhaps making tight circles. It would be expecting too much for one SINS to function continuously—and accurately—for two months.

Therefore, Schock's engineers decided there should be not one, but three, inertial navigators in each submarine. In addition, there would be three other independent systems for monitoring the inertial navigators, to determine whether they functioned properly. These ancillary systems included regular celestial navigation through the sub's periscope, but only as a last resort. Sticking up the periscope might give away the sub's position. Moreover, visual "fixes" need clear skies. So Schock gave orders for radio-metric sextants, which could sense—through radio impulses—the position of the sun, moon, and stars. Other contracts were issued for electronic position-giving instruments.

The task of producing all these systems and putting them together into one neat, completely integrated package fell to the Sperry Gyroscope Company of Great Neck, Long Island. The company also received contracts for the submarine steering equipment, which would work from a "stick" like the steering equipment in an aircraft and actually enable the submarine to be steered much as an airplane is flown.

Sperry did not take over until 1958. It immediately found itself squeezed in the SP time compressor.

Normally, for a job so complicated—the entire navigation system has been estimated to contain more than one million parts—separate pieces of equipment would be lowered into the submarine, hooked up, and tested. This would be, and is, a lengthy, exacting chore anywhere. In the tight confines of a submarine, it is much harder. Tracing a break in one cable can delay a project hours, sometimes days.

But Sperry did not even have a submarine to put anything into. The submarine was still under construction at Groton, Connecticut.

The old art of make-believe opened a way out. A reproduction of the hull section, where the navigation center would be located, was built in a laboratory owned by Sperry at Syosset, Long Island. The equipment was installed in the replica, exactly as it would be in the first Polaris sub, the *George Washington.* The equipment was so assembled that, once it was working properly, it could be transferred to the *George Washington* and literally "plugged in" in a few hours.

Raborn thought so highly of this "Ashore Polaris Navigation Center," landlocked amidst Long Island's split-levels, that he welcomed an opportunity on a hot July day in 1959 to "launch" it. His wife performed the christening with a bottle of sea water.

The difficulty in launching a Polaris missile from a submarine and hitting a target 1,500 miles away has been likened to the attempt of a marksman to knock a beer can off a fence post while riding a horse at a gallop—blindfolded. The variables to be taken into account are fantastic. Location of the submarine is but one. Actually, the most important role played by navigation is in determining the precise direction of true north. For all missiles are aimed along an angle established by the relationship of the target to the North Pole.

But at the moment of launch, the missile—which also is guided inertially—must also contain what is known as a "stable table." This is a round platform controlled by gyros, which align it horizontally with the center of the earth. To achieve perfect alignment, a variety of complex instruments must continuously record every motion of the submarine and simultaneously make compensating adjustments to the "stable table." If the table is tilted when the missile is fired, the guidance system will have a false reference point and the missile will either fall short, overshoot its target, or go astray.

The job of making all these fine corrections rests upon the Polaris fire control system. The manner in which they are made electronically is fantastically complex—an engineering nightmare.

To begin with, adjustments must be made for six ship motions: pitch, the end-to-end movement of the submarine; heave, up and down; roll, side to side; surge, as on a wave; sway; and yaw, which is a sidewise movement caused by a wave when it strikes the bow. Since the submarine normally launches the missiles from below the surface, pitch, roll, and heave are the most serious movements to be encountered. They are caused by underwater currents and the sub's speed. The other three movements would be felt far more in launching from the surface, where there is wave motion.

Fire control also must correct for the earth's rotation and atmospheric influences. And it must even refine some of the information coming from the inertial navigator before giving it to the guidance "brains" of the missiles.

Finally, as conceived by Captain Herold and his engineers, the fire control system needed lightning-fast reflexes that would give it the ability to change signals with a speed that would stagger a football quarterback. It would be expected to give in a few seconds different target directions to the guidance package inside each of the sixteen Polaris missiles aboard a submarine.

Prior to launch, the gyros in each missile guidance package would be "spun up," set in motion to stabilize the "stable table." This activity is part of the Polaris countdown. To insure that each guidance system is functioning properly, the fire control panel had to have dials and gauges telling the operator that all was in readiness.

Most important of all, the fire control panel would contain the buttons that are pushed to send the missiles on their way— at the rate of one a minute!

Little wonder that back in 1957, when they were given their first look at the plan for the "brain," the contractors thought they were being asked to do the impossible.

The General Electric Company's ordnance department, which developed the fire control and guidance systems for Polaris, originally was invited into the fleet ballistic missile program to work on fire control while the Navy was still wrestling with the Jupiter. Fire control at that early date was presenting new complications every day. Just sitting down and drawing the wiring diagrams and listing all the parts that were needed was staggering.

Special Projects, moreover, decided that two similar types of fire control were required for Polaris. One would go aboard the submarines—the other would fire the missiles while they were being tested at Cape Canaveral and aboard the *Observation Island*. The big difference was in size. For the test equipment, which had to be delivered first, there were no limitations on bulk. The second system had to be small enough to fit into a submarine.

Engineers from Captain Herold's SP unit and GE were still in the process of defining what would be needed, when Raborn shifted to the Polaris missile and moved up the deadline to 1963. This decision, in the minds of many people connected with the project, marked a beginning—and an end. It was the beginning of hectic, all-but-limitless workdays and the end to anything resembling normal home life. Babies, wives, newly purchased power tools for the cellar workshop, and personal career objectives were set aside by the plunge into a seemingly bottomless well of work.

It started first for fifteen engineers connected with GE's ordnance and light military electronics departments and a major subcontractor, Librascope. These men were given a locked room where they remained sixteen hours a day, seven days a week, until the complete design of the system was finished. Their work was turned over to other engineers, who sat down at drawing boards to design the individual parts—the internal electronic circuits—for each piece of equipment that would go into the entire fire control system. Only a few months after this phase of the work began in 1957, largely at GE's plant in Pittsfield, Massachusetts, Russia's Sputnik I went into orbit. The new acceleration was on. They would have to deliver three years sooner.

Because of its complexity in installation, and the possibility that something could go wrong that needed major correction, SP decided the combat fire control system should be delivered almost a year in advance of the date when the first Polaris submarine would go on combat patrol. The equipment, in order to meet the schedule, would have to be installed before the submarine first went to sea.

Under the 1963 operational date, this meant the equipment could be made with parts available in 1962. Correspondingly, when the program was accelerated to 1960, the parts would be of 1959 vintage.

This created a crisis. Looking ahead to 1962, the engineers cooped up in their locked room had decided the electronic parts would be better and smaller and would fit into less space. Therefore, they allowed less space for the equipment. Suddenly told they must use 1959 parts, which were bigger, they needed more space.

Back they went into the "think" room at GE. They asked for one month to come up with new dimensions for the equipment. No, was the reply from SP. Work on the submarine would be stopped too long, and the whole program would be delayed. They were given one week.

To their surprise, they met the deadline. They asked for a little more space in the submarine and they got it. But, they were told, no matter what happened, that was all they would get.

And they were told to deliver the first fire control system to the Electric Boat shipyard at Groton by New Year's Eve, 1959— a little more than twelve months away.

# 12 "Green Board—
Pressure on the Boat"

Sputnik's shadow reached out and touched Bill Atkinson on December 7, 1957.

Only a few days before, Atkinson had bought a new home near the Thames River at Gales Ferry, Connecticut, a pleasant old New England town. It was a Christmas present for his wife Martha, who had just given birth to their second son. They were counting on moving in before the holidays, and Atkinson was in the process of trying to sell his first house. But on the day he was pounding a For Sale sign into the front yard, a succession of urgent telephone calls was being made between nearby Groton and Washington. They were to affect his house, his Christmas, and his life for months to come.

The calls were to Atkinson's boss, Carleton Shugg, a former deputy general manager of the Atomic Energy Commission, who now ran the nation's largest private submarine yard at Groton— the Electric Boat Division of General Dynamics Corporation. Officials in the Navy's Bureau of Ships were on the line, informing Shugg they were in a jam. Red Raborn wanted his first Polaris submarine in a big hurry. They had just been told of the acceleration of the Polaris program. The deadline for putting missile-carrying submarines on station had been moved up from 1963 to 1960. Three years were wiped out, leaving almost no time to produce the submarine.

Shugg could appreciate the problem. Electric Boat had pioneered in building nuclear-powered submarines, beginning with the *Nautilus* and *Seawolf,* and now was building the latest class of nuclear-powered attack submarines for the Navy. Bringing in a new submarine—particularly a prototype, the first of a class—was a long and difficult job. From a standing start, the fastest that a new-class submarine can be put to sea is about three years.

BuShips, as the Bureau of Ships is known familiarly in Navy jargon, had been working for nearly six months on the design of the new Polaris sub ordered by Raborn with the switchover from Jupiter. The Bureau's engineers had practically completed the preliminary plans for the huge new submersible called for by Special Projects master blueprints. On paper the sketches showed a sub with a radically different hull, shaped like a football. The streamlined hull would make her almost as fast as the *Skipjack*—then on the ways of Electric Boat and expected to be the speediest underwater vessel afloat. The Polaris submarine would weigh more than 6,000 tons and be more than 400 feet long.

The submarine had to be launched and commissioned—turned over to the fleet—a full nine months before she would receive her missiles and go on station under the timetable imposed by Special Projects. There had been no real squeeze under the original deadline for delivering the Polaris sub by the end of 1962. However, the acceleration to 1960 placed delivery at the end of 1959—just two years away.

Numerous suggestions and approaches were discussed in the cryptic, guarded telephone calls. They all pointed to one inescapable conclusion: start building without further delay.

Shugg's next move, once the Navy got him to agree to shoulder the problem, was to send for Bill Atkinson, tell him to drop everything and take charge. Atkinson left for Washington two days later.

Possessed of seemingly boundless energy, Atkinson at thirty-two was singularly equipped mentally, physically, and by experience to assume what admittedly was a fantastic job. Built like an end, the six-foot, three-inch naval engineer on December 9 lunged into a grinding work schedule. He took over an office in BuShips, practically living in it five days a week. On Friday nights he rushed back to Groton for Saturday and Sunday conferences at Electric Boat. His family saw him only on Saturday nights for a few hours; he headed back to Washington Sunday nights. The new house stood empty for months; there was no time to negotiate the sale of the old one, which meant carrying both at the same time at a personal financial loss. It was just one more worry to occupy whatever free moments he could tear away from the submarine, which had become an all-devouring challenge not only to him but to everyone else who came into contact with her.

To an outsider it might have seemed strange that Shugg should turn over most of the responsibility to a man only thirty-two years old. But not to Shugg. Atkinson had already proved himself to be a man who could do things well and quickly. He had come to Electric Boat eight years before, shortly after graduating from Massachusetts Institute of Technology with a degree in naval architecture, and progressed to assistant chief mechanical draftsman of the yard. Early in his career the company sent him to the Oak Ridge School of Reactor Technology for a year to learn about the new nuclear propulsion system being designed for submarines. On his return, Atkinson went to work on the *Nautilus,* then just on the ways.

One thing that had struck Atkinson when he applied for the school at Oak Ridge was the lack of understandable texts on practical applications of atomic energy. Never having studied nuclear physics in college, he looked in vain for a book that would give him a working knowledge of the field. Back at Electric Boat, he began instructing a course in elementary nuclear physics to his fellow engineers at the plant. The course was a hit. And since there was no text, Atkinson wrote one, which was printed by the company and later sold to a textbook publisher.

Electric Boat's relationship with the Polaris program when Atkinson arrived in Washington is best described as hazy. BuShips had invited Electric Boat to assist in the drawing of the contract plans—the actual working blueprints—for the new sub, under a contract for a nominal $60,000. Atkinson, and the staff of twenty-five engineers and draftsmen who followed him from Electric Boat, were really supplementing the staff at BuShips. Within days, however, the picture changed abruptly.

The change came with the realization that if someone didn't act very quickly, there wouldn't be any steel with which to start building the submarine. Steel producers furnish their products to big industrial concerns on a quarterly basis. New orders are not filled until after a new quarter starts—and one was starting on January 1. If the first of the year passed without a steel order, then three months would be lost—three months that certainly could not be spared.

Using the preliminary drawings, his thumb, the combined guesswork and calculations of his team in Washington, and one thousand more engineers assigned to the project back in Electric Boat, Atkinson began feverishly to prepare orders for steel. There were dozens, running into the millions of dollars.

The thickness of the steel going into the sub's pressure hull was classified a secret. It couldn't be discussed over the telephone. Atkinson couldn't be in two places at the same time, and it was necessary for him to consult with the crew at Groton in making up the orders. He ingeniously skirted the problem by making up a series of coded sketches, which he brought up to Groton on one of his weekend sorties. In Washington, working from a duplicate, he could refer, over the telephone to Groton, to various sections by letter and number—the number standing for the thickness—with no break of security.

Christmas passed in a flurry of figures and paperwork. Time was the only consideration; nothing could wait—not even the customary letting of bids for a contract to build the sub. Since Atkinson and the other members of the Electric Boat team knew more about the new submarine than anyone else, it seemed natural that Electric Boat would receive the job. But the first of the year approached—and the Navy still had not put anything down on paper. Finally, a BuShips official indicated that the Navy would not look with disfavor on Electric Boat's contracting for the steel anyway—adding in the same breath, "But I'm not authorizing you to do it."

Electric Boat's attitude was "The hell with pussyfooting—we'll get the steel." On New Year's Eve, orders prepared by Atkinson were brought to Shugg at his home in Groton. He signed them —around 3 million dollars' worth—and off they went to the steel companies. If the Navy didn't give him a contract, the company was going to be stuck with a pile of steel. "We took a gamble," Atkinson told an associate later, "a real gamble. As it turned out, I made some bad guesses and we ordered some steel we didn't need. But we got started building without losing any time and eventually signed a contract."

At the same time he was computing material requirements, work was proceeding rapidly on the blueprints. Submarines are extremely complicated machines, and they require about four thousand individual blueprints—each measuring 30 inches by 12 feet long. It takes two months to draw and check them, and to ascertain the material needed for each section covered by a blueprint. Although many could be done simultaneously and not all were needed at once, six weeks to two months still were needed for the initial drawings before the keel could be laid.

Someone in BuShips had an idea how to save some of this precious time. Back on November 1, the keel had been put down at Electric Boat for the *Scorpion,* a sister sub of the *Skipjack.* Many of the large curved sections of steel that formed the hull already were in place. Instead of starting from scratch on a new submarine, it was proposed that this one under construction could be adapted to missiles. The keel could be cut and the bow moved forward to permit the insertion of a missile section.

Engineers pondered the idea, and the more they studied it, the more sense it made. All the submarine parts that take the longest time to make—the reactor power plant, the turbines, and reduction gears—had already been ordered for the *Scorpion* long before, and would fit into the missile sub's two-year timetable. The only real question lay in the power plant: would it be powerful enough? It was designed to push a 2,830-ton sub, and the missile submarine would weigh 5,400 tons—a difference of 2,570 tons. More calculations.

Admiral Rickover, the AEC, BuShips, and Atkinson went into a huddle. They emerged with a verdict that the extra weight would not appreciably affect the speed of the heavier submarine. The *Scorpion*'s reactor would do. At most, the top speed of the first Polaris sub might be a few knots less than the *Skipjack*'s.

The decision was made to bisect the *Scorpion*.

Welders unceremoniously attacked the 250-foot keel with torches in mid-January, slicing it like the skeleton of a fish. The cut was made midway in the hull, just behind where the conning tower—now called the sail—would be. A 15-foot section was removed, and the bow was moved forward 130 feet, the length of the missile section that was yet to be built. The effect on the sleek design of the *Scorpion* was not unlike cutting a cigar in two and placing the halves on either end of a matchbox. The missile section gave the sub a rectangular midsection covered by a humpback.

The appearance and the cut didn't bother Atkinson as much as what it did to the Polaris sub's original preliminary designs and blueprints. He regarded them as being "shot to hell." Fortunately, the after end of the *Scorpion,* where the reactor is located—the most complicated part of the sub—was not greatly affected. Fifteen hundred blueprints, a whole year's work, were salvaged.

Submarine builders do not like to cut a keel after it is started. Their antipathy arises not so much from fear of creating a structural weakness, as from the offense to their aesthetic sense. It means they are tampering with a masterpiece. The design of a submarine hull springs from the mind of an architect and from a thousand tests of models in laboratory tanks to determine hydrodynamic characteristics—the equivalent of wind tunnel tests for aircraft and missiles. When the design is completed, the submarine builders believe, that's the way the ship should look when she slides down the ways.

However, since the introduction of the "black box," symbol of ever-proliferating electronic gadgets, submarine designers have become resigned to changes. Flinching inwardly, Atkinson had twice had to order cuts in the *Seawolf* and in her sister sub, the *Skate,* which later became the first sub to surface in the middle of the ice pack at the North Pole. Though it seemed like a radical idea to many people to open up the *Scorpion,* by that time it was nothing new at Electric Boat.

With the remaking of the *Scorpion,* which originally was intended to be a hunter-killer submarine, Special Projects rechristened the hull the *George Washington.* The Navy, going one step further, officially designated this huge new man-o'-war a ship—holding that she was much too large to be called a boat, the traditional Navy nomenclature for submarines.

Bitter cold winds raced down the Thames River. They sawed at the high steel scaffolding standing like a giant crib on the riverbank. Nestled below, the *George Washington* slowly puffed into shape, a rust-red sausage in Electric Boat's south yards.

An electric crane with an operator boxed inside shuttled ceaselessly back and forth on rails 100 feet up in the scaffolding. Its steel hook, dangling at the end of a cable, deftly picked up slabs of steel plate from a flatcar, hauling them to the submarine.

Men moved everywhere about the hull. Carpenters. Steelworkers. Welders. Electricians. Shipfitters. A hundred blue-arced torches spluttered showers of red sparks down the side of the ship. Wind ripped the shouts out of the mouths of crew chiefs, their cheeks raw and red and their noses dripping from under their yellow protective helmets.

Not since World War II had there been such a frenzy of activity at Electric Boat. The yard was going all out. Three shifts, around the clock, Sundays, holidays, overtime. Don't stop, or you'll lose a day. Move. Remember December, 1959, and watch where the hell you're pushing that pipe.

Inside the hull more welders, their faces goggled grotesquely, worked in spaces so cramped they must move like contortionists. They used mirrors to get at some of the joints. They stepped on each other and cursed, but they went right on working.

Mechanic Fred Refo was called away from the Sunday dinner table to attend to a problem in the *George Washington*'s engine room. His wife drove him to the yard, treasuring a few extra moments with him. She said she would wait in the car and take him home. It was very cold, but she didn't mind. Fred didn't expect to be long. Five hours later he returned. She was there, half frozen, but not complaining. They could finish dinner together.

A new shift comes on. The men, hunched in their jackets, walk through the gate opening off Thames Street, clutching lunch pails and bulging paper bags in their arms. They walk down the hill toward the water, past the end of a large brick warehouse. Completely covering the top of the wall of the building are row after row of faded signs—seventy-four in all. Each bears the name of a submarine turned out at Electric Boat in World War II. Across nineteen of the plaques in large letters is inscribed LOST IN ACTION.

"Shipbuilding is the last holdout against the assembly line. It's a crazy but wonderful business," Shugg said earnestly, sitting in his office.

"The men feel it. They see the boat grow from the keel. It has a name. Personality. They even get to see the sponsor's legs. Later on they get to know the crew. The ship's a part of them, even though they've been through hell to get her into the water. And they follow carefully everything that happens to her later."

. . .

138

In a submarine, goes an old Electric Boat saying, there's room for everything but a mistake.

The *George Washington* was the first of a kind, and it was plagued by scores of mistakes. Atkinson became the chief trouble-shooter.

Returning to Groton in March of 1958, Atkinson at last sold his house and shifted from design to construction in the yard. Being completely familiar with all the plans, he could see on the job how well the designs were conceived, or as he put it, "how we goofed."

There were many goofs: a pipefitter cut a hole in a bulkhead and ran a pipe where it didn't belong; one supplier of a piece of machinery placed a valve on the side opposite to where it should have been. Several parts of the sub had to be ripped out and done over again two and three times. It was to be expected in a new ship, but every mistake threatened to delay the launching date set for June, 1959.

The skilled artisans of Electric Boat had a tradition to uphold. During the war they had turned out boat after boat months, sometimes almost a year, before the scheduled delivery dates. They were the ones who made it possible by 1944 for the yard to launch a 1,500-ton sub every two weeks—a magnificent achievement. They were doing all they could to keep the record intact with the *George Washington*.

Atkinson took the phone call himself. It was Herb Kindl in Pittsfield, GE's project manager for the fire control system. Atkinson suspected the worst, but what Kindl had to say was so appalling, it took a moment to sink in. Atkinson had been hurt before by black boxes, but never this badly.

In the original layout of the *George Washington*, the space set aside to hold all the fire control equipment seemed too small to Atkinson, though he was assured that it was adequate. On his own he increased it anyway, making it almost twice as large. Now Kindl was informing him that nine more black boxes had to go in—they were the ones needed to make the system work by 1960—and even the bigger space was now too small.

All Atkinson could mutter was "Jesus, we're dead."

But he found the room. A storage space was eliminated, the officers' wardroom was pared down a few feet, and the serving pantry was moved. The space could not be denied this most important part of the missile ship's equipment.

"The shipbuilder is bottom man on the totem pole," was the way Atkinson put it later. "All the other guys' goofs come to roost on you."

The months flew by, and with winter also came the most trying task of all—the installation of the sixteen tubes to hold the missiles. Each tube weighed several thousand pounds and measured about 30 feet in length and 8 feet in diameter. And each one had to fit into the submarine with the precision of a piston in a motor. Every dimension had to be exact, down to the thousandth of an inch. The slightest error would cost days.

Atkinson watched, a pipe clenched grimly in his teeth, as the crane hoisted the tube high over the deck. Three shipfitters waited around the hatchway as it was lowered to them. The tube descended. They touched it gently, maneuvering it over the hole. At the wave of an arm, the tube sank into the ship. It was in—in six minutes.

Nearby a new keel had been put down on May 27, 1958, designated Hull 153. This was the second Polaris sub, the *Patrick Henry*. The pace increased.

The *Patrick Henry* was an exact duplicate of the *George Washington*. She did not have to suffer the same growing pains, however. All the problems associated with design and construction had been worked out, and her building proceeded at a faster rate than her sister ship's.

A crew of mechanics, once they had accomplished a difficult

installation in the *George Washington,* would move over to the *Patrick Henry.*

Orders flowed out stamped "Top Priority," "Urgent," and "Rush."

"The only thing we're missing is a war bond rally," grumbled a fitter over a beer in a Thames Street tavern.

Nursing along the two subs just as carefully as he attended his first "baby," the *Nautilus,* Rickover assumed complete responsibility for the delivery and installation of the two nuclear reactors. He gave no one at Electric Boat a moment's peace.

"I get calls from Rickover any time of the night," Shugg told an assistant, explaining why he wanted up-to-the-minute progress reports. "And he wants an answer immediately. Rickover's idea of a long time is an hour."

Shugg had known Rickover for years. He had been Rickover's part-time boss when Rickover simultaneously headed the Navy's Nuclear Power Branch and the Civilian Liaison Committee in the AEC. In 1951, when he joined Electric Boat, the tables turned for Shugg. Rickover became his boss.

They came to grips with each other the next year, when the *Nautilus* slipped three months behind schedule. There was no tremendous urgency to produce the *Nautilus,* since she was an experimental ship, and extra time could easily have been granted for her construction. But Rickover's response to the news that she was behind schedule was to shorten the original schedule by another three months—forcing Electric Boat to work twice as fast to catch up.

"You know," Shugg said later, "we found it was easier to do something twice as fast."

Rickover had prepared Electric Boat for the superhuman effort it was able to make to build the new missile submarines.

The *George Washington* rumbled down the ways on June 9, 1959. Just eighteen months had elapsed since a welder's torch had knifed into the *Scorpion.* An entire year had been cut from the time it had taken to build the *Skipjack.*

On her huge sail was painted her number—598. Her bow was gaily covered with red, white, and blue bunting. Mrs. Robert B. Anderson, wife of the Secretary of the Treasury, hit the bow with a bottle of domestic champagne. Under the hull, men pulled out the shoring timbers, and the *George Washington* slid out into the Thames. As the hull tasted water for the first time, the Electric Boat Division band played "Anchors Aweigh."

It was a proud and satisfying moment to almost everyone but Atkinson. The pomp and ceremony, brief as it was, was still a delay. As soon as the ship could be moored to a dock, Atkinson impatiently ordered work crews aboard. Much outfitting and installation and testing of equipment still lay ahead. There were less than six months left to do it in.

Electric Boat was not the only birthplace of the first Polaris submarines. More subs were being built at other yards, to the same specifications as the *George Washington.*

The *Theodore Roosevelt* was going up on the ways at Mare Island, a government-owned yard at San Francisco. The keel had been laid seven days before the *Patrick Henry*'s.

Just outside Norfolk, the Newport News Shipbuilding & Drydock Company was building the *Robert E. Lee,* having laid a keel on September 25, 1958. And at a second government yard in Portsmouth, New Hampshire, a fifth sub—the *Abraham Lincoln*—had been started in November, 1958.

All three yards clamored for information on how to solve the knottier construction problems in a minimum length of time. They looked to Electric Boat, the "lead yard," to supply it quickly. There was no time to wait, not even for the mails.

Engineers from other yards descended on Electric Boat for a look at the *George Washington.* On the same day, they would bundle up plans and head for home by plane. Ship-to-ship telephone lines were hooked up to speed communications. When a description of how something should look was needed, an engineer would snap a Polaroid photograph and have it delivered by courier.

The Navy worried about the fact that the other yards were following so closely. A time lag of nine months to a year was preferable, to catch mistakes in design. However, Raborn's luck held and none developed.

Normal workdays were now twelve and fourteen hours. Men streamed back and forth across the gangplank of the *George Washington* with antlike resolution.

The sub had been out to sea for the first time on November 17 and passed her builders' trials with flying colors. Raborn wired Shugg, "Heartiest congratulations to you and your fine company on the splendid job on the *George Washington*."

She was almost ready. Atkinson and his men had only to make the final tests and adjustments, to plug up leaks and do a thousand and one other painstaking little jobs, and the Navy could have her. There was also one big job left. The fire control equipment. It was due aboard before the ship was commissioned. The date for this formal occasion was December 30, 1959.

But there was trouble at Pittsfield.

General Electric engineers were still feeling the effects of a numbing discovery made back in August, 1958. They had taken the wrong approach in designing a very delicate motor for the fantastically complex fire control system. The motor would control the accuracy of the missiles. They had to redesign it from the beginning.

The heartbreaking mistake was to be expected in producing so complicated a system in so short a time. But through unrelenting effort, the GE crew had succeeded in making up most of the time lost.

They were racing the clock by working sixty- and seventy-hour weeks.

One engineer, Charles E. Kraus, was so absorbed in running fire control tests one night, as the deadline approached, that he completely forgot about his expectant wife. Without calling him, she had taken a taxi to the hospital in Pittsfield and gone into the delivery room. At 9 P.M. a nurse phoned the plant and informed Kraus that his wife had just given birth to twins. He politely thanked her, went back to work, and did not realize at all what she had told him until he stopped at midnight for a coffee break.

Christmas week came, and no fire control equipment had arrived. Everyone began to worry. If one of the black boxes were too big and wouldn't fit through a hatchway, or if they all couldn't squeeze into the fire control room, the *George Washington* would miss her deadline.

Finally, on Christmas Eve, a big trailer truck rumbled to the dock. It was from General Electric, and no Christmas present looked any finer to the Electric Boat crew. All it needed was a red ribbon on it.

The fire control equipment had arrived. To the relief of everyone, when it was swung aboard a few days later, all the boxes fitted to the inch.

Except for the missiles, the first fleet ballistic missile submarine was now in being.

Fort Griswold stands on a hill overlooking Groton and the Electric Boat shipyard. Most of the fort is in ruins. A tower, which has been made into a monument, stands a lonely watch over the place. A plaque at the base notes that on September 6, 1781, the British under command of the traitor Benedict Arnold burned both New London and Groton.

The Revolutionary troops who gallantly defended the fort were commanded by Lt. Col. William Ledyard. On a gatepost at the entrance to the fort is another weathered bronze plaque depicting the last moments of the defenders. A bas-relief shows Ledyard offering his sword to a conquering British officer, who is not identified.

Below it is inscribed:

"British officer: 'Who commands this fort?'"

"Ledyard: 'I did sir but you do now.' "

The British officer thereupon took the sword and ran it through Ledyard. Eighty-seven of Ledyard's men died with him.

Nearly two centuries later, on December 30, 1959, a group of small boys played in the old fort and looked down on a crowd gathered at an Electric Boat pier. The *George Washington* lay alongside it.

Before microphones set up on the ship's missile deck stood Dr. George B. Kistiakowski, President Eisenhower's scientific advisor. A pale winter sun glinted on the crowd gathered on the dock. Kistiakowski's voice echoed from the loudspeakers:

". . . it was 160 years ago this month that George Washington died, but this spirit—his spirit—has never foundered. It has been built into this ship to maintain peace and to preserve our precious way of life. . . ."

The men of the *George Washington,* dressed in blues and with campaign medals strung along their chests, mementos of World War II and the Korean War, stood rigidly at attention in a mass formation on the after end of the missile deck. A motion picture camera whirred impassively in the press section.

"Like her namesake, this *George Washington* will be in the hearts of our countrymen, particularly in the hearts of the men and women of the Electric Boat Division of the General Dynamics Corporation. . . ."

Four sea gulls flapped noisily off an adjacent pier and headed out over the water toward a passing barge. In the front row of the spectators' stand a young wife thought of long vacant days to come, as she looked at her officer husband, resplendent in his white cap and gold sword.

"Let us remember that under this stout hull there are now hidden—or soon will be—the most advanced and diverse products of our technology: turbine and rocket propulsion; nuclear power and nuclear weapons; electronics tailored into sophisticated radar, radio, sonar, and many other applications. . . ."

In a row of chairs behind the speaker sat Raborn, a smile pulling up the corners of his mouth; Shugg, looking solemn; and several high-ranking Naval officers. At one end was Comdr. James Osborn, the new skipper of the sub. A smart breeze whipped the American flag flying on a temporary mast raised on the low-lying stern. Wind blowing into the microphone smothered some of the words.

"Yours is a glorious heritage. . . . We know that you will be brave, be loyal, be faithful to the ideals of George Washington. To each of you we wish for every dive 'Green board'— 'pressure on the boat,' and on every cruise smooth sailing. . . ."

# 13   The Ghost Walks

In the spring of 1957, half a year before Sputnik, the House Military Appropriations Subcommittee ended a rather long day with a few words from Admiral Raborn. The admiral had been waiting for several hours in the ornate Victorian hearing room in the House Wing of the Capitol. The subcommittee was listening to other military men talk about a grab bag of other defense matters. Raborn sat patiently, half listening, half gazing out the window at the hazy April sky and the budding trees on the Capitol lawn. Finally, his turn came.

Raborn swiftly outlined the Polaris system that the Steering Task Group had blueprinted the last few weeks.

The missile would be powered by a solid propellant. It would have a range of 1,500 miles. It would be launched from a nuclear-powered submarine. It would be all but invulnerable.

"It could subject any target, including submarine pens and bases, to powerful Navy retaliatory action from the sea," Raborn said carefully. Then he added, "Despite the uncertainties that we face, we have maintained a conservative approach. We are also taking a calculated risk in not providing full-scale backup programs in certain major components."

Congressman Harry Sheppard of California, who was sitting in the chair, asked if there were any questions. There were none. The congressmen had other things on their minds.

"Thank you very much for your appearance," Sheppard said. "We are sorry to have had to keep you waiting so long."

"It is always an education and a pleasure, sir," Raborn said. His testimony had taken just five minutes.

Few groups of congressmen have greater influence on the fate of the United States of America than the House Military Appropriations Subcommittee. The most influential member of this pivotal group during the formative years of Polaris was its chairman, George H. Mahon of Texas.

Every dollar voted by Congress for a missile or a bomber, a warship or a bullet, had to be approved first by Mahon's subcommittee. Each new defense budget sent to Congress by the President was passed on to the sixteen-member subcommittee. When the spending bill emerged from the subcommittee, its dimensions were set. There might be dickering over some items, but the final defense budget passed by Congress generally was not much different from what the subcommittee approved.

Mahon, a tall, soft-spoken Democrat, and his colleagues always set about their work in a subdued and orderly manner. As soon as Congress convened each January, they began calling in the nation's military leaders to question them on their programs for the coming fiscal year beginning on July 1. Only the subcommittee members and the military leaders, with their respective staffs, met around the old heavy table in the subcommittee hearing room. The sessions were closed to the public, for they dealt with the nation's military position and its top secrets. Much of the testimony and discussion was made public later, however, by the subcommittee in a censored version. In the case of the Polaris program, recorded testimony contains indelible evidence of how the Eisenhower administration repeatedly undercut the most important phase of the whole project—the number of submarines.

In November of 1957 the Mahon subcommittee did an extraordinary thing. As Sputnik II followed Sputnik I into orbit, the subcommittee decided to hold hearings on the United States ballistic missile program without waiting for Congress to convene in January.

Mahon and his subcommittee on November 20 faced the new Secretary of Defense, Neil H. McElroy, and a dozen top military officials. Mahon opened the hearing bluntly:

"The spectacular developments of recent weeks have captured the attention and imagination of the people of the nation and the world. All of our people are interested. Many of them are puzzled. Some, if not all, are concerned, and some are alarmed, you well know, Mr. Secretary. Mr. McElroy, you are Secretary of Defense in perhaps the most critical moment in several decades. You are confronted with the making of very grave decisions."

McElroy replied that one of the decisions he was thinking of making was to accelerate the Polaris program.

"If we can, in fact, accelerate the availability of a reasonable submarine operational capability without throwing the program out of balance, we intend to do so," he said. "It looks as if we can."

"You just stated you thought that we could accelerate the Polaris program?" Mahon asked. He emphasized the word "thought."

"Yes."

"Some of us looked at it in the California area, and we were very much impressed with the possibilities."

"We are, too," McElroy said.

The next day Raborn appeared before the subcommittee. Under questioning, he disclosed an interesting new development. He had received final approval from the Secretary of Defense to accelerate the Polaris program.

"When did you receive it?" asked Congressman Robert Sikes of Florida, somewhat amazed.

"Last evening," Raborn said.

The first payment for the speed-up of the Polaris program was 350 million dollars. That was 30 million dollars more than had been authorized for the entire fleet ballistic missile program up to that time.

The bulk of this extra money would be used to build the first three Polaris submarines. The Navy felt so sure that Congress would go along with the idea that, with approval of the Secretary of Defense, it began the acceleration in December with funds borrowed from some of its short-range missile programs. The request for extra money came officially before the Mahon subcommittee on January 8. McElroy included it as part of a request for an extra 1 billion dollars, mostly for speeding up the long-range missile programs of all three services. This was the administration's answer to Sputnik.

The following Monday, Secretary of the Navy Thomas S. Gates and Admiral Raborn explained the details of the Polaris acceleration. Admiral Burke, the Chief of Naval Operations, and other high admirals joined in. The first operational submarines would go to sea in 1960—three years earlier than planned. The only penalty to be paid was that the Polaris missiles would have a range of 1,200 miles instead of 1,500. The increased range would come later.

The subcommittee was impressed. But it wanted to know more.

"What is your reason for requesting funds for three Polaris submarines instead of, say, seven or ten or some other number?" asked Congressman Sheppard.

"Mr. Sheppard, I do not think we know the answer to that question," Gates said. "We are looking at this program every day after every new development breakthrough occurs. Within the last thirty days we have had meetings with our principal contractors involved in this program. I believe on a tentative basis we can build more submarines, and I am quite sure within the very near future we will make a recommendation to this effect."

"Do you have in mind at this time approximately how many additional submarines?" Sheppard persisted.

"I would say the maximum we have in mind of submarines is nine."

The subcommittee members did some mental calculations. Nine submarines, each armed with sixteen Polarises, would give the United States 145 big missiles around the Soviet Union: 145 unstoppable, all but invulnerable, ballistic missiles, each capable of destroying a city. This was a force that would make the men in the Kremlin pause.

The verbal ping-pong game continued across the hearing room.

Congressman George Andrews of Alabama asked Raborn if he felt he had the "bugs out of the Polaris at this time."

"I think I can best answer that by saying all our basic research problems have been solved and what we have now is essentially an engineering job," Raborn said.

"You have made considerable progress since you appeared before our committee last year?"

"Yes, sir. We certainly have."

Congressman Edward Miller of Maryland inquired of Admiral Burke whether a Polaris fleet would "not duplicate or at least greatly fortify" the Air Force's Strategic Air Command.

"It would increase the retaliatory power of the United States," Burke said innocently.

"And might it not make it possible to reduce the bomber force of the Strategic Air Command?" Miller persisted.

"Yes, sir. It might. I do not want to go on record, though—"

"I do not want to start another round of interservice argument," Miller interrupted. "But if you can reach targets from a submarine, would it not to an extent duplicate what the Air Force can do through SAC?"

"It would augment it. Yes."

The answer was significant. Suddenly, the Navy no longer was talking about knocking out submarine pens and shore installations. Polaris was emerging as a great strategic striking force far superior to the Air Force's intercontinental jet bomber, and certainly comparable to the Air Force's intercontinental ballistic missile.

Then a ghost from the past entered the hearing room. Congressman Daniel Flood of Pennsylvania introduced it by asking the Secretary of the Navy how much of the money now sought for Polaris had been requested by the Navy in 1958, but had been thrown out by the administration.

"None, sir," Gates said.

"Why not?"

"Because the development program of the Polaris was not far enough along to justify it."

"Well, it should have been," Flood snapped. "If the Navy tells me that they could not see through this Polaris program six months ago, beyond where they are today, and are going to refer me to a sudden breakthrough last month as the reason for not asking for more than they asked for, I think they were wrong. I think that is bad vision."

"You ask the man who is running the program. He had absolute freedom to ask for anything he wanted," replied Gates.

"All right, Red, go ahead," Flood said, sitting back and waving his hand toward Admiral Raborn.

"He asked for it when he was ready to do it in an orderly fashion," Gates put in.

"All right," Flood said, turning up his hands in a helpless gesture. "Here come the semantics. What do you mean by 'orderly'? The lawyers have a habit of saying this. What is an orderly manner under the circumstances?"

"I am not a lawyer."

"I am sure of that." Flood turned to Raborn. "But now, Admiral, why did you not under the circumstances ask for more?"

"First," Raborn began, "let me say when this program was approved a year ago this last December, we sat down and thought about our problem for an intensive three months to develop the performance characteristics of the weapon as a whole, the missile, the submarine, and all the things."

"The system?" Flood put in.

"Yes, sir."

"That is what I am talking about," Flood said. "Are you talking about the missile or the system?"

"I am talking about both."

"The missile is part of the system," Flood said suspiciously.

"It certainly is," Raborn said.

"I am talking about the system now, not just the missile. Do not trap me on the missile."

"I was talking system."

"All right."

"We sat down," Raborn continued, "with the help of the best technical brains in the country, in our opinion. We studied out the performance characteristics of the entire Polaris weapons system for three long months, an intensive study around the clock, seven days a week. At the end of that time, April 1 of this past year, we had the parameters, performance parameters of the entire system, which we felt might reasonably obtain a few years down the road when we would bring this weapon system to fruition. That is, making it ready to go to sea. I say this because I want to emphasize the rapidity with which the ballistic missile program and allied programs are moving these days."

"What do you mean by 'allied'?" Flood asked.

"Technical progress. It is bewildering even to our best scientific brains, and since April 1 of this last year, when we formalized the performance characteristics of the entire system—"

"Oh, oh." Flood laughed. "You said a bad word: 'formalized.' "

"Let him pick out his bad language if he wants to use it," Sheppard said irritably. "Go ahead and answer the question."

"I mean when we were deciding," Raborn said.

"Go ahead," Flood said, nodding approvingly and winking down the table at Mahon.

"Having decided on the weapons system, we have had some most significant breakthroughs—some people like to call them breakthroughs; we call them technical advances. I enumerated some of those in my classified, off-the-record talk this morning. Now, we did not know how to do those. We started in April of last year, but we decided by the aid of the best brains in the country that the way we were going to tackle them was the best way, and we were right. Secretary Gates has mentioned that he has left that up to our judgment, and this is a matter of judgment when you come in for money. I do not like to run too fast. I want to go just as fast as the technical progress will allow us."

"That is your answer?" Flood asked. He dilated his nostrils over his small waxed mustache as if he were smelling something slightly overripe.

"That is my answer," Raborn said.

"You stick by it. I do not accept it. There is something the matter with it. I do not know what, but my viscera tell me that it is not a good answer. I cannot argue with you, because I do not know the technical end."

"I have previously invited you to come down and see our office," Raborn said with only a touch of the tone of a put-out host in his voice. "It has been called the best in the country. I would like to repeat the invitation."

Flood was not to be put off.

"You told Mr. Andrews that you entered into this thing first in 1956. Five years ago, when Admiral Radford was sitting in that chair over there, I asked him about firing IRBM missiles from American submarines under water. I said to him, 'Do you not know'—and I say to you, Mr. Secretary, do you not know—certainly Admiral Raborn knows, and half those sailormen back there know—'that at the end of the war the Germans had this set up?' The Navy knows that. They had the plans made to fire missiles from submarines, inside the submarine, through the torpedo tubes at different angles and on the deck in combinations of three."

Gates, at whom Flood had been looking as he talked, simply nodded and said, "Yes, sir." The "sailormen" in the back of the room—a row of admirals, captains, and commanders—said nothing.

"The Russians grabbed those plans," Flood pressed on. "We have known for years that there are missile launchers and inventoried, stored missiles at German naval stations on the Baltic. Admiral Radford said to me that he knew about that. Why have you not been at this for the last five years? Why did you wait until 1956 to have a program with submarines to launch 1,500-mile missiles, IRBMs—not rockets, not guided missiles—ballistic missiles? Why is it so new?"

Congressman Flood's viscera were working very well. The ghost that Congressman Flood had brought into the room now joined the group. It had come all the way from Peenemünde.

Gates said nothing.

The subcommittee was ready to rush through approval of the 350 million dollars for the three Polaris submarines. But Mahon and others thought three were not enough. If the country ought to build three, it ought to build more. Probably nine, the number the Navy wanted, should be built.

Mahon went across the Potomac to the Pentagon for a private talk with McElroy. The essence of Mahon's question was simple: Why not more submarines now?

They sat in the long hall-like office of the Secretary of Defense. McElroy, the suave, clever soap manufacturer from Cincinnati, sat behind a polished desk that had once belonged to General of the Armies John ("Blackjack") Pershing. Mahon, the courteous, intelligent lawyer from Lubbock, Texas, who had watched Cabinet officers come and go for twenty-five years while he served in the House, sat in a large, leather chair. Behind the two men, beyond a long table that once belonged to Gen. William Tecumseh Sherman, tall windows overlooked the Potomac and the gleaming white buildings of Washington.

McElroy told Mahon that there was no need to complicate the present supplementary appropriation bill by adding more than the three Polaris submarines already in it. There was no question that the administration would be asking for additional Polaris submarines this year. But, for the sake of orderly procedure, it would be best to include them in the new budget for fiscal year 1959 rather than add them to the old 1958 budget.

Mahon agreed. He would wait. The supplementary defense bill, with only three Polaris subs in it, was approved by the Mahon subcommittee, and final Congressional action followed quickly.

The Mahon subcommittee was closeted again on February 10 in its hearing room with Secretary Gates and Admiral Burke. This time they were discussing the new budget for fiscal 1959. It included 391 million dollars for the Polaris program. This would cover a continuation of the accelerated effort. But it would not buy any more submarines. The number still stood at three.

Congressman Richard Wigglesworth of Massachusetts, the ranking Republican member of the subcommittee, wanted to know why.

"Is the money you received for Polaris in the 1958 supplemental plus the 1959 request sufficient to bring about the maximum acceleration, in your opinion?" Wigglesworth asked Admiral Burke.

"No, sir," Burke replied, and a whisper went around the table. "We could accelerate even further with more effort, more money."

"How much?"

"We could get nine submarines during the same time that we can get the present three submarines, and we could get the first submarine about five to nine months sooner."

"Can you get the missiles any sooner?" Wigglesworth asked.

"Yes, sir. The missiles and the submarine, the whole weapons system."

"You can get one submarine with missiles six months earlier than is now contemplated?"

"Yes, sir. About that."

"You could get nine submarines—"

"In the same time that we can now get three, sir."

"At what additional cost?"

"Roughly a billion dollars, sir."

"A billion dollars over the full period?"

"That is the total cost, sir."

The significance of what Burke was saying was very clear. The Navy could dispatch its first Polaris submarine with sixteen missiles to the Soviet coast by early fall of 1960. Eight more would follow within the following half-year.

The next question was whether the White House would approve it. Secretary Gates informed the subcommittee that the matter was before the Secretary of Defense and the Joint Chiefs of Staff. But they would have to take their cue from the President.

Now came the money squeeze.

President Eisenhower and his closest advisers were determined to balance the Federal budget. The President was convinced a "sound economy" ranked in importance with weapons. He was fully committed to the theory that Russia was trying to bleed the United States to death economically. Moreover, 1958 was a congressional election year, and the top Republican political strategists had seized on the phrase "fiscal stability" as a party slogan.

The President used two means to accomplish his goal. One was to begin as few new domestic programs as possible. The other was to maintain an arbitrary ceiling of about 40 billion dollars on the annual defense budgets—approximately half the total Federal budget.

To increase the defense budget by 10 or 20 per cent, as many critics advocated, the President would have to commit one or more politically unpalatable acts. He would have to unbalance the budget and thereby increase taxes. Or he would have to cut some congressmen's favorite programs. Or do a little of both.

President Eisenhower, as President Truman had done before him, chose the easier path by clamping down on defense spending. He conveniently convinced himself that the money being provided was adequate.

The Pentagon was forced onto a tightrope. The three services had to trim their programs to fit a mold prescribed not on the basis of military necessity but of budgetary necessity.

The Eisenhower administration each year distributed the defense budget to the three services in pie-shaped wedges that seldom varied at all. The Air Force received the largest wedge: about 48 per cent. The Navy came next: about 28 per cent. The Army received what was left.

With the services forced to operate within these restrictions, interservice and intraservice rivalries became damagingly fierce. The effect was further heightened by myopia and flabbiness at the top decision-making levels. Repeatedly, the Pentagon's civilian bosses and the White House temporized instead of killing a program or even adjusting it to meet new circumstances.

The Navy found itself in particularly difficult straits. Although many of its leaders appreciated the potential greatness of Polaris, they deplored seeing their scarce dollars spent on it. For the most part, the Navy received no extra money for the increasingly expensive Polaris program. Instead, it was financed with money that normally would have been spent on other Navy activities.

The Navy's carriers and other ships mostly dated back to World War II. If the Navy were to maintain its carrier forces, they had to be replaced. The threat of Soviet submarines was growing daily. Better antisubmarine weapons were desperately needed. But these and other programs were skimped for Polaris. Repeated pleas to increase the Navy's 28-per-cent share of the defense budget went unheeded.

Therefore, not everyone in the Navy found a warm place in his heart for Polaris. It was even possible for many Naval officers who had spent their lives on carriers and cruisers and destroyers to scoff at the new weapon. As Chairman Clarence Cannon of Missouri, chairman of the House Appropriations Committee, put it dryly, "The carrier admirals just don't like the idea of going to sea in pig boats."

In the end, the administration gave the appearance of initiating much-greater efforts as a result of the Sputniks. But this was only a façade.

On April 2, the administration proposed some half-hearted increases, including another 336 million dollars for the Polaris program. This included enough money for just two more submarines. The Navy proposal to build six more had been rejected.

The next month the Mahon subcommittee made its decision. It increased the number from two to six. An additional 638 million dollars was put in the defense appropriation bill to pay for them.

Nor was that all. The subcommittee issued a biting report on the bill.

"The Polaris's importance to the security of this nation and the free world can hardly be minimized," the report said. "The committee feels that an increase of only two fleet ballistic missile submarines at this time is insufficient to meet the requirements for this weapons system and fails to take proper advantage of the scientific and technical progress which has been achieved. Accordingly the committee has increased the number of additional submarines to six. . . ."

The report added that when it had approved the first three submarines earlier in the year, the subcommittee had stated that "Polaris must be made a part of our missile arsenal as promptly as possible." The subcommittee made clear that nothing that had occurred in the last three months had changed its mind.

The House agreed. It passed the bill with the extra six submarines. The fight moved to the Senate.

On June 27 Raborn sat before the Senate Defense Appropriations Subcommittee. The hearing was open to the public, and the large room in the Senate Office Building was crowded. Senator Leverett Saltonstall of Massachusetts, the ranking Republican on the subcommittee, was asking the questions in his upper-class dry Yankee drawl.

"May I ask this sixty-four-dollar question? Or maybe it is only a thirty-two-dollar one," Saltonstall said. "The House recommended the number of fleet ballistic missile submarines to be increased to a total of nine. Is the Polaris sufficiently along in development to make it necessary to start these submarines this year, or would it be wiser to wait until next year?"

Raborn grinned.

"That's bordering on the sixty-four-dollar question with me, sir," he said. "I think from my point of view, and I can only speak from a technical point of view, we have the utmost confidence that the program which was recommended can be met and met safely. Our assurance, in other words, from a technical point of view is very good."

The questioning droned on. The issue was outlined again. Raborn already had authority to build three submarines. He could build six more in the same time period, bringing the total to nine. But the President had asked for only two more, thereby holding down the cost at least for the present. The House had approved six more submarines anyway.

"May I put it this way?" asked Senator John Stennis of Mississippi. "According to your present development, you probably will be ready for the use of these submarines by the time they will be built?"

"Yes, sir," Raborn said.

"Probably?"

"There is no question about that, sir."

The Senate approved the six more submarines, too.


# 14    Countdown for a Wake


A countdown may end in the middle of a blazing afternoon on the coast of Florida while vacationers are swimming a few miles away in the surf. Or it may end in the blackness of three in the morning along the California shore on a steel stage bathed in floodlights.

Depression, anger, tears—backslapping, laughter, bursting elation—the full range of human emotion is run at one time or another at missile launchings. No man can watch a great rocket ignite and roar into the sky without identifying himself with its fate. If it lives and soars through the heavens, the human spirit soars with it. If it dies, the pain of those who built it is shared by all.


The first hot launching in the Polaris program took place barely a month after the program was under way.

Lockheed engineers were ready to test in the air a new theory of how to lick the all-important problem of thrust termination —the control of the power of a burning solid-fuel-propelled rocket. The methods they proposed were a carefully guarded secret. Years later they were still a secret.

On January 11, 1957, test engineers set up a small, slim rocket near the beach at Point Mugu, a flat triangle of land jutting from the Southern California coast about fifty miles north of Los Angeles. The rocket—called Phase V-1—looked nothing at all like a Polaris.

Phase V-1 was a specially modified solid-fuel-propelled rocket manufacured by the Thiokol Chemical Corporation. It was used because it was reliable and readily available.

The countdown was brief, and the rocket streaked out over the Pacific. At the proper moment its motor ceased hurling it forward, and it plunged gracefully toward the sea.

The first launching was a success.

There were six firings from Point Mugu between January and April. All involved similar rockets modified in various ways to test various designs. All but one firing was considered successful.

Engineers working on the program were satisfied that they had found a way to shut off a solid-propellant motor in flight, exactly when they wanted.

The Polaris test program moved that summer from Point Mugu to the Atlantic Missile Range at Cape Canaveral.

The Cape's greatest days still lay ahead. This once-barren strip of eastern Florida beach was on the threshhold of assuming its role as America's first spaceport. Testing of the huge Atlas ICBM was still in its early stages. The Vanguard was being readied to attempt to launch the world's first satellite into orbit around the earth.

Polaris was a novelty. The Air Force, which operated the Atlantic Missile Range, had never before dealt with a large solid-fuel-propelled ballistic missile. The problems were not inconsiderable.

*Polaris!*

All the big missiles tested at the Cape had been powered by liquid propellants. Until the highly explosive propellants were pumped into the missiles shortly before launching time, the missiles themselves were inert and could be handled with safety in congested areas. Accordingly, facilities for all the big missiles were divided into two areas: one—the industrial area—was at the main base; the other—the launching area—was stretched out along the isolated beach.

The industrial areas contained administrative offices, machine shops, storage buildings, and hangars where missiles were assembled. At the launching areas were the launching pads themselves, the steel gantry work towers that surrounded the missiles, the thick concrete-walled blockhouses, and other installations necessary for testing a big missile. If a missile filled with propellant exploded, the damage would be confined to the launching area only.

This arrangement was satisfactory for the liquid-fuel-propelled missiles. But it would not do for Polaris.

Polaris missiles were transported to the Cape loaded with thousands of pounds of propellant. No one was used to this sort of thing. No one was certain how stable the propellant might be. Some people thought a jolt along the Cape's bumpy roads might cause it to explode. If it fell while being assembled in the crowded industrial area, half the physical facilities and the programs dependent upon them at the Cape might be destroyed.

Maj. Gen. Donald Yates, the Air Force commander of the Atlantic Missile Range, shuddered at the thought. Yates had made safety into a religion. The accident rate at the Cape compared almost favorably with that along an abandoned highway. Yates decided that in the interest of safety all Polaris facilities would have to be isolated.

They were.

Cape Canaveral is a wedge-shaped stretch of flat beach and palmetto-covered wasteland lying on the eastern shore of Florida about halfway between Jacksonville and Miami. At its front stretches the Atlantic Ocean. At its back is the wide Banana River.

The land is hot and low. Water lies only six to eight feet beneath the sandy surface. Mosquitoes abound. Day after day the sun blazes from a vast blue sky. Only the swelling sea and a few palm trees in the distance offer any hint of relief.

This is what the Air Force calls Capebase.

The piece of this real estate that was assigned to the Polaris program by Yates lay a few miles south of the Cape's point. At the time, the principal inhabitants were snakes. The nearest neighbors were some Jupiter launching pads just south of the Cape's point. On the far side of the point rose the tall gantries for the Atlas ICBMs.

Raborn was given about seventy acres. The Polaris industrial area was to be built about 800 yards from the launching pads. If a Polaris blew up, only the Navy facilities would go with it.

The Navy constructed nearly a dozen buildings, including a large hangar, an engineering laboratory, a machine shop, and a heating plant. There was room for three launching pads and the ship-motion simulator.

But that summer there was nothing but the beach and the palmettos and the heat.

The first Lockheed test engineers to arrive found themselves operating out of an old one-story shed borrowed from the Air Force. The shed was a sheet-metal shack in an isolated area south of the proposed Polaris site. Engineers working inside baked as the Florida sun beat on it. The only sound outside the shed was the sea on the shore.

Standing in the sandy grass near the shed, they launched the first Polaris test rocket from the Cape on July 17. The rocket was part of the FTV—the Flight Test Vehicle—series. In all, there were sixteen of them launched over the next eleven months. All were successful.

The FTVs looked little more like a Polaris than had the

Phase Vs fired at Point Mugu. They were strange, lean missiles with fat noses and fatter tails. The earlier ones had fins. The later ones didn't. None were particularly impressive to look at. But they accomplished what they were designed to do.

Essentially, the FTVs were used to test two major parts of the Polaris: the nose cone and the jetavators. To do this, Lockheed used all or part of an old test rocket originally designed for Air Force research. It was called the X-17.

The X-17 was a three-stage solid-fuel-propelled rocket. It carried a nose cone to about 120 miles. Then it turned the nose cone back toward the earth and drove it into the atmosphere at the speed of an IRBM. The tests sought to find a nose cone that could survive the tremendous heat caused by air friction.

Only the first stage of the X-17 was used for testing the jetavators. The one nozzle at the base of the rocket was removed, and replaced by the four nozzles of a Polaris, and equipped with Willie Fiedler's magic metallic rings.

The first of these test vehicles—called the FTV 1-7—was launched on October 15. The FTV 1-7 not only had jetavators but also had large fins to stabilize it in flight. But when the FTV 1-9 was launched on December 10, the fins were removed.

Engineers not connected with the Polaris program gaped as the FTV 1-9 was rolled to its launching pad. Some laughed. Some hooted.

"It'll never fly," one shouted.

"I give you five to one it goes blooey," someone said in the crowd.

The FTV 1-9 flashed from its launcher into the clear sky. It flew like an arrow. The jetavators were a success.

A hot breeze occasionally moved up the sandy Cape and brushed the scrub grass at the Polaris launching complex. A year before, there had been nothing here. Now a half-dozen satellite buildings were clustered around a huge barn called Hangar Y where missiles were assembled. Along the shore, one launching pad and blockhouse were complete. The ship-motion simulator was still under construction. A second launching complex had not been started.

This was no ordinary day. The area was crowded with visitors from the Special Projects Office in Washington. All kept watching the completed launching pad—Pad 25A. It was in use. A fat 28-foot missile that looked like a champagne bottle sat on it. The date was September 24, 1958.

This was the first full-scale Polaris. It did not carry a combat guidance system. It did not carry a lot of things. But it was a Polaris all the same.

Five minutes dragged by. Smith, Raborn, and Rod Middleton, his missile chief, watched from the blockhouse. Kirchner and Bednarz stood near them. Others watched from in front of Hangar Y. The sun-baked launch area was quiet. Everyone felt the tension. Twenty-one months of work sat out there on the steel test stand. There had been thousands of laboratory tests, twenty-two hot test launchings, dozens of static firings. Now all this work had been put together in one missile. Raborn was about to witness the proof or disproof of a thousand technical puddings.

If all went well, the missile would rip skyward for several miles, tilt toward Africa, and soar over the Atlantic. About 10 miles out the first stage would drop away. At some 20 miles out, the second stage would follow it. The re-entry body would fall into the sea about 700 miles from the Cape.

The technicians made the final adjustments with the precision of watchmakers. Now the launch area was clear. The range safety officer nodded to the test conductor and said, "Check." The test conductor pushed the button in front of him. The countdown needle on the block-house dial jogged to zero.

Outside in the sunlight the Polaris emitted a shattering roar and shot into the air. Great clouds of white smoke shrouded the launcher. Flame gushed from its nozzles. The missile roared higher and higher into the sun-bleached sky. Onlookers at the hangar cheered and looked upward, shielding their eyes. Sound numbed the area. The missile continued to climb straight up. Then suddenly, more than 40,000 feet over the launching area, it shuddered and blew apart.

The loudspeaker barked, "All personnel on the Cape, take cover. Take cover."

Onlookers dashed into buildings as parts of the missile showered the area. One large piece crashed in flames near the launching pad and appeared to explode.

Inside the blockhouse the range safety officer still sat with his finger on the destruct button. The Polaris' programmer—a $25 piece of electronic equipment that should have made the missile turn and fly out to sea—had failed to work.

Middleton and Bednarz looked at each other but said nothing. Both wanted to cry.

Kirchner and Bednarz attended a wake later that afternoon at the bar of a Cape motel. Half-a-dozen similar wakes were held in other bars and motel rooms in the area. Raborn and members of his staff flew back to Washington. Raborn wanted to get back as quickly as possible. He knew what would be waiting for him.

The next morning the newspapers served up the story for breakfast for every top official in Washington.

The headline on the front page of the *Washington Post* said:

POLARIS GOES
OFF COURSE
IS DESTROYED

The *New York Times* headline said:

POLARIS BLOWN UP
OVER TESTING SITE

Raborn hustled to the Pentagon. He had a lot of calls to make.

# 15 "Smelling Like a Rose"

October, 1958. Men in the Polaris program held their breaths. Tempers were short. The September test had failed because of one cheap part. Similar problems appeared everywhere. No one knew it better than the men who sat behind the bolted doors of the Management Center. The charts told the story. The bars were down in a dozen different places.

Pehrson stood at the lectern. Raborn sat in the front row. The officers and civilian officials of his staff and the industrial representatives from throughout the country crowded the room. Pehrson talked.

"I've been trying to think how to say this, Admiral, and I think the best way would be a little story. When I left college, I went to work for the government as a bank examiner, the very lowest-grade bank examiner. And part of my job was to go around with a team and count money. Of course, as the very lowest-grade bank examiner, I was assigned to count the change. In the first bank that I went to, I was taken into the vault by a bank official, and he kicked a pile of money bags and they jingled. 'There they are,' he said. 'You can count 'em if you want, but we usually just kick 'em, and if they jingle, that means they are okay.' Well, I decided I didn't like that idea too much, so I opened them, and do you know what I found? I found the shiniest washers that you've ever seen. And this is what is happening now in the Polaris program. We've started kicking these bags that these contractors with high reputations have handed us, and we're looking inside, and unfortunately we are finding plenty of washers."

Then Raborn spoke.

"We've had a lot of criticism here today, and that's good. That's what these meetings are for. We have to criticize ourselves if we are going to get anywhere. That's how we find out our weaknesses. But let that stop here in this room. Now, let's get the hell out of here and get to work."

Two weeks later they made a second try.

Raborn again sat in the blockhouse. So did Middleton, Bednarz, and Kirchner. Capt. John Refo, who directed all Polaris testing, watched from his usual place outside the big hangar.

The AX-2 Polaris test vehicle stood on the small frame launching stand. The missile was painted with stripes to allow cameras to record movement of the missile in flight. It looked exactly like its ill-fated predecessor, the AX-1.

The test conductor pushed the firing button. There was a pause as the countdown moved swiftly to zero. A great roar shook the blockhouse. Raborn rushed to a periscope window and shouted that something had gone up. But no one in the blockhouse was certain what had happened. Television cameras showed only billowing white smoke.

Outside, the view was better.

The first stage of the Polaris sat on the pad, spouting flames from its top like a Fourth of July fountain. The second stage had ripped away and was soaring erratically into the sky.

Onlookers bolted for cover. One spectator standing on top of a nearby building jumped off and broke his leg. A Naval officer with a well-padded rear dashed into Hangar Y and dived under a low-slung pickup truck, trapping himself. An engineer dived for safety under a trailer on which a Polaris motor lay.

Meantime, observers reported the runaway to the range safety officer. He pressed the destruct button, which set off an explosive in the missile, and blazing parts of the second stage rained on the Cape. A brush fire started nearby, pouring more smoke into the area.

The fountain of fire erupted for more than five minutes. Then it sputtered out. Firemen dumped water into the brush and used their axes to kill dozens of snakes that crawled onto the road in flight from the smoldering palmettos. The atmosphere in the blockhouse was heavy.

"I guess it's like the newly married ensign," Raborn said. "It just doesn't want to go to sea."

Newspapers across the nation the next morning carried a dispatch that began:

CAPE CANAVERAL, *Oct. 15—(AP)—A temperamental Polaris experimental rocket twisted crazily over the Cape and exploded today when the missile was deliberately destroyed after an abortive launching.*

Another dispatch being widely published the same morning reported an interesting statment made by Vice-president Richard M. Nixon. The Vice-president said the United States was now ahead of Russia in exploration of outer space.

Nixon's assertion, with little basis in fact, was explainable. The Vice-president was in the midst of an election campaign in which the Republicans rather hopelessly were trying to regain control of Congress. Repeated Russian successes in space were not helping the administration. Repeated missile failures at Cape Canaveral weren't political capital, either.

Hence, the wind blowing from the White House toward the Navy Department turned decidedly chilly with the Polaris failures.

Raborn pushed ahead regardless of the critics. Engineers found that the freak launching on October 15 was caused by the misfiring of an explosive bolt, a safety device that held the igniter for the first-stage motor in place. As the first stage ignited, the bolt had blown apart prematurely and blasted the second stage into the air. The first stage, unable to build up any power because it was burning on both ends, didn't move at all.

The problem was relatively simple to solve because they knew what had caused it.

Tighter controls were ordered. All contractors were alerted. Random failures could not be tolerated.

Raborn, meantime, sought to ease the publicity-induced strain on the Polaris technicians at the Cape. He called Robert Gibson, the Lockheed liaison man in Washington, and asked him whether the "brass factor" at the Cape might be creating too much tension at launchings. Gibson replied as diplomatically as possible that the presence of high-ranking Navy officers could put some men on edge. Raborn immediately prohibited all "sightseers" from the Polaris complex during tests. He included himself.

But new trouble continued to dog the firing of the full-sized Polaris. This time it was important. The kind that can be fatal.

On December 30, 1958, another missile was ready, designated the AX-3. Raborn stayed in Washington. Middleton and Bednarz watched from the blockhouse.

The missile took off beautifully from the launching pad. For forty-five happy seconds it climbed on its course. Some hats already were in the air. But the cheers broke off as soon as they started. The missile began to pitch erratically and wiggle over the Atlantic like a cootch dancer.

The test conductor signaled that it was time for the second stage to separate from the first. It did, with a drunken lurch. The end came a few seconds later. The range safety officer pushed the destruct button.

This was no random failure. Something very strange had happened. A large part of the Polaris team flew back to California to try to figure out what it was.

In Washington, Raborn was wading through hot water. He had to convince the Navy and the administration that there should be no cut in his big share of the new Navy budget despite the sudden uncertainty of Polaris' future. And he had to talk the Navy into letting the tests continue no matter what happened.

The admirals in the Pentagon had been getting increasingly anxious. The memory of Vanguard still haunted them. There were only so many times that you could go to the Cape and launch a missile and have it fail. Failures not only reflected on Raborn; they besmirched the entire Navy. Raborn suddenly found himself conducting a running defense of his program.

Nor was the news from the West Coast reassuring.

Something most unexpected had happened to AX-3 on December 30. Information, radioed from the missile while it was in flight, clearly showed that heat from the burning propellant was causing the tail of the missile to fall apart. The materials could not stand the strain. Polaris suffered from what the missilemen called "hot bottom."

Here was a physical problem that the Steering Task Group had never anticipated. Nor had anyone else. If a solution were not found, the Polaris program was finished.

Raborn would have been justified then in halting further testing. It would have relieved some of the pressure. But it also would have wrecked the schedule. The launchings were needed to test a wide variety of Polaris parts. Raborn decided to gamble.

"I don't care if we have five more blowups," he told his staff. "I want to lick this and I want to stay on schedule. Now let's do it."

Raborn smiled at the Pentagon admirals and assured them they need not worry. Then he went home at night and worried for everyone.

Again the Cape. The date: January 19, 1959. The AX-4 stood on the launching pad.

The firing button was pushed. The missile roared from the stand, flashing skyward. For thirty seconds all went well. Then it happened again. The missile began to pitch, it wiggled, it rocked. The second stage separated from the first in a puff of smoke, but continued the wild pitching and rocking. Before the range safety officer could push the destruct button, the missile broke up and tumbled into the sea.

Everyone went back to the plush new Polaris Motel on the Cape to get drunk.

"We tried everything," Bednarz recalled later. "We tested all kinds of metals. We had the problem, we knew we had it, we thought we knew what we needed to solve it, but we still had to come up with the right material."

Nearly two months of laboratory tests followed. At last they believed they had found the answer. And what they hoped would be the answer immediately became one of the nation's top secrets.

But it didn't come soon enough to avert another blowup at the Cape.

On February 27 the Polaris test engineers erected AX-5 on the launching pad. The missile was practically the same as its predecessors. Everyone in Special Projects knew it would perform poorly. But there were components that had to be tested in flight if the program were to remain on schedule. Information received from the early stages of flight would be sufficient. Middleton and Bednarz went ahead with the test.

AX-5 performed exactly as they had expected.

The missile flew normally for twenty-seven seconds. Then it began to gyrate violently. Eleven seconds later it disintegrated.

"You might say this is the stiff-upper-lip approach," Bednarz said, shuddering.

Plenty of stiff upper lips were needed in Washington

The latest bad news from the Cape got very little attention in the newspapers. The disintegration of a Polaris in flight was no longer news. But the latest Polaris disaster, as some referred to it, was well noted in the outer rings of the Pentagon.

Air Force generals merely grinned. It was too bad. Everyone knew this big solid-fuel-propelled missile was a weird idea anyway. Not that those fellows over in Raborn's shop weren't a dedicated lot. But it was too bad the Navy had to waste so much money on the project.

Admirals found grins very difficult to muster. Raborn had to stop this before it got worse. The Navy was getting into another Vanguard for sure. Something had to be done, and the admirals tried to do it. In the weekly admirals' meeting in the Pentagon, one after another came up to Raborn with the same friendly advice.

"For Christ's sake, Red, why not knock off the testing for a while? You're just trying to go too fast."

Raborn smiled. He explained. He refused to budge.

Some of the admirals tried a different route. They got their objections to Adm. Arleigh Burke, Chief of Naval Operations. Burke heard them out. But Burke, also, refused to budge. He continued to back Raborn.

At least for the present, the crisis passed.

AX-6 was something new. In many ways, it was generally like the five Polaris test missiles that had preceded it except in one important respect: AX-6 had the "new fix," the special changes designed to prevent the disasters that had sent its predecessors to premature deaths.

On April 20, 1959, everything was ready to test whether the "new fix" would work. All indications from laboratory tests showed that it would. But no laboratory test is the equal of actual flight.

Middleton, Bednarz, and Kirchner waited nervously in the blockhouse. Middleton had been commuting to the West Coast and Washington for months. Bednarz had all but lived at his office. AX-6 was the result. The missile waited on the launching pad for final adjustments to be made.

The countdown resumed.

"Sequencer start," the test conductor said.

"12 . . . 11 . . . 10 . . . 9 . . ."

*Polaris!*

"No hot bottom today, please," someone said quietly.

"8 . . . 7 . . . 6 . . . 5 . . . 4 . . ."

Middleton crossed his fingers.

"3 . . . 2 . . . 1 . . . 0"

AX-6 ripped from the launcher and thundered straight up. Then it gracefully tilted toward Africa and headed over the Atlantic. A few miles out, a puff of smoke surrounded its middle and the second stage soared on as the first stage dropped away. Minutes later its nose arced toward the sea 300 miles from the Cape.

The blockhouse went wild.

Men pounded each other's backs. They hugged each other. They cheered. Outside, engineers and Naval officers tossed hats in the air and whooped.

Fifteen hundred miles away in Washington, a short heavy-set admiral with red hair smiled the smile of the delivered.

Within an hour the celebration moved to the Polaris Motel. When the Polaris team entered, everyone stood and applauded. Signs everywhere celebrated the triumph. A huge sign in the crowded bar said:

CONGRATULATIONS LOCKHEED

POLARIS FINALLY MADE IT

Out at the motel swimming pool, the usual honors were performed with the Polaris team. One by one they were shoved in by engineers from other projects.

Bednarz, being a man who thinks ahead, took elaborate precautions. He meticulously removed his glasses and wrist watch and handed them to a bystander as he happily approached the pool. Seconds later he was in the water, struggling to the surface. As he came up, the first thing he saw was the helpful bystander being pushed in a few feet away.

Bednarz didn't even swear.

# 16   The Men:
## From Nuky Poo to Sunnyvale

Comdr. James Butler Osborn, skipper of the *U.S.S. George Washington*, blew a cloud of cigar smoke toward an empty coffee cup on the wardroom table. He wore a black crew-neck sweater and Navy suntan pants. As he talked, he occasionally rubbed his right hand across his close-cropped skull. Two new officers of the *George Washington* sat across from him and listened.

"The trouble with this country is there is too much intellectual overhead," Osborn said. "They talk. They draw beautiful pictures and beautiful formulae. But no one wants to do anything."

His large jaw jutted forward, and the corners of his mouth turned down, baring his teeth as if he had tasted something sour.

"What do we find on this ship? These smart fellows have put a knob that we touch once a week right here in a handy spot, and a knob that we have to turn four times a day is down where you can't reach it. These are the things you find when you try to operate a ship. There are thousands of them. Thousands of them. Of course, the people who dress these things up aren't worried about operating them. All they worry about is that sailors are going to mess up their beautiful systems. And in their minds there is nothing lower than sailors—either in this world or the next."

Osborn grimaced again and lit another cigar.

"Facts. That's what we deal in here. Doing things. Sailors are executors. They don't plan ahead. They don't worry about strategic concepts and the mission of this ship and whether the Navy is going to get forty more Polaris submarines. That doesn't affect them. Sailors worry about what they have to do today. They worry about doing a good job and getting a pat on the back. And sailors know if they don't do a good job, they'll be reaching over their heads to pat their tails. If this program is a failure, it will be because it is a technical failure. If it is a success, it will be because of the people who are working here on this ship. You couldn't hire people to do what you will be doing. This is a sexless, whiskyless life. The only vice we have is cigar smoke. I make everybody share that."

The officers and men who were to man the Polaris subs gathered long before the fleet ever took shape. Their training started in 1958.

The *George Washington* was a skeleton on the ways at Groton. The Polaris missile was still a blueprint; nothing that looked anything like it had ever flown.

But at Washington—and Sunnyvale, California—and Pittsfield, Massachusetts—and Idaho Falls, Idaho; at Syossett, Long Island—and Cape Canaveral—and Dam Neck, Virginia—the men who were to take Polaris to sea were watching its parts take shape.

Men who would form two complete crews for each submarine were sent to school—two crews because the endurance of the nuclear submarine is so much greater than that of the human beings who run her. With diesel power, both the submarine and the crew were ready after a cruise of two months to head back to port for overhaul and rest. The new missile subs capable of covering 100,000 miles and more on a single charge of fissionable fuel could stay out on station almost indefinitely. So the Navy decided in the spring of 1959 to rotate the personnel with a Blue Crew and a Gold Crew, each numbering ten officers and ninety enlisted men.

The Blue Crew would take out the submarine first. Toward the end of their sixty days on station, the sub would rendezvous briefly with a tender, and the Gold Crew, flown overseas to an advance port to meet the tender, would go aboard. Both crews would work side by side for about two weeks to effect an orderly turnover of duties and to resupply the sub. Then the Blue Crew would leave aboard the tender and fly home.

Total time away from their home port for each crew would be about 110 days.

Training for most Polaris submariners began at either of two places. One is Nuky Poo—the Nuclear Power School classes at New London, Connecticut. The other is Dam Neck—the Navy's Guided Missile School outside Norfolk, Virginia. Some attended both.

From these they moved on to Idaho Falls to the Arco reactor —a land-based nuclear power plant similar to the one on the *Nautilus*. Or they went directly to one of a half-dozen schools operated at the factories of companies developing parts of the Polaris system.

Still later they went to Cape Canaveral to observe the launching of test missiles. The technicians made trips on the *Compass Island* with the Polaris navigation system and the *Observation Island* to work with the fire control and launching equipment.

Their final schooling came in the submarines themselves. Even as equipment was being installed aboard the *George Washington* and *Patrick Henry,* officers and men began to work with it.

In all, an officer of a Polaris submarine was obliged to spend more than a year studying nuclear reactors and another year learning about the submarine's other complicated equipment. The training was as lengthy for many of the ratings.

They learned the mysteries of a new world. A world of transducers and servomechanisms, of critical atomic piles and inertial navigation, of Boolian algebra and specific impulses.

Excellence is the standard that the Navy used in picking the Polaris submarine crews. Operating the submarines was to become one of the Navy's most exacting jobs. Only men of rare abilities could make them fulfill their pivotal missions.

Many of the officers and men were veterans of the submarine

Polaris!

service, an elite arm of the Navy. The Polaris submarine service had to be the elite of the elite.

As might be expected, the Navy exercised the most meticulous care of all in choosing Polaris fleet commanders.

Records of the candidates were examined with hair-splitting thoroughness down to the pettiest detail by critical officials in the office of Arleigh Burke. Each candidate was subjected to the penetrating questioning of Admiral Raborn and Admiral Rickover in personal interviews.

One high-ranking officer admitted at the time, "It'll be a damn wonder if we find anyone to meet the qualifications."

But they did.

The man who was to become the skipper of the nation's first Polaris submarine was born in Stockton, Missouri, on May 5, 1918, in one of the darkest periods of World War I. He was graduated from the Naval Academy just in time to take part in World War II.

James Osborn became an ensign twelve days after the Japanese attacked the Pacific Fleet as it slept at Pearl Harbor. Osborn quickly married a pretty Missouri girl named June Hanna and in a matter of weeks reported for duty aboard the battleship *Tennessee* back in service after taking two bombs on December 7. He fought through the Aleutian and the Gilbert Islands campaigns. Then, in January, 1944, he was ordered to the Submarine School at New London.

This was a turning. Little in his life was ever to be the same again. In June, 1944, he left New London and reported to the submarine *Perch* as gunnery officer. Before the history of the world was changed at Hiroshima, Osborn had made six war patrols.

Another turning came for Osborn less than a year after World War II ended. He became interested in the possibility of adapting guided missiles to naval warfare. By this time he was commander of the *Perch,* and he brought her into port in May, 1946, to place her in the moth-ball fleet. A month later he was back at the Naval Academy attending postgraduate courses in guided-missile engines. The next year he pursued his studies at Rensselaer Polytechnic Institute and received a master's degree in mechanical engineering.

His studies served him well. In 1952 he took part in converting the diesel-powered submarine *Tunny* into the Navy's first guided-missile submarine. The missile was the relatively slow-moving Regulus I. In March 1953 he assumed command of the *Tunny* and for the first time in the history of the Navy fired a guided missile from an operational submarine. Later he took command of the Navy's first squadron of guided-missile submarines.

At the very time that Raborn was making his crucial decision to kill the Jupiter program and put the Navy's money on Polaris, Osborn left sea duty and began a year of study at the Naval War College at Newport, Rhode Island. Then, in the summer of 1958, he was assigned to Admiral Rickover's Nuclear Power Division in Washington. His appointment to command the Blue Crew of the *George Washington* followed the next year.

Osborn arrived at the Electric Boat yards shortly before his forty-first birthday. Years of war, years at sea, years of classrooms, had left him still young-looking, still filled with drive and fight. No one who watched this square-built sailor in a black crew-neck sweater commanding his new ship in the chilly New England spring could lack confidence in his ability to carry out the task that lay ahead.

No two men could be more opposite types than Comdr. James Osborn and Comdr. Harold Edson Shear, first skipper of the *Patrick Henry*.

Superficially there were many similarities. Shear and Osborn had been classmates at Annapolis. Both became ensigns the same day. Both were thrown into World War II in a matter of weeks. Both had married and each fathered two daughters. Both proved themselves highly intelligent, able officers. Both rose relatively rapidly in rank.

But they were very different men.

Osborn came from a modest background. Before winning an appointment to Annapolis, he supported himself at the University of Missouri by working as a printer's devil. He came from a hard world where those who worked succeeded—sometimes. His naturally buoyant personality combined with an early knowledge of reality to make him an outgoing, gregarious person.

Shear had more opulent beginnings. Born in New York City, he grew up on Shelter Island, near Long Island's pleasant northern tip. Before entering the Naval Academy, he attended the Cochran Bryan Preparatory School. He won a letter in yachting while in the Academy. Shear observed the world as well as Osborn, but from a more comfortable position. Where Osborn was outgoing, Shear was quiet, from a native reserve that permitted him to be demonstrative only on rare occasions.

Regardless of differences, both men were fighters.

A month after leaving Annapolis, Shear reported as a gunnery officer aboard the destroyer *Stack,* which was convoying merchantmen through the North Atlantic. His wartime career began with fighting Nazi U-boats. The Germans seemed to be everywhere. All through that cold, wild winter in the North Atlantic the U-boats sank more than eighty ships despite the efforts of the Navy. In the first six months of the war the Allies sank a total of twenty U-boats. That was less than one month's production in the big German shipyards.

That summer the *Stack* switched oceans and in August took part in protecting the landings of Marines on Guadalcanal and in the bloody, slugging struggle that followed. The *Stack* fought on through the naval battles that wrested control of the southern Solomons from the Imperial Japanese Navy. Then it joined in the blows at the big Japanese naval base at Rabaul and at the Gilbert Islands. The balance of naval power in the

South Pacific slowly swung to the United States. The drive back to Japan began.

As the Pacific offensive gained force, Shear was detached from the *Stack* and ordered back to the United States to attend the Submarine School at New London. In May, 1944, he returned to the Pacific as a gunnery officer on the submarine *Sawfish* and for the first time in his life helped to hoist a broom to his submarine's sail, celebrating a clean sweep of a war patrol.

Shear participated in four war patrols aboard the *Sawfish,* including the battle of Leyte off the Philippines and the invasion of Okinawa. Before the end of the war he was awarded the Silver Star for "conspicuous gallantry and intrepidity."

With the war's end, Shear moved from submarine to submarine, beginning with the *Becuna* where he served as executive officer. Later he returned to the *Becuna* as her commander. His career as a submariner was interrupted twice. Once to serve as a personnel planning officer in Washington. The other time to attend the Armed Forces Staff College and subsequently serve in the Navy's Strategic Plans Division for two years.

In June, 1958, Shear was transferred from submarine duty to the Naval Reactor Branch. Eleven months later he was named commander of the Blue Crew of the nation's second Polaris submarine.

Shear, although seven months younger than Osborn, looks older and more stolid. His heavy-set, finely cast good looks and innate reserve give him the air of a successful lawyer in suburban Connecticut. But when he talks, he speaks with the authority of the veteran warrior and commander.

Shear, as did Osborn with the *George Washington,* watched his submarine rise on the building ways at Groton. He devoted himself day after day to her problems. The *Patrick Henry* became not a job to be done, but a passion.

When the *Patrick Henry* sailed down the Thames on her builders' trials, Shear told Electric Boat engineers on board, "We're not going back until everything is right."

*Polaris!*

Everyone laughed, but they knew he meant it. Fortunately, no underwater endurance records had to be broken. The *Patrick Henry* performed beautifully. As she swept back up the Thames to the yards, Shear had a broom hoisted on her sail.

Osborn and Shear. In their hands, the Navy placed the first of a mighty fleet. In each of the magazines of these new underwater ships of the line was more destructive power than had been dropped by aircraft in all of World War II. This would no longer be the old submariner's game of cat-and-mouse with surface ships. This would be cat-and-mouse on a global scale with the defense of the Free World in the balance.

No one could question that the hands in which this power was placed were capable of that trust. Osborn spoke for both himself and Shear when one day, standing by the *George Washington,* he told an inquirer:

"Am I prepared to push the button if necessary? I've been preparing for this job all of my life."

The crews of the Polaris submarines are made up of brave men and smart men. They like the challenge of these great ships. They like their work.

But there are problems, too.

Some men have trouble with their wives. A hundred days is a long time to be away.

Some men worry about being cut off from the world. A hundred days is a long time to spend mostly under the sea.

Some men wonder whether their sacrifices are appreciated. A hundred days is a long time to spend in what at any time could be the most hunted ship in the world.

These are some of the things that the Polaris crews think about when they have time.

David B. Coates, a young guided-missileman from San Jose, California, had spent nearly a third of his life in the Navy.

At seventeen he quit high school to enlist. Eight years later, he was training to go on station with the *George Washington*.

Coates was a short, sturdy fellow with a shock of black hair and a face that girls in most ports would find appealing. He had a tattoo on his forearm, but he wore horn-rimmed glasses that gave him a studious look.

"I put in for submarine school back about '55," he said, standing by a missile tube in the *George Washington*. "When I got it finally, I got into this. I've been working ever since."

Coates said he had been to submarine school, then to missile guidance school. He had been to Sunnyvale and Cape Canaveral.

"The last four months, we've been at it eight hours a day seven days a week. It's interesting, all right. I'm learning plenty. But I wouldn't recommend it. I have a wife and two kids. Working like this doesn't make you popular at home. And then come the hundred-and-ten-day cruises. The way I see it, the Navy has a problem. You have to know a lot to do this job. I already know more than some of these factory jokers that come around, more about actually doing the job. But they're getting big money and going home at night. In three years, when my enlistment's up, I'm probably going to get out and get a job in the industry. I'm not the only one, either."

Lt. John R. Olson, an Annapolis graduate in his late twenties, was an instructor at the submarine school in New London when he was reassigned to the *Patrick Henry's* Blue Crew. His post: fire control officer, the man who pushes the last button to launch a Polaris.

"I have a good wife," he said. "She feels someone has to do this job. She's glad I'm out there doing it for her."

Olson, father of two children, has a young-looking serious face. It became more serious as he talked, standing in the shadow of the *Patrick Henry's* sail.

"If they say fire them, we'll fire them. But that's not our real mission. Our real mission is never to have to fire them but to serve as a deterrent. If we ever had to fire them, I guess we'd have a feeling of despair. After all, you'd know they were coming the other way."

Stephen Kmiec was a young friendly seaman. He was a little shy because of a complexion that gave him trouble. He used to be an electrician on the diesel-powered submarine *Croaker.* Then he was transferred to the Gold Crew of the *George Washington.*

"They sent me to nuclear power school for a half year, and after that up to West Milton, New York, where they have a reactor you can train on. I was up there six months too. After that I came back to help get the ship ready. My job is checking all the electrical connections here for the power plant and fixing them if something goes wrong."

He waved his hand at the maze of piping and cables around him.

"I'm not married, and I live in town in an apartment with two other guys from the ship. It's a pretty good deal. Of course, a hundred days is a long time, but it's okay for a single guy. The skipper is all right, too."

Guided Missileman Arlan Boyd spent nearly seven years in the Navy before he came to the *George Washington.* He was a slim, twenty-five year old sailor with sad-looking blue eyes, a couple of intricately designed tattoos, and an almost shaved scalp.

"I used to be a cook on the *Barbero,* a Regulus sub. But I switched to missiles when my chief told me I was too bright to be a cook. I'm glad I did. I don't want to be a short-order cook when I get out of the Navy. I've gotten more than seventy weeks of school since I've been in this."

He stopped and fumbled a moment with a meter that he was carrying.

"It's cost me, though," he said. "My wife just couldn't keep up. She's left. The day after I got married, I had to get up at six in the morning in a hotel in Atlantic City and fly to the

West Coast for some more training. I haven't had a day off in four months. I'm not much different than lots of others, though. There are plenty of guys from the *George Washington* crews whose wives have quit. But that's the way this thing is. You've either got to give yourself to the program or tell the chaplain you want off."

Charles E. Wollenweber, Jr., of Indianapolis, Indiana, joined the Navy at seventeen. At twenty-three he became a computerman on the *George Washington*'s Blue Crew. He was a smart, good-natured fellow with short-cropped hair.

"What I want to know is what I'm going to be doing for sixty days," he said. "I come here and watch the computer. Then I walk seventy-five feet to my bunk, or I can play some cards in the mess. Or, maybe, I can do a few laps around the missile tubes."

He shook his head as if all life amazed him.

"Maybe the time will go, though. If I'm going to get my dolphins, I've got a year to be checked out on the rest of the ship. There's plenty to be checked out on."

He shook his head again. The lights on his computer winked at him in the semidarkness of the attack center.

"Look, I've just gotten married. But this business about hundred-day cruises isn't going to cause any difficulty. It's going to be good because it's going to be predictable."

Lt. Glenn C. Merritt threw his head back and laughed.

"Everyone likes to bitch. But you won't find many who want to get out of it."

Merritt was a tall, good-looking officer with prematurely gray hair. He was thirty-one. His job was Gold Crew engineering officer on the *George Washington*. He was in charge of the reactor.

"I started out on a destroyer. Then I went to a diesel guppy sub. Then I graduated to nuclear power. Before the *George*

*Washington,* I was on the *Swordfish.* I guess the most unforgettable part of getting into the nuclear-power subs was an interview that I had with Admiral Rickover.

"The first thing he asked me was whether I played football at the Academy. I said, 'No.' And he asked, 'Why not?' And I said, 'Because I didn't go to the Academy. I went to Duke.' Then it got worse.

"The funny thing is I was accepted."

He threw his head back and laughed again. Then, sobering, he said:

"I'm glad I was. I think this is the most important job that I could be doing. This is one of the few times in my life I've felt like that. It's soul-satisfying. I think this is really big."

# 17    The Ships: From the Hanging Gardens to Sherwood Forest

The *George Washington* glided slowly up the Thames through wisps of early morning fog. Osborn stood in the tiny bridge wedged in the top of the sail. He was bareheaded and wore a green pea-jacket. A cigar jutted from his mouth.

Osborn was taking the sleek gray sub back to Electric Boat after three days of testing the missile tubes on Long Island Sound. The firing of 2,500-pound slugs called Sabots had gone well; the *George Washington* was tuning up, but she still had a long way to go.

The blade-shaped sail in which Osborn perched loomed high over the hump-backed missile deck. The stubby winglike planes, outspread from the sail, gave the ship a weird appearance. She might have been a fabled monster rising from the sea. The seemingly disembodied rudder, riding the white wave far to the rear, looked like the tip of a dragon's tail.

As Osborn ordered the helmsman to point the *George Washington*'s blunt snout toward the Electric Boat pier, the thought passed through his mind that it was a pity few Americans would ever personally look upon this Missile Age man-o'-war. They would never know the incredible amount of work that had gone into her. If they could but see her and appreciate her for the masterpiece of ingenuity that she was, combining the atom for power with the atom of destruction, perhaps their fears of war would be eased. Russian leaders should see her, too. They would tread more softly.

But there was no time for sightseers. Every day was a workday, and in a few months the *George Washington* would be heading south to Cape Canaveral. The tubes would be loaded with real Polaris missiles for the supreme test—the first 1,200-mile shot of a ballistic missile from a submarine. This was the test Raborn, the thousands of engineers and craftsmen, and Osborn and his ninety-nine-man crew, were driving for; it had to be a success. Nothing must be allowed to go wrong. This was not the proving-out of one ship and her armament, but the proof of an idea.

Anyone who did take a walk through the *George Washington* after she docked that early spring day in 1960 might easily have thought her ready for action then. Below decks all was taut, from her forward torpedo room to the steam turbines nestled around the propeller shaft in the stern. The members of the crew moved about the ship, tending her equipment with a confidence and ease born of long familiarity. They were getting to know her good points and shortcomings better all the time.

At that moment, the biggest shortcoming of all was space. Every conceivable place was filled with extra bunks, for on practically every trip to sea the *George Washington* was taking along passengers. There were technicians who wanted to watch over a newly installed black box. There were members from both crews, who were being trained simultaneously. And occasionally Navy brass hats and congressmen were wedged in so they could inspect her progress. Extra bunks were on top of lockers. They hung above the torpedoes. They were squeezed between the missile tubes.

For all of her 380-foot length and 32-foot width amidships, no one would ever call the *George Washington* roomy. At first glance it seemed impossible that a hundred men could fit aboard, much less live in her for months without ever coming to the surface. Yet at times she had taken out more than two hundred men for a night or two.

On these occasions, even with the extra bunks, the crew had to suffer through a throwback to the days of cramped World War II submarines—"hot bunking." There were enough bunks in small subs for only two-thirds of the crew to use at any one time. The other third would be on watch. When they came off duty, they would have to crawl into a bunk that had just been vacated by a man going on duty—a bunk that was still warm. Provision was made in the *George Washington* and the other FBM subs for an individual bunk for every man, so that there was no hot bunking unless extra people were aboard.

A Polaris submarine is divided into four main sections. The forepart, except for the 24-foot torpedo room in the bow, is devoted almost exclusively to living quarters, the dining hall, and galley. Next comes the attack center—the command post of the ship—which lies directly below the sail. Next is the 130-foot missile section, and after that, the engine rooms in the stern. Through the middle of the ship, which is about 30 feet deep, there are three main levels, or decks. In the bow and in the stern they taper down to one deck.

The torpedo room has six tubes from which the Navy's most modern torpedoes can be fired. The long, deadly projectiles, each type painted a different color, are stacked against the bulkheads on both sides of the room. Directly over the tubes is a great steel hatch through which torpedoes are loaded aboard or the crew can escape in time of disaster.

Besides the extra bunks jammed into the room above the torpedoes, there is a gallery overhead known as the "hanging gardens." Here a dozen bunks, accessible from the torpedo room by a straight steel ladder, dangle amid some electronic gear. Asked whether he minded sleeping over the torpedoes, a member of the Blue Crew said, "A bunk over the pickles is better than no bunk."

A watertight door covering a narrow 20- by 30-inch hatch leads from the torpedo room into the crew's mess. The door is just wide enough for a man to run through when called to his battle station. A relatively trim man.

For the crew, the mess compartment is the focal point of the ship. On one side is the galley, an amazingly compact stainless-steel kitchen complete with automatic dishwasher and automatic ice cream dispenser. The remainder of the compartment is fitted with two rows of tables that serve not only for eating but also for studying, card playing, and other off-duty recreations. At sea full-length movies—a different one each day—are shown twice daily. A jukebox provides a wide variety of music. A TV set is available for use when the ship is in port.

On the port bulkhead of the mess is a shiny bronze plaque that reads:

*U.S.S. George Washington*
*SSB (N) 598*
*Named for the first President of*
*the United States of America*
*Built by General Dynamics Corporation*
*Electric Boat Division, Groton, Conn.*

| | |
|---|---|
| *Authorized* | *20 January 1958* |
| *Keel Laid* | *1 November 1957* |
| *Launched* | *9 June 1959* |
| *Commissioned* | *30 December 1959* |

Above the crew's mess is the officers' wardroom. It is just large enough for a table that seats ten. A glass-enclosed bust of George Washington—a gift of the ship's sponsor—looks down on the table. The bust sits on a walnut base from Mount Vernon. A plaque on it reads "Courtesy of Mt. Vernon Ladies Association of the Union."

Running next to the wardroom is a narrow passageway leading into the officers' quarters. There are three compartments opening off each side of the passageway, resembling those on a railroad Pullman car with railroad-type washstands that pull out from the wall. The captain and his executive officer have individual compartments. The other officers double up in the remaining four. At the end of the passageway is the officers' "head" with toilet facilities and a shower.

Most of the crew sleep on the lower level under the mess area and attack center. The bunks—each with a reading light—are double-tiered, offering little privacy. However, bulkheads and other interior equipment divide the compartment into several small alleyways where there are just four or eight bunks together. Each bunk has a locker where a man can keep his clothing and personal belongings. The crew's quarters also contain another item to make life more bearable—a bank of four automatic clothes washers.

Perhaps the greatest luxury of all to these new missile submariners is an almost unlimited supply of fresh water. Two "stills," which convert sea water into fresh water, produce a total of 8,000 gallons a day: more than enough for the steam turbines and the crew's showers. This is a great improvement over old submarines where showers had only salt water, which rendered the skin and hair scummy and was no inducement to cleanliness.

Abundant water also means, of course, as one *George Washington* officer told a seaman pointedly, "There's no damn excuse to go around smelling like an arab."

In a compartment adjoining the crew's head sits one of the

strangest machines in the ship. It looks something like a huge top, and, in a sense, it is. It is a 62-ton gyroscope, a big brother of the delicate little gyros that go into the missile's guidance brain. Its purpose is to stabilize the whole submarine, for the sub conceivably might want to fire its missiles from the surface. In a rough sea the gyro would hold the sub steady so the missiles could be aimed accurately. A few ocean liners have gyros like this one, but in ships like the *George Washington,* many sub builders feel they are excess baggage.

This is a tender subject with men like Electric Boat's Bill Atkinson, who has observed repeatedly, "Somebody is always trying to put another gadget in a submarine, but no one ever wants to take anything out. So you end up with two, three, even four machines for one job."

Atkinson's barb was directed chiefly at the attack center, which is jammed from deck to ceiling with dozens of electronic gadgets. The SINS inertial-navigation gyros hang at the center of the compartment in three individual cases, each about 3 feet by 2 feet. They are relatively small. But the computers, which store up and sort all the information on the ship's movements from these three devices, take up dozens of feet of floor space.

In the middle of the attack center, where the sub's three periscopes descend, is the commander's station. His post is raised about three feet off the deck, enabling him to survey everyone in the compartment. At his left are two large panels of instruments. One is for operating all the navigation gear, which includes radio directional finders, star trackers, and a number of secret devices. The other panel monitors the countdown of missiles and many of the critical operations of the ship, such as the operation of the nuclear reactor and the ballasting of water to keep the ship on even keel.

The helmsmen—there are two—sit facing a bank of dials and gauges in front of the commander's station. In much the way an airplane is steered, they guide the sub with identical "sticks"

—small wheel-shaped handles mounted on posts that disappear into the deck. These sticks can be locked together and the sub steered simply by one man if necessary.

It is a strange electronic world beneath the sea, where men appear to be serving the machines rather than machines the men. However, packed in among the computers is one that demonstrates how man remains the essential cog. It is called NAVDAC—the Navigational Data Assimilation Center.

On NAVDAC's control board are three buttons. One is labeled C (for calculate); a second is labeled I (for insert of new figures), and the third U (for use). The man running the machine can pump in figures from all three SINS and the other navigational aids and watch the numbers and lights click by. But only he can decide which of the three give the best reading—perhaps after rubbing his nose and looking at the ceiling; then he presses the "use" button to determine where the ship is at that moment.

Aft of the attack center, the missile fire control and missile launching control centers face each other on either side of a narrow passage. The doors to these rooms are kept locked at all times, and only the operators of the equipment and the officers are allowed entry. At the end of the passage is a hatch that leads to the missile tubes themselves.

The crew on the *George Washington* call it Sherwood Forest.

The sixteen big gray-green tubes rise through the deck in a column of twos down the length of the 130-foot missile compartment. The outsides of the seven-foot steel trunks are padded and wound with painted canvas. Inside each is a metal liner. Inside each liner stands a Polaris.

The tubes extend from the bottom of the sub through two decks to the top of the pressure hull. The decks themselves serve as a gantry from which men can gain access to various parts of the missiles through double steel hatches.

At the lowest level—known throughout the ship as the "mushroom factory"—the air is chilly and damp. Beside the base of each tube stands a ball-shaped steel flask that contains pressurized air. This is the source of the power that drives the missile out of its tube. From these steel flasks comes the force that can hurl the 15-ton seabirds upward through many feet of ocean and far above the surface where they ignite.

The tube hatches on the lower two levels give missilemen access to the Polaris' first and second stages. The hatches on the upper level open on the Polaris' "brain" and nose cone.

Above the upper level on top of the tubes are metal doors, which swing back like the lid of a coffeepot. Just prior to the launching of missiles, the covers open simultaneously with a muffled clang. Water is prevented from rushing into the tubes by an opaque diaphragm through which the missile is catapulted when the launching button is pushed.

Between the tube's lid and the "brain" of the missile is the nose cone—the so-called re-entry vehicle. At its base, imbedded in the missile's white skin, is a slotted metal disc. This is a keyhole to a lock which the world prays is never turned, for to turn it would make the mighty bomb inside ready for its deadly mission. The captain is the sole possessor of the key.

A step through the hatchway in the watertight bulkhead at the end of the missile section leads into a passage above the nuclear reactor. There is a round metal plate in the floor of the passage, which can be lifted back on its hinges, revealing a lead-glass porthole. Through the glass, with the aid of a movable mirror, the reactor room can be observed without being entered. The room is bathed in an eerie reddish light that illuminates a maze of pipes and machinery. The reactor, entirely encased in lead to protect the crew from radiation, is hunched on the floor; within burns the power of the universe. The entrance into the presence of this universal power is through a narrow metal door in the side of the passageway.

The *George Washington* is a self-contained, self-sufficient world. Whatever its crew needs to live and fight the submarine must provide.

The air that the crew breathes is made from sea water by electrolysis. The carbon dioxide that the crew exhales is removed from the air by $CO_2$ scrubbers. Air conditioners maintain the temperature aboard at a constant 72 degrees.

The food the crew eats flows in an unending stream from the sub's refrigerated lockers and storage bins. Garbage is ejected in plastic bags that are weighted to prevent giving away the sub's position.

The machines that the crew tends are repaired from an inventory of more than 60,000 spare parts, including new guidance "brains" for the missiles. Maintenance is a never-ending job. Besides the jungle of electronic equipment, the submarine contains 70 miles of cable, 24 miles of pipe, and 118 electric motors.

The lives of the crew are protected by emergency equipment housed throughout the ship. Special protective clothing for use in case of damage involving the reactor is available in every compartment. Nearby are air-breathing masks that can be plugged into oxygen lines in case of fire.

The morale of the crew that must live in this sealed environment for more than sixty days at a time has received equal attention.

The man put in charge of studying crew morale for Special Projects was Dr. Jack L. Kinsey, a Navy psychiatrist, who wears steel-rimmed glasses and a harried expression around his short mustache. Kinsey—no relation to the late sex researcher of the same name—began probing into the psyches of nuclear submariners during the transpolar crossing of the *Nautilus*. He always has appeared more concerned with what the ballistic missile submariners will do with their time than they have been. He also has worried about such things as weight and exercise.

To keep the men in shape physically, Kinsey argued for the installation of gymnasiums aboard the new *Ethan Allen* class of

FBM subs. These craft will be about 30 feet longer than the *George Washington* and weigh about 1,500 tons more. Captain Monroe Hart, SP's shipbuilding branch head, responded by pledging to make room for "something that can pass for a gym."

But the submariners themselves have been skeptical. They thought it hardly worth while. One of the *George Washington*'s officers said with a laugh, "If we think anyone is getting flabby, we'll put 'em to turning some of the valves down in the scuppers. You can get a real sweat up in no time." Unmindful of this cool attitude, Kinsey prepared plans to clear a space in the crew's quarters, measuring 6 by 20 feet. He proposed setting up in this area weight-lifting and rowing machines, chin bars, and punching bags.

Another idea advanced by the doctor, to provide "motivation" as well as exercise, was to divide the crew into teams and stage bicycle races. The bikes would be stationary and equipped with timers and mileage recorders. During a tour on station the teams would pedal away, and the one piling up the most mileage would receive a special seventy-two-hour pass in a foreign port on their way home as a prize.

None of these proposals were adopted, at least for the first Polaris submarines.

Kinsey also saw a likelihood that the men may put on weight. The submariners get vegetables and other rations in a "dense"—partially dehydrated—form, which tastes better than completely dehydrated food. The frozen-food compartments hold enough deboned meat for the men to eat beef or steak once or twice a day. The cooks, who are sent to some of the country's best hotels to learn the art of fine cuisine from master chefs, daily turn out copious amounts of fresh baked breads and pies and pastries.

All this was fine for morale, but bad for the waistline, and served to underline Kinsey's demand for exercise facilities. At one time he suggested putting in a handball court, but conceded the rounded hull and low ceilings made the engineering of one a little difficult.

One of the *George Washington*'s biggest morale boosters is her movie supply. Kinsey suggested movies might also have another use. In the *U. S. Armed Forces Medical Journal,* he wrote:

"The selection of a few poor-quality pictures is advisable. The purpose of this is not so much to show the contrast between good and bad pictures but to mobilize, activate, and release anxiety, particularly that occurring from a more or less repressed feeling of hostility" of the crew members to one another.

He noted that aboard the *Nautilus,* "the first few poor pictures, in a sequence of poor pictures, produced many sarcastic comments and much infectious laughter. The evidence that this provides a tension-reducing effect is strengthened by the observation that after several poor pictures were shown in sequence, the tension was reduced to the point where there was little or no comment or laughter. . . ."

Kinsey's researches produced this picture-preference rating among submarine crews:

"1) 'Good' Westerns; 2) Mystery and 'good' Science Fiction; 3) Comedy, classical drama and musicals are grouped at approximately the same level of preference. It should be noted that a pretty girl, particularly if scantily clad, will be most favorably received and provoke prompt reactions in any type of picture."

At one point the good doctor favored rendering Osborn and his men cigarless. Noting that the carbon-monoxide level was raised by smoking, and the concentration of tars in the air increased, Kinsey suggested smoking should be severely limited or eliminated while submerged. However, he admitted "this would probably create a morale problem of greater dimensions than the contaminant problem."

Osborn's cigar eventually was saved by another machine—an improved air-filter.

# 18   Give Us the Subs!

Congress may hand the President money to spend, but Congress can't force him to spend it.

Polaris, in the fall of 1958, ran into just such a situation.

The budget for the year held 600 million dollars extra, which Congress had put in so that four more missile submarines could be started. This would have increased the number to go on station in the 1960-61 winter to nine in all.

President Eisenhower decided, however, to stand pat on five submarines.

The keel for a fourth—the *Robert E. Lee*—was laid in September at Newport News Shipbuilding & Drydock Company in Virginia. The keel for the fifth—the *Abraham Lincoln*—went down in November at Portsmouth Naval Shipyard in New Hampshire. The *George Washington, Patrick Henry,* and *Theodore Roosevelt* were well under way.

As the year closed, the White House relented and released enough of the extra congressional money to build a sixth Polaris submarine—the *Ethan Allen*. It also allowed enough for the conversion of a merchantman into the first Polaris submarine tender. It was called the *Proteus*.

But that was all. Eisenhower left the rest of the money sitting in the Treasury.

The major argument of the administration to beat down the Navy's requests to release all the money was that the Polaris system was still unproved. The administration's budget men wanted to see more evidence before spending more money.

The Navy countered that the cost was relatively small com-

*Polaris!*

pared to many other military programs, and the gains would be tremendous compared to the slight risk involved. The Navy found itself repeating this argument for the next several years as billions of dollars were poured into Air Force antiaircraft missiles, which later were discarded, and billions more into fixed ICBM bases.

The administration's answer was always the same: No.

Moreover, in the fall of 1958, the administration received support for its position from the Air Force, which by this time was becoming increasingly uneasy about Polaris. The Air Force had won the battle with the Army over control of Jupiter. Now it had control of all long-range missiles—except Polaris.

At first, the Navy had guardedly talked about Polaris as a weapon designed for shore bombardment. But within the last year this nonsense had been dropped. Polaris had the reach of an Atlas ICBM. The Air Force could see a fight ahead for dollars that formerly had "Air Force" written all over them. Therefore, the Air Force missed few opportunities to remind the administration that Polaris was unproved.

The news from Cape Canaveral did not help the Navy either. Beginning in September with AX-1, one unhappy report followed another. When the administration talked of wanting more assurance, all it had to do to support its arguments was point to the morning papers.

So shortsighted was the White House, it took little notice of an event far more significant than exploding Polarises at Cape Canaveral.

Late that summer, 4,000 miles from Washington, the dark shape of the *Nautilus* moved cautiously beneath the Arctic ice pack. Comdr. William R. Anderson stood in the attack center and spoke to his crew over the ship's loudspeaker system.

"Stand by," Anderson said, watching a dial. "10 . . . 8 . . . 6 . . . 4 . . . 3 . . . 2 . . . 1. Mark. August 3, 1958. Time: 23-15. For the United States and the United States Navy, the North Pole."

Two days later, the *Nautilus* emerged from the ice northeast of Greenland, and Anderson wired to Admiral Burke three words: "Nautilus 90 North."

The *Nautilus* had traveled submerged beneath the ice pack from the Pacific to the Atlantic by way of the Pole. What the *Nautilus* could do, so could a fleet of Polaris-launching submarines. The way was open to surround Russia with missiles. Here was the proof. Yet the White House kept its eyes shut.

In January President Eisenhower put 611 million dollars for Polaris in the new budget for fiscal year 1960. However, no money was provided for any more submarines. Only funds for some submarine parts that take a long time to produce were included. These "long leadtime" items were parts for nuclear power plants and reduction gears. The budget included enough to pay for long leadtime items for three additional submarines.

The administration made one other concession. It told the Navy that the rest of the money that Congress had appropriated the year before would be released about July 1—the beginning of the new fiscal year.

In effect, this arrangement put the Navy on a schedule that would enable it to send to sea a total of twelve Polaris submarines at the rate of about three a year.

Many within the Navy were unhappy with this arrangement. The explanation came when Admiral Raborn and Rear Adm. K. S. Masterson, Navy director of guided missiles, appeared before the Mahon subcommittee April 6. Mahon asked Masterson if the Navy had asked for more Polaris submarines in the 1960 budget.

"The Navy originally requested that six submarines be in the 1960 budget request with long leadtime items for enough submarines to where we could schedule twelve in fiscal year 1961," Masterson replied. "That is, in addition to what was given to us by the 1959 Congress."

"To contrast that and clarify the record, what do you actually have in the budget?" Mahon asked.

"We actually have in the 1960 budget only long leadtime money for three submarines."

The subcommittee was generally not pleased. The more it questioned, the less pleased it became.

The administration had refused to spend the money Congress appropriated. It had refused to begin building a large fleet of Polaris submarines that would have added another 800 million dollars to the 1960 budget. It had spent more than 2.5 billion dollars on the Polaris program so far, and proposed to spend more, yet it kept saying it wasn't sure of it. Finally, many felt the administration was deliberately attempting to obfuscate what it was doing, for it talked about long leadtime items as if they were more submarines. There is no question that the situation was confusing. Many congressmen never were able to untangle it. Many of those who could were left feeling as if reason had fled the Capital.

"I think all of us are more or less enthusiastic about the Polaris program," Mahon told Masterson. "It appeals to our judgment and to our imagination. I think it is a very popular idea with the people as an extra-special type of deterrent. I know we cannot do everything and do it simultaneously, but it concerns me that the Navy would think enough of this to ask for six additional submarines, and that you would be able to persuade the Defense Department to give you none at all. What is wrong here? Is it purely a budgetary matter, or is it lack of confidence on the part of the Office of the Secretary of Defense, or what is the trouble, Admiral?"

Masterson looked at Mahon. Certainly this man didn't need an answer to his question. Certainly he must know, just as he must know that Masterson or any other military man couldn't tell him in an open hearing without destroying himself.

"I am afraid I am not speaking for the Secretary of Defense in this matter, sir," Masterson said, avoiding a reply. But any military man would have told Mahon privately what the problem was. It was the budget.

The budget! The budget! The Eisenhower budget! And before it the Truman budget! Russia had been arming for years, but the United States kept hoping the nightmare would go away.

Eisenhower had strangled the Army. If the nation had to fight a war, it no longer could fight with nonatomic weapons. Eisenhower had allowed the Navy's fleet to deteriorate. Ships were being held together with luck. Eisenhower had staked all on the retaliatory forces of SAC, but then had skimped for years on giving SAC the big missiles that it needed to remain strong. Now Eisenhower was doing the same thing with Polaris.

Secretary of Defense McElroy did speak for himself.

He told Congress and the American people that there was nothing to worry about. He said it was true that the Soviet Union by 1962 or 1963 probably would have three times as many intercontinental ballistic missiles aimed at the United States as the United States would have aimed at the Soviet Union. This was the Missile Gap.

But McElroy said the United States did not have to rely on its ICBMs alone. The United States had and would continue to have a great array of forces that would deter the Russians from striking. He called the American forces a "mix" that included the SAC bomber fleet, Navy bombers based on carriers at sea, Air Force fighter bombers based around the world, some Thor IRBMs based in Britain, and a squadron of obsolescent Snark missiles based in Maine. He said that in the next few years this force would be augmented with Atlas and Titan ICBMs on land and Polarises under the sea.

Many in and out of uniform were not reassured.

Gen. Thomas Power, the commander of SAC, said the nation's retaliatory strength was deteriorating. He urged that the United States build more bombers and more Atlases.

Critics showed where McElroy's mix contained a lot of chaff. All America's overseas bases were vulnerable to a surprise attack by Soviet IRBMs, and SAC bomber bases and the relatively few

ICBM bases under construction in the United States were also increasingly vulnerable to surprise attack as the accuracy of Soviet ICBMs improved. As for the slow-moving *Snark,* Congressman Flood said he could knock it down "with a rock."

The Pentagon had already begun to look toward launching missiles from mobile bases as the answer. The Navy, of course, was developing Polaris. The Air Force was developing a solid-fueled ICBM called Minuteman, which could be put on trucks or trains, and another solid-fueled missile called Skybolt, which would have a 1,000-mile range and could be launched from a bomber.

But Minutemen were not scheduled to be ready for deployment in quantity before mid-1962, and Skybolts not before 1964. Polaris would be ready in 1960, but there would be few submarines from which to launch it.

The Navy said the Missile Gap could be plugged to a great extent by building a fleet of forty-five Polaris submarines. If the United States started even in mid-1959, a fleet of twenty-seven submarines could be on station by 1964. Such a fleet would ring the Soviet heartland with more than four hundred missiles carrying nuclear warheads.

At the Bethlehem Steel shipyard at Quincy, Massachusetts, the Navy had under construction its first nuclear-powered cruiser, the *Long Beach.* The 14,000-ton ship was scheduled to join the fleet the following year. At Quincy and other United States shipyards the Navy also had more than a half-dozen cruisers that were being converted to carry short-range missiles.

Operating on the theory that what armament it put on its ships was strictly its own business, the Navy ordered Polaris tubes aboard the *Long Beach.* There were to be eight tubes installed in the ship's superstructure.

The Navy also made plans for installing eight Polaris tubes in several of the smaller cruisers that were then being converted to missile ships. On these the tubes were to be installed in the space occupied by gun turrets.

Eighteen cruisers were available for use as floating Polaris bases. Naval architects had designs for installing still more tubes on Victory ships that had been in the moth-balled reserve fleet since the end of World War II.

Just as work on the tubes for the *Long Beach* was about to begin, a high-level admiral prepared a speech telling about the plan. It was a mistake. A copy of the text came into the hands of McElroy, who immediately picked up the phone and ordered the installation of tubes stopped pending a review by the Joint Chiefs of Staff.

That was the end. The Chiefs shelved the plan until the Navy could give a fuller demonstration of the workability of the Polaris.

Space for Polaris tubes was left on the *Long Beach* and the other cruisers, but the ships went to sea without them.


Secretary of the Navy Gates was in the witness chair. Congressman Flood shot the questions in the hearing room, just off the floor of the House.

"You said, Mr. Secretary, that when you went topside you asked for six new Polaris systems plus the nine you gaily thought you were going to get," Flood said.

"Yes, sir," said Gates.

"But the budget, as it is now, talks about only three, and even then not all the money for all the submarines of those three."

"No, sir. Only long leadtime items. Minor money for components, Mr. Flood, not for the ships."

"There is nothing in the budget asking for three Polaris systems including three submarines?"

"The three in the budget are a carryover from the 1959 Congressional action."

"Yes, but these are not three of the six you asked for?"

"That is correct."

"I wanted to make that clear," Flood said. "We thought we

gave you the nine. You did not get them. I heard the Director
of the Budget say last week—and my mustache nearly dropped
off on the floor—he said, 'I think that the national defense
budget is adequate.' He thinks. Some glorified bookkeeper down
there. We are going to give him a half-dozen more stripes, you
know. We are talking about that. The Director of the Bureau of
the Budget is going to get three or four more of these stars up
here. He thinks everything is all right. That's great."

Flood paused a moment, grimacing.

"You did not get any part of the six you asked for?" he asked
again, his voice overflowing with mock amazement.

"That is correct," Gates said.

"Of course, you emphasize all through your testimony the
manning levels of the operational fleet have never been this low
before in percentage. Is that correct?"

"Yes, sir," Admiral Burke interjected.

" 'Austere' and 'minimum,' " Flood said, opening his hands
in an expression of helplessness. "This is great. Of course we
are all right. We have never been in this shape before, but we
are all right."

"Will you yield right there?" Congressman Charles Boyle of
Illinois interrupted. "I have considerable trouble following the
numbers. Are these additional Polaris submarines?"

Commander Middleton was ready to try the next big step in
testing the Polaris on July 15, 1959.

Until then, all Polaris test missiles had been guided in flight
by an automatic pilot that received its orders by a crude tape-fed
system. It was now time to try flying a Polaris with its inertial
guidance system inside it.

The inertial guidance system would not operate the missile
on this first flight. An autopilot would still be in command. But
the inertial guidance system would operate throughout the
flight as if it were directing the missile, and special instruments
would radio back how well the new guidance system was doing.

The guidance package was installed in Polaris test missile AX-11, and the brightly painted missile roared into the Florida sky. Seconds after it was in the air, it was in trouble. A piece of one of the jetavators that steer the missile broke away.

The missile soared gracefully to about 40,000 feet over the ocean, slowly turned downward, and did a full loop. Observers on the shore were stunned. The range officer reached for the destruct button, but stopped. The second stage had separated from the first with a puff of smoke. As the second stage reoriented itself and headed again down the range, safety observers made conflicting reports on stray parts flying about. The range safety officer had had enough. He pushed the destruct button.

But the launching was a tremendous success. The inertial guidance system had operated perfectly under the most extreme circumstances. No one considered sane would have suggested that the guidance system be tested by making a missile perform circus tricks. However, this is precisely what had happened. Any guidance system that could function well during the flight of the AX-11 could function well anywhere under any conditions.

The White House had a political hex on Congress that summer.

The huge Democratic majority that took over Congress in 1959 was looking for political blood—and the White House in 1960. There was much proposing of big new programs that would need big new appropriations. Democrats talked in terms of bold approaches and the need for giving the country leadership.

But Republican Eisenhower met the Democrats on their own ground. He said he would balance the budget, and anyone who wanted to do anything that would unbalance it was a "spender." The "spender" label stuck and burned. By summer, the Democratic host was in flight.

Congress passed a defense budget for fiscal 1960 that gave Raborn the entire 611 million dollars that the administration had permitted him to request. But not a dollar more.

.   .   .

*Polaris!*

The Polaris test program, which had been so crippled with troubles less than a year before, suddenly began to leap from success to success.

During the second week in August, Polaris AX-13 was lowered with a watchmaker's care into the tube of the huge ship-motion simulator. A Polaris test missile was about to be launched for the first time from this enormous cocktail shaker that could simulate the six motions of a ship at sea.

However, the purpose of the test was not to see if a missile could be launched while the tube gyrated. That would come later and was of little importance anyway, since the motion of a submerged submarine is very slight. The purpose of this launching was to see if a live Polaris could be successfully ejected and fired from the tube, which was a duplicate of the tubes in the *George Washington*.

Everything was ready for the launching on August 14. The missile bolted from the tube in a great white cloud of ice crystals, and a sharp report reverberated along the coast as the missile climbed into the air. Then a roar drowned the area in sound as the motor ignited and the missile plummeted down the range. A cheer swept the complex.

The launching was a complete success.

Thirteen days later the same thing was tried for the first time from a tube on the *Observation Island* test ship.

The converted merchantman moved slowly in a prescribed race-track course about seven miles off the Cape. The day was unusually hot. The crowds of bathers far away on the shore did not know what the ship was doing. There was no advance announcement to the public. Bill Pearl, Refo's chief civilian assistant, paced the beach.

There was good reason to worry. Middleton knew the rocket motors that he had been using had some flaws. These had been corrected in later models, but the later models were not available yet. Rather than delay the test program, the available motors were used. However, Middleton's luck had held for so many months that he felt he was stretching it.

A man who knew Pearl stopped and chatted with him on the beach. A little girl with a beach ball ran past them. Pearl looked at his watch. It was almost time. He slowly pivoted as he talked, so that he faced the sea and his companion faced the land. Far out Pearl saw a white puff, then an orange flash, as the missile ignited in the air and headed out over the Atlantic.

The launching was a success. The way was clear for the A1X series, a new family of Polaris test missiles that incorporated a whole bundle of improvements. They looked exactly like the AXs. But inside, they were the result of a year of heartbreak and success.

The A1X-1 roared from a test pad at the Cape on September 21, almost exactly a year from the day when the first AX missile had soared straight up and been destroyed. A1X-1 did much better. It soared gracefully above the complex, tilted toward Africa, and soared 900 miles down the range—the longest flight yet made by a Polaris.

The Navy, Raborn, the Special Projects Office, all were elated. Apparently the Air Force was impressed, too. A number of Air Force generals began to hammer harder for favorable action on an Air Force proposal that the Polaris fleet be made part of a Joint Strategic Air Command.

# 19    Battle Stations on Capitol Hill

On the 18th day of January in the year A.D. 1960 the President of the United States sent to the Congress, duly convened at the seat of government, his annual budget message.

"With this message, transmitting the budget of the United States for the fiscal year 1961, I invite the Congress to join with me in a determined effort to achieve a substantial surplus," the President wrote.

*Polaris!*

The economy theme of the final year of the Eisenhower administration had been announced.

"While seeking the true road to peace and disarmament we must remain strong," the President added.

However, the new defense budget was frozen at the usual 40 billion dollars. The President was ready to spend anything needed up to 40 billion dollars to remain strong. This included, as the budget disclosed, enough money for three more Polaris-launching submarines and long leadtime parts for three more. The Navy had proposed building nine more submarines and buying long leadtime parts for twelve more.

The Republican President sought to support his position by sending his new Secretary of Defense, former Secretary of the Navy Thomas Gates, to Capitol Hill with a very special piece of information. Gates informed one Congressional committee after another that they no longer had to worry about the Missile Gap. New intelligence estimates showed that Russia would not build as many missiles as it had been thought capable of building. Therefore, the Missile Gap would no longer be big enough to mean much.

Gen. Nathan Twining, chairman of the Joint Chiefs of Staff, added an interesting overtone. The white-haired Air Force general implied with the subtlety of an atomic bomb that anyone who openly questioned this new estimate was bordering on disloyalty.

The Democratic majority in Congress was furious.

In the first place, they didn't believe what they were told. In the second place, they smelled a political rat that many felt might have been loosed by the Vice-president.

The Democrats called in the nation's top intelligence experts. Closed hearing after closed hearing was held; bits of information were released day after day. It became increasingly clear that United States intelligence estimates did indeed show that Russia would produce fewer missiles than it could. But they also showed that Russia would have as many missile launchers as had been previously expected, if not more. The Missile Gap in late 1962 and 1963 would be as great as ever, if not greater.

Gen. Thomas Power, commander of SAC, warned publicly that the United States already was in great danger. He said Russia would soon be able to obliterate America's retaliatory power with missiles and, until many more United States missiles could be built, hundreds of SAC bombers should be kept in the air at all times.

President Eisenhower called General Power's approach "parochial." The country remained prosperous and unalarmed.

Adm. Arleigh Burke sat in a crowded hearing room of the old Senate Office Building. In this room the Senate Preparedness Subcommittee and the Senate Space Committee had for nearly two weeks been holding joint hearings on the state of the nation's defenses. Lyndon Baynes Johnson of Texas, chairman of both the subcommittee and the committee, majority leader of the United States Senate, and unannounced candidate for President of the United States, presided.

Edwin Weisl, a special counsel to the committees, looked at some notes and then asked quietly about what the notes before him so clearly said.

"In fiscal years 1958 and 1959, the Congress provided funds and authority to proceed with nine Polaris submarines; isn't that correct?"

"Yes, sir," Admiral Burke said.

"Despite this, is it not true that the Executive Branch refused to release the funds for submarines 7, 8, and 9 during fiscal year 1959?"

"Yes, sir," Admiral Burke said.

"Is it not also true that the 1960 budget contained no funds for construction of additional Polaris submarines except for advance components for submarines 10, 11, and 12?"

"That is correct, sir," Admiral Burke said.

"Isn't the withholding of the funds appropriated in 1959 and the failure to request additional funds in 1960 resulting in a sharp decrease or a gap in the deployment of Polaris submarines after the first nine?"

"Not a sharp decrease, sir," Admiral Burke said. "What we can do, of course, is to deploy about three submarines per year, because that is what we are building per year."

"I understand that," Weisl said, some slight impatience coming into his voice. "But if you had used the money that you asked Congress to give you and for which you pleaded so eloquently, you wouldn't have had that gap, isn't that true?"

"Yes, sir; that is correct."

"Obviously you cannot make up that leadtime now. Once leadtime is lost, it is lost forever, isn't it?"

"Yes, sir."

"Are you fully satisfied with the funds in the 1961 budget for the Polaris?"

"No, sir. We will ask for a supplemental, I believe, sir. I also believe that the Department of Defense will look favorably on it, sir, although I am not sure."

So much for the past. Weisl had made the record clear. The next question obviously related to the future and the number of additional submarines that the Navy would request. Senator Leverett Saltonstall asked it.

"We haven't completely got our figures in line, sir," Admiral Burke replied. "I can tell you what we can do. We can build six additional submarines in 1961 and then after that year, in 1962 we can build one Polaris submarine per month. In addition to that, there is the question of Polaris on surface ships. We have cruisers which can take the same suit of Polaris missiles as are on submarines: in other words, sixteen missiles. We think it would be advisable to put Polaris missiles in cruisers, too, so that more missiles would be available."

Admiral Burke said the cost for the first additional six submarines, including sub tenders and related equipment, would be close to 1 billion dollars.

.   .   .

A week later another admiral, Vice Adm. John T. Hayward, deputy chief of naval operations for development, put the case for Polaris more bluntly. Hayward, an outspoken man with a biting style, accompanied Raborn in an appearance before the House Committee on Science and Astronautics.

Congressman Ken Hechler, a West Virginia Democrat, asked Raborn if there were any reason why the United States "might want to push the Polaris program to a greater extent than programs that are going on in other areas."

"I would answer that," Admiral Hayward broke in. "If you had had faith in Admiral Raborn in 1956, when we came and presented this program, and you had gone forth with our program then, today you would begin—this particular year you would begin—producing these submarines at the rate of one a month, and there would be no argument by anybody then that you didn't have the power or that there was any so-called gap, whether it is missile or deterrent or anything, because they would be coming off the line. Those are the hard decisions that have to be made. Each year, as we go along, they say, 'Well, maybe it will work, and maybe it won't.' This is the decision-making process. It is not the technical lead time."

Congressman John McCormack of Massachusetts, the House majority leader, had been listening carefully with his ear cupped in his hand. Now he sat up and interrupted.

"Will the gentleman yield right there?" he asked Hechler in a tone that indicated the gentleman had better.

"Yes," Hechler said. McCormack turned to face Hayward and squinted at him cannily.

"You mean if the decision had been made then?" he asked.

"Yes," Hayward said.

"You understand that the decision is not purely Congressional?"

"No, it is not purely Congressional. If the decision had been made then that the United States required a deterrent force of this nature, and that you were going to fund it and build it at a rapid rate, you would have those coming out this year at one a month."

"As a matter of fact, several of the Polarises have been on the Congressional level," McCormack persisted.

"Yes, sir," Hayward said. "More of them have been added by Congress."

"I say that with pride for all members without regard to party," McCormack said. "Congress has apparently seen the value of this and has had the vision and the courage to go ahead making appropriations over and above the budget."

McCormack nodded emphatically and sat back. Hechler resumed his questioning.

"And you are personally convinced, from the standpoint of national security, that one-a-month production of Polaris would be not only feasible but necessary?"

"Personally," Hayward said, "I am convinced that the Polaris system is the best deterrent system that we have in the world today."

The political fight over construction of more Polaris submarines was not the only political fight in which the Polaris program was embroiled at this time. Another of equal ferocity involved the United States Air Force.

Congressman Flood brought this second struggle clearly into the open as Admiral Burke and the new Secretary of the Navy, William Franke, testified before the House Military Appropriations Subcommittee.

Flood began with an attack on General Twining's condemnation of people who describe the nation's defenses as not being all they might be.

"Mr. Secretary, I am about to aid and abet the enemy," Flood said. "You are now looking at somebody who, under this new yardstick of the budget and the Defense Department, is not quite 100 per cent American. I probably have elements of treason in my soul, all that kind of thing, because this budget does not come to me as sacrosanct. I think there are some things the matter with it. *Mirabile dictu*. Can you imagine that? I fly in the face of the gods. It is a heedless abandon to reason. I am a very bad guy. I remember from my Blackstone, a hundred years ago there was an expression: *Rex non potere est.* Literally translated, as lawyers translate such things, it means 'The king can do no wrong.' My ancestors came here from Ireland 220-some years ago because we did not believe it then, and I do not believe it yet. There is another old, moth-eaten legalism: *Omnia homines non est perfectum*—'Men are not perfect.' Believe it or not, that includes you and me, which is going pretty far, but I think it is so."

"I would be the first to admit it," Franke squeezed in.

"Yes, I would break down and admit it," Flood said. "I just think this attitude that is presented here by the Department of Defense, as espoused by the Secretary and General Twining, is unbelievable. You people say in effect, 'If you dare to question the propriety and the sufficiency and the quality and the quantity of our weapons system and our posture—you must not do that; the Russians are liable to believe you, Flood. And if they do, there will be disaster to pay. You will bring war and missiles. You would be responsible for a cataclysm and World War III. They are liable to misconstrue the facts and think we are weak and puny and poor. Do not talk about these things. That is not right. We know what we are doing. We know more about this than you do, you Congressional morons, that sit up on that committee there for ten years and see presidents and generals and admirals come and go like Greyhound buses.' But the fact is we do sit here, and some of this rubs off on us."

Then, catching his breath, Flood turned to Admiral Burke and Polaris.

"I am shocked by what my spy system sends to me from the Pentagon and throughout the country—that the Air Force is actually serious about this Polaris business. I think that is more important than whether the President is the greatest military leader in the United States or not. Here is a great weapon system that these flyboys are not fooling about. I thought they were kidding. I thought it was a diversionary operation last year, to get more bombers or something on a deal with the Joint Chiefs of Staff, like you fellows do every once in a while. I did not think they meant it. But, by golly, they do. It has gone to Secretary level. It is going to be there in the next thirty days again for the Secretary of Defense to decide whether or not the Polaris system, your pigeon, should or should not be assigned to the Air Force as a strategic bombardment weapon. Without being profane, will you comment about this?"

Burke, whom Flood on occasion called "Skipper," nodded.

"The proposition that the Air Force proposed was not that the Air Force take it over exactly," Burke told him, "but that they provide a strategic commander in command of all delivery systems including Polaris, SAC, ICBMs, IRBMs, and all the rest."

"Strategic bombardment weapons?"

"That is correct," Burke said. "They base that on the need for co-ordination. That is the reason for submitting the proposition."

"It is obviously a planned and determined effort to incorporate this Polaris system of the Navy into some strategic bombardment concept of the Air Force," Flood said. "No question about that, in my opinion. That should not be done. I personally hope that if and when this reaches the Joint Chiefs level for final action, before it goes to the Secretary level, if your name is Burke, I think you know how to handle the Navy's case."

"Yes, sir," Burke said.

"I expect you would and I am sure you will. Do not let these jokers push you around. That is nonsense."

On Flood's invitation, Admiral Burke later submitted to the subcommittee a statement that concluded:

"The Navy has behind it generations of experience in the

operation of sea-based weapons systems. To depart from the principal of the integrated, balanced fleet at this critical time in history, by assigning Polaris submarines to a command charged with operating land-based strategic bombers and missiles, would weaken our nation's ability to strike back. It would reduce the effectiveness of our Polaris submarines by artificially creating many serious operational problems. The enemy will create enough problems for us at sea as it is. Let us not deliberately create more of our own. The proposal to remove Polaris submarines from our fleets and lump them into an over-all strategic command is both impractical and dangerous."

The internal political struggle between the Air Force and the Navy was inevitable. Polaris was already challenging the future supremacy of SAC as the nation's primary retaliatory force, and Raborn was talking of extending the range of Polaris missiles to 2,500 miles by 1964.

The Air Force had some of its best salesmen at work. They kept the Navy's salesmen busy.

Influential people in Washington were informed publicly and privately that one of the shortcomings of Polaris was that the Soviet Union could put its huge diesel-powered submarine fleet on the tails of the Polaris subs. No one explained how the diesel-powered Soviet subs would ever catch up with the much faster Polaris ships.

Word was spread that Polaris could not possibly be as accurate as a land-based missile; that the Polaris warhead, which is many, many times more powerful than the bomb that destroyed Hiroshima, was "rather small" compared to the more powerful warheads carried by the Atlas and Titan; that the missile could not ignite after passing through water; and, most important of all, that Polaris was "untried."

The Air Force quietly leaked to the Washington press corps a critique of Polaris written by an unidentified scientist. Its principal criticism was the size of the warhead. It did not mention that the warhead is approximately the same as would be put on the Minuteman, the Air Force's solid-fueled ICBM, which was then nearly three years behind Polaris.

One Washington newsman arrived at Special Projects Office with a list of Polaris drawbacks provided for him by Air Force officers around the country. One alleged drawback was that the Polaris submarines leave a tell-tale radioactive trail in the water —a ridiculous notion. Another alleged drawback was that the Polaris submarines, which can remain under water almost indefinitely, would have to surface to recharge their batteries.

There were murmurings that Polaris submarines also were vulnerable to a sneak underwater attack: that pattern missile bombing of key ocean areas could knock out the Polaris fleet. The Navy called the idea farfetched at best. In the same breath, Navy strategists added that any missile system was vulnerable to some degree—if an enemy wanted to pay the price. And they said the price to wipe out the Polaris fleet, if such a move were possible, would be staggering.

An Air Force contention more damaging to the Polaris program in congressional eyes was that Polaris was extremely expensive. Comparative figures presented to congressmen showed that each Polaris missile on station cost nearly $10 million while each Minuteman in an underground silo would cost about $2 million or less.

The Navy countered that the Air Force estimates for Minuteman were low. The Navy also pointedly added that whatever the cost of Polaris it had the decided advantage of being here while Minuteman was still two to three years away.

The charge that hurt most was that the Polaris was "untried."

The administration wanted to believe that the best thing to do was to do very little. And, even in the Navy, many influential officers hesitated. They did not want to push too hard in case they were wrong.

One Naval officer recalled that during World War II, the Navy had developed a new torpedo that, before it had been fully tried, was produced in quantity and distributed to the fleet.

"A sub would slip into a convoy and fire a load of these pickles and they'd go rat-tat-tat against a hull of a Jap destroyer and not explode, and then there you were on the bottom while the Japs dropped things on you," he said.

Raborn sat in his office and talked about his program.

"It's true I've been impatient at times because of my detailed knowledge of the technical assurance of the program. But I am also fully aware that these things must fit into the over-all military picture. And I would like to make this clear: It has been my consistent stand before Congress that the pace at which the program has been supported by the Administration is necessarily based on the decisions of those who have a broader view than I of over-all defense needs. Because of this I have always endeavored not to be critical of decisions handed down. However, now, we're coming down to the end of the road, and when you get there, you just have the end of the road. I've been punching doorbells for the last two years, and people have been patting me on the head—and I know that's why I've got that bald spot —and saying, 'Show me a little more, sonny, and when you do, we're really going to get in this one.' I told a gang the other day that we're like the girl stripper who's down to her G string and she's saying, 'What else do you want to see?' "

Raborn laughed wryly, leaning back in his leather-cushioned desk chair. He paused to see how the words registered on his listeners. At his right elbow was a globe of the earth in a floor stand. The map of Russia was turned toward him. Raborn leaned forward, stabbing the top of the desk with the tips of his strong, blunt fingers.

"Over the past four years," he continued, "the ebb and flow of what we need has been somewhat influenced by understandably enthusiastic proponents of one system or another. At one time it was thought in this country that we only needed ICBMs.

*Polaris!*

And then about two years ago, we started thinking about hardening, about putting these things underground. Well, what are we going to do next?"

He shrugged, then raised his head and looked up questioningly. It was a gesture that signaled he was about to make a point.

"I think they are going to come right down to the dock and jump aboard the submarine. And I think very properly so. But they could have jumped on this submarine earlier. They could have put the band aboard some time ago. Maybe there are some bad things about our program. I don't know. We haven't been able to find them. I think we have had some rather expert help from other folks, too. This is good. Maybe they will convince themselves. If we get enough convinced people, maybe the country will get a share of this weapon system which we sincerely believe it needs."

# 20    The Homestretch

March. A cool Monday morning. The Management Center at Polaris headquarters is crowded as usual. The clock says 8:14. In Moscow, it is midafternoon. In Peiping, it is the middle of the night. The minute hand on the Management Center clock jumps to 8:15. The steel door of the room swings open, and Admiral Raborn enters. Capt. K. M. Tebo, the director of program evaluation, says, "Good morning, Admiral." Everyone stands. Raborn takes his seat in the front row. Another of the weekly reviews of progress has begun.

Captain Tebo, as always at these meetings, speaks first. He talks briefly about the coming month.

"We are going to be dealing an awful lot with BuShips, particularly at the Naval shipyard, to get current on the installation program. We have a very tight schedule of about three shipyard tests out of the other six activities next month. You may not see very much of me . . ."

He talks on. There has been a problem about getting training publications on time. Now it is solved. The training publications project is in "good shape."

Raborn crosses his legs. Several officers around him make some notes. Captain Ela speaks next.

"Good morning, Admiral, gentlemen. We have a minor weakness, but this is not necessarily going to be this way all our lives. . . ."

The clock on the wall says 8:45. Now it's 8:55.

"Admiral, your next report is from Commander Sanders," Captain Tebo says.

"Good morning, Admiral," says Commander Sanders. "This morning I have some pictures pertaining to the umbilical cable and the connectors problem on the West Coast."

And the talk goes on.

Transmission items are being delivered to the *Theodore Roosevelt*. No gains were made the week before on the Model-A gyros. Two SINS systems are installed on *Patrick Henry* and "are being groomed." A bearing on a periscope was damaged and returned to the factory for repair.

Some reports are good. Some are very good. But everywhere there are problems.

Captain Herold says, "What we don't know is what these bars below the line will look like a month from now. One of our problems is people who don't know what they're doing and who think all of these controls are silly. But we will have some pretty tight controls on these things. You can really damage these things when they're in the hands of people who don't know what they're doing. . . ."

Captain Middleton says, "The test failed. There is perhaps a faulty design, or perhaps some damage was done in installation. . . ."

After all his branch directors have spoken, it is Raborn's turn. He rises and stands before the lectern. He grins and then looks soberly over the room.

"Each of you is captain or boss of a certain area," he says crisply. "You can't expect anyone else to do your job. If you don't do it, something is going to slip so far behind, you can't do anything about it. And then you're going to have to come up here saying, 'Somebody let me down.' Now, you must jump on these things like a hawk and really see that they get done. You're coming down the homestretch now. By God, if anything looks a little soft, you get after it. Don't assume somebody is taking proper action. You see that he takes it. This is the only way you can run a show, boys. You've got to twist a tiger by the tail every week."

Raborn smiles. He tells his men they are doing a "grand job —so far." Then he shifts the subject to the missile, still speaking like a coach to a football team.

"On Capitol Hill they think we're doing a good job. But they need to set a sight on significant events. They ask me, 'What have you really got your eye on?' I think the thing I have my eye on, and I pass it along to you for your information, is the fully integrated systems test on the *Observation Island*. The series of tests on that ship will show how all of the equipments work together as an integrated unit. True, we've worked them out in subsystems and many combinations of subsystems and done very well. But if people have to hang their hat on something tell them that.

"Also, Admiral Burke has said that we ought to have Polaris in surface vessels. If the time comes when they want to put up some money and get these missiles overseas in a hurry, surface vessels look pretty good. Therefore, drawing people's attention to the *Observation Island*'s forthcoming tests is, I think, very proper. It is an integrated missile base. The mere fact that we can shoot from the surface is, of course, significant because the submarine also must be able to shoot from the surface. You don't require the submarine to pull the plug in order to shoot.

"The so-called wet match test out on the West Coast, where we shoot a cut-grain [partially fueled] missile from the Pop-up and ignite it, is significant only in the minds of some people. Not in my own, because we have tested our ignition devices many times, as you know, and we are quite sure that they will ignite. I remind people that we learned how to keep our powder dry back in Revolutionary War days while fording streams. Certainly we know by this time. But there are still some non-believers."

Raborn rubs the palms of his hands together. His tone becomes serious again.

"Time is our biggest enemy, gentlemen, and I encourage you to take an aggressive attitude. Go on a seven-day week if necessary. Don't stop at five days a week or five and a third. And I want you to be in your shop here Saturday mornings. Get all your people to come and don't let them wear Sloppy Sue dress, either. Saturday morning is a working day. I'd like to see your secretaries show that they know it's a working day, too. One more point: If you want to do your shopping, do it when I do, on Saturday afternoon. Or better still, get your wife to do it. That's showing leadership."

This, then, was the homestretch.

Thousands of contractors . . . tens of thousands of engineers . . . millions of parts . . . an industrial complex spread from coast to coast . . . all aimed at putting the *George Washington* on station by fall.

Each day the job became still more complicated. But Raborn and his staff continued to keep track of it all. Wherever someone faltered, new efforts were put forth immediately. Whenever someone gained a day, the gain was exploited immediately. More than two years after the program had started, it remained on its killing schedule.

Gordon Pehrson's management systems continued to be the sharp tools with which Raborn so successfully worked. They enabled the staff of the Special Projects Office to function knowledgeably with freedom and efficiency. But as the program had gained momentum and had become increasingly complex, even Pehrson's early systems were not good enough. Something even better was needed. Again Pehrson provided it.

In January, 1958, Raborn, at Pehrson's urging, initiated a special study of whether computers might be put to work in planning and controlling the Polaris program. The study group included representatives of the Special Projects Office, Lockheed, and a management consulting firm, Booz, Allen and Hamilton. Ideas put forth by Pehrson formed the basis of the system that was worked out during the next six months.

The new system was a managerial marvel nicknamed PERT —for Program Evaluation Review Technique.

Essentially, PERT operates on the basic, simple truism that it usually takes longer to do one part of a job than another part. Find the part that takes the longest time, and the time that the whole job will take can be determined.

For a job involving only a few steps—sharpening a pencil, for instance—the problem is relatively simple. The human brain can solve it in a reasonable length of time. For a job involving billions of steps—developing Polaris, for instance—the problem boggles the mind. But PERT can solve it by using a computer.

The steps needed to develop each part of the Polaris system were put on huge blueprints 15 to 20 feet long. The blueprints were translated into numbers and fed into computers. The computers swiftly told Raborn when each job would be finished, and he could act on this information.

Change a step. Lose a day. Lose an hour. Gain a week. Invent
a new kind of anything. The new information was fed into the
computers. The computers gave Raborn a revised estimate.
The Special Projects Office used the system first. Lockheed
soon followed. Then other members of the Polaris industrial
team tried it. The Special Projects Office computer began ex-
changing information with the company computers. The computers talked with each other.

Pehrson called PERT a "management breakthrough." He predicted it would revolutionize bidding on government contracts.

"Contractors will tell us what they have in PERT terms," he
said. "They'll stop talking like bond salesmen and start talking
like boxcar salesmen. PERT gets behind the enthusiasm of the
sales department. A company forced to go through this exercise must know more about its problems—not just take diagrams
from its engineers. At the very least, a company using PERT
must become a more deliberate liar."

Nor was this all.

Pehrson felt PERT was the kind of tool a modern democ-
racy needed in order to compete with autocracy in the twentieth
century.

"We must come to this," he said. "Missile Gaps, expensive
programs canceled, confusion and fumbling: these things happen because we can't see ahead. PERT can show us where we are
going. With PERT giving us the information, when we say we
can do something, by God, we know what we're talking about.
We have cut through the guff."

Many agreed with him.

Business schools, universities, foreign countries, industrialists,
Air Force and Army officers, all became interested. Pehrson was
not alone in recognizing how thick the guff had become.

On the placid Cooper River, eighteen miles north of Charleston
and the ruins of Fort Sumter, is an old South Carolina plantation
called Liberty Hall. In the evening warm breezes blow from

the winding, broad river. Spanish moss hangs from the trees, moving slowly in the heavy air. The country is old and quiet. Nothing seems ever to have changed.

This is the land where Raborn chose to build the first missile supply depot for the Polaris fleet.

Geographically it is ideal. The climate is moderate throughout most of the year. The river is always free of ice. The area is protected from the open coast, yet it is easily accessible to the sea.

Nearby is the Charleston Ammunition Depot, which services the Atlantic Fleet. A few miles down the river is the Charleston Navy Yard, home port for some of the Polaris submarines.

The Navy took nearly 900 acres of the plantation for the missile depot. Some 27 million dollars were spent erecting and equipping what has become one of the most important naval supply bases in the world.

The Polaris missile depot links the industrial complex producing the Polaris missiles and the submarines. From here all Polaris submarines take their missiles on board before going on station somewhere in the world's oceans.

All parts of the missiles—the great motors, the delicate guidance and hydraulic systems, the re-entry vehicles—are flown to the depot and stored until needed. Nonexplosive parts are kept in ordinary warehouses. The other parts are placed in special underground magazines evenly spaced at safe distances across the fertile countryside, like a cemetery built for giants.

When the time comes to assemble missiles, the parts are taken to a complex of buildings that have been erected in a small park. Each part is minutely checked. The motors are examined by X ray and bore scope machines. The guidance packages are checked by an array of computers. The re-entry vehicles are worked on in a building that looks like a hospital. They are moved to operating tables on little carts. The floor is tiled and the technicians wear white smocks.

Once approved, the parts are taken to a main assembly building where the operational Polarises are put together on three assembly lines. Then the missiles are placed inside double containers that protect them from shock and provide the necessary environment in which they must be kept.

The containers are placed on flatcars and hauled to a 1,000-foot pier three miles away on the Cooper River. Here a crane, which cost a half-million dollars, picks up the missiles as if they were Chinese porcelains and tucks them into the tubes of waiting submarines or submarine tenders.

More than two hundred Navy officers and men operate the depot with the help of about one hundred and fifty civilian technicians. Most of the civilians are from Lockheed, but a handful are from General Electric and Aerojet.

They work surrounded by the tightest possible security measures. The depot is enclosed by a high steel fence. Marines guard it at all times. Passes are checked and checked again. No one who knows what is done at the depot forgets for an instant that the Polaris fleet could be crippled in the coastal back country of South Carolina.

The depot was commissioned only a few months before the *George Washington* first went to sea loaded with nuclear-tipped Polaris missiles. The ceremony took place on March 29, 1960. The day was warm, and the azaleas and camellias were blooming in Charleston.

When the invited guests gathered in front of the assembly building, the land around the depot was still as raw as the bulldozers had left it. Raborn had flown down from Washington with a planeload of government officials, Navy brass, and newsmen. Prominent Charleston men—and their wives with large, pretty hats—turned out. Gen. Mark Clark, the retired hero serving as commandant of The Citadel, also came up for the day.

L. Mendel Rivers of South Carolina, a veteran of the House Armed Services Committee, was the principal speaker. He stood on the bunting-draped platform with his long white mane bare to the spring sunshine, and told Charleston the meaning of the depot.

"Today Charleston becomes a potent thorn in the side of the Soviet Union," he drawled pointedly. "Today Charleston becomes the deterrent capital of the world. We make an indelible mark on the planning maps of the Soviet Union. This is the penalty we must pay for this great honor."

Later a cocktail party was held under a tent on the lawn of the commanding officer of the Charleston Ammunition Depot.

The commanding officer's house overlooking the Cooper River is relatively new. But it is built on the site of another plantation house called Red Bank. The old gardens that remain were filled with blooming red camellias. Ancient live oaks, covered with Spanish moss, shaded the tent. A few hundred yards down the lawn was an old family graveyard covered with wild flowers. The principal tombstone marked the grave of an eighteen-year-old girl who had died in 1828 a few days after giving birth to a son. The infant also had died and was buried nearby.

Music from the tent floated over the long lawn and out over the Cooper River. The river was empty. But soon the great dark Polaris submarines would pass by this place to pick up their missiles and then pass back again, back down the river past Red Bank and the old oaks, past Charleston, past the ruins of Fort Sumter, and slip secretly beneath the surface of the sea.

Waiters moved through the crowded room with trays of drinks. Conversation of a hundred voices flailed the smoky air like broken wings. It was another Embassy party in one of the big brownstone mansions off Washington's Massachusetts Avenue. As at parties before it and those that would follow, there were some new faces present. But most of the guests knew one another.

Raborn, clad in his dress uniform, picked up a passing drink, noticing as he took a sip that the Soviet Ambassador, Mikhail Menshikov, was standing a few feet away. The suave, white-haired diplomat, handsomely attired in a dinner jacket, looked more like a Berlin banker than a Communist. The admiral moved over to him and introduced himself.

"How long will it be, Mr. Ambassador, before your country will have Polaris-type submarines available?" Raborn asked cordially.

Menshikov hesitated before replying, his eyes narrowing only slightly.

"I really can't say, Admiral," he said. "They don't keep me informed of these—uh, technical developments. Why do you ask?"

"Oh," said Raborn, smiling, "I just wondered how long it would be until Russia could restore the balance of power."

# 21   Proving a Pudding

The crucial tests that many awaited came in March and April, 1960. They took place at Cape Canaveral, off San Clemente Island, and in the North Atlantic.

The first took place on March 9. A new-model Polaris—an all but operational bird—was launched for the first time from the Cape. The missile included extensive modifications made on the basis of tests in the A1X series. It also included a number of newly introduced parts that made the missile lighter and accordingly increased its range. The missile soared more than 1,000 miles down the Atlantic Range. Crucial Test No. 1 was a success.

Shift the scene to some hundred miles off the New England coast. The date is nearly mid-March. The *George Washington* dives beneath the surface while a tug circles the area. For months the *George Washington* has been successfully launching from her tubes the big, 2,500-pound Sabot test slugs along with tubefuls of water. These have been launched from dockside while the submarine lay on the surface, and later at sea while the sub was submerged. But this was something different. The *George Washington* has in her tubes some dummy operational Polarises called Dolphins. The Dolphin is the exact shape and weight of a Polaris, but its insides are filled with water instead of propellant. It is designed for testing launching tubes and for training.

A few minutes go by. The tug continues to circle clear of the area. Suddenly a Dolphin broaches the surface; then another; then another. Crucial Test No. 2 is a success.

Shift again, this time across the country to the Polaris launching tube beneath the surface of the Pacific, off San Clemente Island. The date is March 27. A Polaris test missile is in the tube. Its motor is a so-called cut-grain. That means there is just enough propellant in the motor to carry the missile about 300 yards. Never before has a Polaris been launched from beneath the surface of the sea and its motor ignited. The same thing has been done with black powder, but some skeptics have insisted that propellant is very different. This was the test Raborn had referred to as the "wet match" trick.

Everything is ready. The launching button is pressed. The missile is ejected from the tube, plummets into the air, and falls back without igniting. In the last seconds before the launching, a crossed circuit in the blockhouse has turned off the missile's internal power. Because of a random breakdown that had nothing to do with the missile, Crucial Test No. 3 is a failure.

Two days later the action shifts again to the Cape. The *Observation Island* test ship slowly plies a race-track course some 14 miles off the coast. This time almost the entire missile system is involved. For the first time, the Polaris navigation, fire control, and launching and guidance systems are integrated for a firing.

The missile in the *Observation Island's* tube is one of the new all-but-operational models. Here, except that the integrated system is in a surface ship and not a submerged submarine, is the finished product.

Range difficulties hold up the test. The afternoon wears on. Because it is firing into the range, the *Observation Island* has to be in a prescribed position, or the range safety officer will not permit the shot. The *Observation Island* goes around the track again and again. The sun sets. A small chilly wind comes up. Finally, the countdown reaches zero.

The Polaris rushes from the tube with a loud crack, soars clear, ignites with a crashing thunderclap, and roars down the range. A minor difficulty in the second stage cuts off the second-stage motor prematurely and shortens the distance the missile travels to about 900 miles. But this is nothing. Crucial Test No. 4 is a tremendous success.

Two weeks later the frosting is spread on Raborn's cake. Another cut-grain missile is launched from the underwater tube off San Clemente. This time the missile rips from the water, ignites, and arcs back into the sea a few hundred feet away. Crucial Test No. 3 is a success on the second try.

Only one test of any significance remained: the actual launching of a Polaris from a submerged submarine. Raborn and his staff felt it was anticlimactic. Everything had already been done, checked, proved. The *George Washington* could go on station as soon as Osborn was satisfied that all her equipment was in good working order and her crew was ready. But for unbelievers the final test would be made. Sometime in midsummer the *George Washington* would sail from Port Canaveral with her tubes full of missiles and fire them 1,200 miles down the range.

The Coast Guard Academy band played martial music as the guests took their places on the Electric Boat pier and the flag-draped deck of the *Patrick Henry*. A cold wind swept up the Thames and chilled the crowd despite the intermittent March sunshine. The officers and men of the *Patrick Henry* stood in ranks on her deck. In a slip on the other side of the pier lay the *George Washington.* An honor guard also stood on her deck. A few hundred yards away on the dock lay empty Dolphin shipping containers.

Senator Clinton Anderson, chairman of the Joint Atomic Energy Committee, sat on the *Patrick Henry*'s deck behind the microphones. Frank Pace, chairman of the board of General Dynamics, sat near him. Admiral Raborn came aboard and joined them. Other flag officers followed. All officers wore blue dress uniforms with swords and medals.

Admiral Rickover, wearing civilian clothes and a Navy raincoat, sat on the pier with Senator Henry ("Scoop") Jackson of Washington and other members of the Joint Committee. Wives and children of the *Patrick Henry*'s crew sat around them.

The ceremonies were brief. The *Patrick Henry*'s ensign, union jack, and commissioning pennant were hoisted to the tall sail. Senator Anderson spoke. So did Raborn and Pace. But the most pointed comment came from a man who has been dead nearly three hundred years. Rear Adm. Lawrence R. Daspit, deputy commander of Atlantic Fleet subs, paraphrased Oliver Cromwell by saying, "Put your trust in God but be sure to keep your deterrent mobile."

Commander Shear, the *Patrick Henry*'s skipper, standing in his ship's attack center, later added everything else that needed to be added.

"This ship is ready," he said.

Behind him there was a bronze plaque that read:

*U. S. S. Patrick Henry*
*"I know not what course others may take, but as for me,*
*give me liberty, or give me death."*

Across the pier, Raborn, Rickover, and members of the Joint Committee boarded the *George Washington* for an overnight cruise.

"Well, you must be very proud," Rickover said to Raborn as they went aboard. "This is your day."

"So should you," Raborn said. "This is your day, too."

Inside the sub, Rickover took Osborn aside.

"Hey, Os," he said. "How many Sabots are you going to fire?"

"Oh, a couple," Osborn said warily.

"You're going to fire four. These are important people."

"All right, we'll fire eight," Osborn shot back with a laugh.

The two submarines got under way within minutes of each other and moved out into the channel. The band played "Down, Down Underneath the Ocean."

The *George Washington* slipped down the river toward Long Island Sound and the sea. The *Patrick Henry* followed a thousand yards behind. The sky was cold and gray. The choppy water swirled over the ships' bows. Two huge white waves spread behind them.

About a mile from Groton the *Patrick Henry* closed the gap, and the two sister ships sailed abreast. Between them they could launch thirty-two great missiles—more than twice as much destructive might as had been dropped from the air in all of World War II. Between them they alone could hold in their magazines the power of life or death for whole nations.

Far out in the Sound the deadly sisters parted: the *Patrick Henry* to go for her acceptance trials, the *George Washington* to fire not eight but ten Sabots.


Less than twenty-four hours later, the *George Washington* was back. Osborn and his officers sat in the wardroom, across from the bust of Washington.

"You want to know how I feel about the mission of this ship?" he said. "This is a great deterrent. I don't want to ever have to push that fire button. That doesn't mean I wouldn't—any time. If I have to launch them, I'll launch them. This is no canoe club we're running. But the big value of this ship is that if the Russians realize what we have here, it ought to deter them. The Russian people, not just the leaders. It's Ivan we want to get to. Tell Ivan his leaders are stupid. Tell Ivan it's going to be his butt we're going to get, no matter what happens."

Osborn lit a cigar and ran a finger around the collar of his black turtle-neck sweater.

"If I had my way, every time a Polaris sub comes off station, it would announce that it was going to launch a missile without a warhead at 10:53 and that the missile was going to land off Block Island at such and such a spot. And make sure Ivan hears about it. We ought to bring Khrushchev in and show him the atomic stockpile and have all the bombs marked: three for Leningrad, four for Moscow. Then we could stage a big scene and shout at someone, 'Whatsa matter, stupid? I told you to paint all that over.' Don't misunderstand, though. I don't think this will end competition between Russia and the United States. Polaris can only take it out of the area of big bombs and throw it into something a little less obliterating, like trade or education. Hell, they might switch from H-bombs to *épées,* and then where would we be? There probably aren't a half-dozen decent fencers in the whole country."

Raborn chatted with newsmen outside a Congressional hearing.

"What about this business of Soviet subs following our subs and killing them all at the same time?" someone asked.

"It's a neat trick if you can do it," Raborn said. "But we have a hard-enough time finding a sub with our hunter-killer task groups with carriers and shore installations. You get two subs out there in an area the size of Texas—I say Texas because I can't think of anything bigger—and tell one to try to find the other, and he'll look a long time. If anybody says anything different, they never hunted submarines.

"You can tell them ——!"

The reporters stopped writing at the expletive.

"You may quote me," Raborn said, grinning. Everyone laughed.

"How about the warheads?" someone said. "Polaris's warhead is much smaller than Atlas's."

"Megatonitis. I don't believe in it. What do you do with a bigger warhead? All you do is pulverize the same target several times over. You grind the powder a little finer. If you want to hit a bigger area, send two missiles or three, and increase your odds of getting one there."

"But what about hitting Soviet hardened bases? Don't you need the bigger warheads for that?"

"Are there any hardened sites? I don't know of any. There are industries and cities and centers of government. If there are any hardened missile-sites, the missiles will have already flown. As for our hardened sites, remember that all you have to do to harden a submarine is pull the cork and go down."

"What happens if the Russians get Polaris subs?" the same man asked. "Do you think they're working on them?"

"Oh, I think they'll try to keep up with the Joneses. They have a prideful submarine force. This is the pride of their navy. Also they won't want to put all of their eggs together, either. But in this area of Polaris we have a five-year jump on them."

"So then if they get a Polaris sub, we'll all go down together anyway."

"Why talk about going down? We want to keep their finger off the button. We don't want all these fine-pencil calculations on how many minutes we'll have so I can push the button and get them before I die. Get a deterrent that they can't get at. That will keep us all here together."

"Admiral, what do you think of putting Minutemen on railroad cars?"

"Better than at a fixed base, but these railroads have problems, too. If I had missiles on a railroad, I'd want to put a fence around it. Anyone can walk down to a railroad. You can walk down there with a hand grenade, too. You know where trains are going. A spy looks out the window and picks up a phone and says to his pal, 'There goes No. 7.' 'Where's it going?' 'Right where the track is going.' "

"Well, thank you very much, Admiral."

"Not at all. Thank you. I like to talk. Of course, my favorite subject is girls."

The administration made its next move on April 6. Secretary of Defense Gates went again before the Mahon subcommittee. The hearing room in the Capitol was warm. Across the city by the tidal basin the cherry blossoms had begun to bud.

"Again the Polaris program, of course, has been under continuous review," Gates said. "We have been following very carefully the tests that have been made in connection with it. They have been most successful. We have had something like eleven land-based tests, and recently we have had several from the ship's-motion simulator at Cape Canaveral. We have also had a test from a surface ship known as the *Observation Island*. We have had a great deal of work done on the melding of the missile to the *George Washington*—which is the first nuclear Polaris submarine—so that the people concerned now have confidence that the merger of the missile and the submarine, and all of the intricate equipment involved, is in very good shape. In view of this we are prepared to recommend that the program as originally presented to you for three new Polaris ships and long leadtime items for three more—what I mean by ships is really weapons systems—be changed. We would not still only ask for the three complete Polaris weapons systems, but we would ask for long leadtime items for six additional ships, which would mean a program of three and nine; three complete weapons systems and long leadtime items for nine more."

Once again the administration rejected the Navy's plan to begin immediately to build a large fleet of Polaris submarines. Again the administration said it wanted to wait. It hadn't seen enough.

No extra submarines would be added to the budget beyond the three already there. The administration would buy only parts which might be used later. Moreover, the administration proposed to pay most of the 153 million dollar cost of the parts by canceling an earlier request to build two more nuclear-powered attack submarines.

As Flood summed it up, "Let us see: You are going to sacrifice two actual attack submarines for antisubmarine warfare to buy leadtime only for Polaris."

"Yes, sir," Gates said.

"Oh, I am against that now," Flood snapped angrily.

Gates sought to explain.

The administration felt it was taking a "prudent" approach. If all went well and the *George Washington* and *Patrick Henry* went on station on schedule, then the administration "would ask for the full funding of some part, or all, of the nine long leadtime ships" in January. He didn't bother to mention that by then the administration would no longer be in office, and that whoever succeeded Dwight Eisenhower would make the decision then.

The Navy had asked for a great fleet with which to defend America. Many in Congress agreed it was needed. The administration responded by buying the oars. The making of bold decisions—if any—was left to those who would come after.

Dusk. Sunday picnickers in bathing suits and men fishing for salt-water trout crowded the narrow sand spit. Across from them at the man-made harbor of Port Canaveral lay the black hull of the *George Washington*. Moored nearby was the *Observation Island*. Three gray pelicans coasted over the water searching for food. The submarine's missile hatches were thrown open like the petals of some dangerous jungle flower. Slowly a giant crane lowered a Polaris—the A1E1—into one of the tubes.

The A1E1 was one of the first Polarises to be assembled at the new Charleston depot.

Two weeks before, at the beginning of July, the *George Washington* had slipped quietly into the small harbor. Since then, underwater cameras had been temporarily installed on her deck. A tall cumbersome telemetry mast needed for communications on the Atlantic missile range had been temporarily attached to the top of her sail. Now she was almost ready for her most crucial test—the underwater launching of a live Polaris from her tubes for the first time.

The test was scheduled for the following day—July 18. If successful, the *George Washington* would make naval history.

Throughout the broiling Florida afternoon, participants and witnesses arrived at Cape Canaveral in little groups. There were naval officers and industry representatives, congressional staff members and newspapermen. Raborn made a holiday of the occasion and drove down from Washington with his wife.

The Admiral and his associates exuded optimism.

"If anyone sleeps better than I do tonight, they're drunk," Raborn said, grinning.

But despite the outward show of confidence they were uneasy. All tests showed that what the *George Washington* would try to do could be done. But she still had to do it. All agreed that this was the proof of Raborn's pudding, and much depended on the proving.

During the summer of 1960, the cold war had entered a new and ominous phase. The second summit conference had failed before it started. The Russians had become openly contemptuous of the United States. And as Americans became distracted with the coming presidential election campaign, Khrushchev increased Communist pressure on the West throughout the world: in Cuba, in Japan, in the Congo, in Berlin.

The adequacy of the Americans' defenses became a pivotal issue at the Democratic national convention. The crucial underwater test of the *George Washington* fell only days before the

Republican convention began. Many felt that the result of the test would affect the outcome of the election as well as the balance of power in the world.

At sea on the morning of July 18, the *Observation Island* dropped anchor about twenty-five miles east of Cape Canaveral lighthouse. A few thousand yards off her port bow, the *Kittiwake,* a submarine rescue ship, stood by. The destroyer *Gearing* circled the area, patrolling for Soviet submarines and "spy ship" reconnaissance trawlers that had been sighted all summer along the coast.

The *George Washington,* with two live Polarises in starboard tubes, arrived shortly before noon. Both the Blue and Gold crews were aboard. So were Raborn, the program's technical masterminds, Smith and Bednarz, nearly a score of engineers from the Polaris program's major contractors. In all, about 250 people crowded the submarine as Osborn and his Blue Crew prepared to launch the A1E1.

The submarine submerged more than a mile from the *Observation Island* in about 250 feet of water. In a few minutes, people crowding the rails could see only the tip of the telemetry mast as it cut through the royal-blue sea. A voice rasped over the ship's intercom: "T minus 60 and counting." Osborn would push the firing button in one hour.

The sky was clear and the sun was hot. Newsmen and cameramen sought good viewpoints on the *Observation Island.* A *Life* photographer set up a camera with a two-thousand-millimeter lens that looked like a cannon. The intercom voice said: "Condition Zebra"—the order to put the ship in watertight battle condition in case the missile should hit it. The countdown had reached T minus 30 minutes.

The *Observation Island* launched a helicopter. Radars high on the ship turned silently in the sunshine. The time was 1:27 P.M. The intercom voice said: "T minus 4 and holding." An adjustment had to be made aboard the *George Washington.* At 1:42 the countdown resumed.

"T minus 4 . . . T minus 3 . . . T minus 2 . . . T minus 1 . . ."

The submarine released a bright-green smoke signal. The countdown went forward in seconds.

"T minus 60 . . . T minus 30 . . . T minus 10 . . ."

Movie cameras clicked on all over the *Observation Island.* The only sound now was the rush of air from the ship's ventilators.

"T minus 5 . . . 4 . . . 3 . . . 2 . . . 1 . . . ZERO . . ."

Nothing happened. No one spoke. Cameras whirred in a vacuum. Life seemed to stop between the hot sun and the sea.

The intercom voice finally spoke: "We have not fired yet. . . . Standby . . . Standby . . . Standby . . ."

Again silence.

Then: "We have recycled to T minus 40 minutes and are holding."

Aboard the submarine, as the seconds had run out, one light in the mass of instruments had shown that the voltage in one part of the missile was somewhat off. Some experts who were present said the missile would have worked anyway; the chance was worth taking.

Tremendous pressure was on Osborn to fire. But Osborn played the test by the book. He would take no unnecessary risk. He said **no.**

The *George Washington* switched to its second missile and resumed counting at 3:45. This time the countdown reached T minus 5 seconds and stopped. Instrumentation problems involving the range forced another hold.

The Blue Crew tried again at 5:05 and again at 7. Both times weather conditions interfered with range communications. By 7:44 the sun had set over the Cape. Red streaked the west. The intercom voice said: "T minus 5 and counting. All problems have been cleared up."

But it was too late. The telemetry batteries—installed only for tests on the range and not part of the operational system—had run down.

"The test has been terminated for the day," the intercom voice announced. "The *George Washington* will not launch."

The submarine sent up a green flare as if in defiance, as rain squalls closed in again on the area.

The next day a Polaris defiantly roared from a land launching pad and hit a target area more than one thousand miles down the Atlantic missile range, while the exhausted men of the *George Washington* slept. On the following day, they returned to sea.

Once more the submarine carried two Polarises. Once more the ships assumed their positions in the hot sun beaming down on the empty sea. Once more the countdown began.

There were only two brief holds; one caused by a minor technical problem, the other by a merchant ship that strayed into the target area lying between Puerto Rico and Bermuda.

The countdown moved into seconds. The mechanical sound of the voice on the intercom once again took command of the silent *Observation Island.*

"T minus 5 . . . T minus 4 . . . T minus 3 . . . T minus 2 . . . T minus 1 . . . ZERO!"

A great mound of water appeared in the sea two thousand yards away. The Polaris burst through at an angle. It looked off course. But, even as observers gasped, the white-nosed missile ignited and righted itself. It tore into the summer sky on a white tongue of flame. A thunderous blast cracked over the sea.

At T plus 54 seconds, the second stage separated from the first with a puff of white smoke and ignited. Moments later, the now practically invisible missile's second stage motor cut off and the warhead sailed down the range more than one thousand miles.

A wave of pent-up cheers swept through the submarine beneath the water and the ships on the surface.

"Right down the pickle barrel," the Cape reported to Washington.

But Raborn and Osborn weren't through yet. The range

made the necessary adjustments in two hours and the count-down began again on A1E2. At 3:32 the intercom voice barked: "T minus Zero." Again the swirling bubble appeared on the sea, this time only one thousand yards away. The Polaris ripped through it, moving straight up and dragging a spout of water behind it. The motor ignited and it was gone.

"Right down the pickle barrel," the Cape reported a second time.

Osborn sent a wire from the sub to President Eisenhower, who was vacationing at Newport, Rhode Island: "Polaris— from out of the deep to target. Perfect."

In less than an hour, the Navy disclosed that the administration had finally agreed to release funds for two additional Polaris submarines, both added to the Defense Appropriations Bill by Congress over the administration's objections. That brought the total number of submarines authorized to fourteen.

Raborn wired from the *George Washington* to Lockheed: "We know how to fire them. Send us more missiles."

The *George Washington* surfaced, and, with Raborn and Osborn standing on her bridge, she sailed by the cheering watchers aboard the *Observation Island.* Then the *George Washington* headed back to the Cape.

By the time the great missile submarine reached the channel leading to Port Canaveral from the sea, word of her triumph had already spread throughout the Cape, and cheering crowds jammed the channel's banks. Members of the Blue and Gold crews stood at attention on the deck as the submarine moved into port. Raborn's two-star blue flag flapped proudly from the sail.

# 22    On Station

The exact date when the *George Washington* would depart for her station with a load of nuclear missiles aboard was never made public by the Navy.

Secrecy was planned long in advance. There was a strong possibility Russian submarines would be lurking off the coast of the United States and would try to follow her or possibly even torpedo her. If the *George Washington* left for a sea tour and never returned, who would know whether she had been sunk by another submarine or had met with some accident in the depths of the ocean? The Navy was alert for anything.

Because of her speed under water—well over 20 knots—the best opportunity Russian subs would have to fire at the *George Washington* or try to follow her would come just as she was leaving port and still in relatively shallow water. The plan, therefore, was to confuse enemy agents watching her movements by having the new sub make repeated short runs up and down the coast during the summer of 1960, and to ply her in and out of Port Canaveral once every few days.

One day she would depart as usual. But instead of coming back in a few days, she would head for her station. Only after she arrived out "there"—with missiles zeroed in on Moscow, Leningrad, Stalingrad, and other cities—would it be announced that the first Polaris submarine was operational: the new "big stick" of the high seas was now policing the world from a secret hiding place.

The *George Washington* could be in the Norwegian Sea, the Arctic Ocean, the Mediterranean—anywhere.

Raborn sat on the patio of his home and patted his dachshund, Heinz. A few miles down the Potomac the floodlights of

*Polaris!*

Washington picked out the city's monuments in the early evening darkness. Raborn gazed unseeing over his roses, and he thought of the mighty power that the United States was sending to sea.

What had been accomplished in only a few years was enormously satisfying. It was a tribute to his staff and the Navy, to American industry, to thousands of men and women whom he had never seen.

He had always tried to convey the message of this weapon; to stop at a factory and tell a man at a machine tool that he was doing a good job; to call the president of a huge corporation, trace him from city to city, and thank him personally for his help. If people were going to make sacrifices and give their best, they had to feel that they were a part of a great thing. They had to be told and told often.

It was, indeed, a great thing, this submarine, this missile. But still there were so many persons in high places who weren't convinced, so many who didn't want to be convinced. Was this a breach of faith with the man at the machine tool? With the engineers at Pittsfield and Sunnyvale? With the Naval officers at the Munitions Building and the Cape? With the country itself? It was part of Raborn's job to follow through and sell this weapon. And not just this one but the still better one that his people were already designing.

Raborn winked at Heinz.

"Heinz," he said, "would you rather be an Air Force dog or a dead dog?"

Heinz flopped over on his back and stuck his short paws in the air.

"Okay, Heinz, now when I say, 'How about the Navy?' you stand up and salute."

Raborn sat Heinz on his hindquarters and raised the dog's paw to his ear.

"Like that," Raborn said.

On Station

He patted Heinz again, got up, and walked inside to his electric organ. Heinz followed as Raborn sat down and began to play loud and clear.

The making of Polaris was done. In the mid-'50s it had been only a hope. In the 1960s it was in being.

Most of the thousands of people who created the Polaris system will never have their names recorded anywhere except in old service records. Their reward is in the great weapon itself and its success.

For the story of the creation of Polaris is a success story. Nothing can change that.

More, of course, was to follow. In 1960 the fight to build a large Polaris fleet still had to be won. Plans to extend the missile's range to 2,500 miles already were under way. But the hard struggle to create Polaris was over.

It is fitting, therefore, to look at that struggle as a whole and at the questions that it raises about America in the latter half of the twentieth century.

Can anyone knowing the history of Polaris not wonder why there should have been a struggle at all? Can anyone knowing the supreme value of Polaris not wonder why the administration was not ready to take advantage of it and build the submarines that were needed?

Americans have always been willing to sacrifice in the face of danger. Have Americans really become so fat and so comfortable that they are not willing to defend themselves? Or is it that they have been so poorly led by tired men that they have not been aware that more effort was needed?

Americans have long been famous for their ability to get things done. Has this talent generally been lost? Or is what Raborn and his small organization did in a few short years something that can be repeated many times?

*Polaris!*

Fate has been kind to the United States.

For fifteen years after World War II, mankind moved steadily into the new age of rockets and nuclear power. The United States went along, but always reluctantly.

Thus by 1960 Russia had outstripped the United States in the early exploration of space. Russia had outstripped the United States in building a vast land-based arsenal of long-range missiles. And Russia was using these advantages everywhere to press home more victories in the Cold War.

But, by luck, the United States began to develop Polaris. Here was a weapon that was three to five years ahead of anything that Russia had. Here was another chance—possibly a last chance—for the United States to reverse the running trend toward catastrophe.

With Polaris at sea, with other missiles on the land to keep Russia off balance, perhaps the United States could meet the coming challenge in the vast stretches of space.

This was the new frontier. The control of space could mean control of the earth. But, here again, was there a lack of vision? Was not the United States holding back, playing with limited experiments, while Russia struck out for the prize? Was not the answer to cut through the bureaucracy of modern America, pick a man like Raborn, and tell him to go ahead and do the job?

Possibly the problem was lack of faith and lack of courage: courage to do what had never been done before; faith that the impossible could be achieved.

For anyone lacking this faith and courage, Polaris was a guiding star.

Most of the world is water and the continents are islands.

Far from any shore, the vast sea rolls endlessly on. Nothing can be seen in any direction but whitecaps and the ocean swell. From here life first came a billion years ago; here life, in a strange cycle, returns to defend itself.

Beneath the empty surface lies America's new line of defense, deadly and ready, all but untouchable.

One week Polaris submarines can be in the Arctic; the next they can be in the Sea of Japan. The Indian Ocean . . . the North Sea . . . the waters off Arabia . . . the Pacific . . . the Atlantic . . .

The Polaris ships keep the watch.